# CREATIVE DRAMA IN A DEVELOPMENTAL CONTEXT

Edited by
## Judith Kase-Polisini

Consulting Editors —
Robert Colby, Charles Combs,
Richard Courtney, Ruth Beall Heinig,
Lin Wright

UNIVERSITY
PRESS OF
AMERICA

LANHAM • NEW YORK • LONDON

Co-published by arrangement with
The American Theatre Association

A PUBLICATION OF THE CHILDREN'S THEATRE
ASSOCIATION OF AMERICA, A DIVISION OF THE
AMERICAN THEATRE ASSOCIATION

All University Press of America books are produced on acid-free
paper which exceeds the minimum standards set by the National
Historical Publications and Records Commission.

Creative drama in a
developmental context

Dedicated
to the
memory
of
Winifred Ward

# TABLE OF CONTENTS

Page

v

PREFACE

This is the first of a series of publications resulting from the Children's Theatre Association of America (CTAA) Symposia on Creative Drama in a Developmental Context. CTAA is a division of the American Theatre Association. In 1981, President Lin Wright appointed a committee of five to develop a national symposium on creative drama. The committee then selected fifteen creative drama leaders who agreed to meet for a full day prior to the 1982 American Theatre Association Convention to develop the objectives and determine participants for such a symposium.

Those who attended that first national planning meeting were Roger Bedard, Robert Colby, Charles Combs, Richard Courtney, Ruth Beall Heinig, Judith Kase-Polisini, Kay King, Nancy King, Virginia Koste, Margaret McKerrow, Helane Rosenberg, Bernard Rosenblatt, Barbara Salisbury, Julie Thompson, and Lin Wright.

CTAA sponsored the symposium to stimulate fresh discussions, generate more information, and determine future research questions about crucial issues in the field of creative drama. The committee determined that to do this, it would be helpful to view the field from the perspective of scholars from other fields working towards similar professional objectives. Thus, it was decided to invite colleagues from education, psychology, related arts, anthropology, ritology, etc., as well as scholars from the general field of theatre to consider creative drama from their point of view. In turn, some of the leading creative drama researchers were invited to present their views.

Plans for a single symposium evolved to a series of five -- four in North America followed by an international symposium. The general theme of the series would center around "creative drama in a developmental context."

ix

This series of papers emerged from two symposia. The first, "Towards a Developmental Psychology of the Theatre: an investigation into the nature and origin of dramatic intelligence," coordinated and chaired by Robert Colby and Charles Combs was held at Harvard University on November 19, 1983. The meeting was co-sponsored with the New England Theatre Conference. Two prominent psychologists, Howard Gardner and Dennis Wolfe, from Project Zero, offered insights into their work and how it might effect child drama. These presentations were followed by addresses by two theatre scholars, Virginia Glasgow Koste and Jonathan Levy.

The second, the Toronto Symposium, was coordinated and chaired by Richard Courtney, and co-sponsored with the Ontario Institute for Studies in Education, November 25 to 27, 1983. Presentations focused on the general topic "Drama and Learning" from the various perspectives of the speakers. The range of fields was wide, with a psycologist (Weininger), education specialists in the fields of reading, (McInnes), curriculum development (Russell), gifted education (Shiner), as well as scholars from the fields of dance (Silver and Baird), ritology (McLaren) and drama (Courtney and Bernstein). In addition, a multi-cultural panel presented views of drama as it relates to the Kathak (Singha), the Japanese Tea ceremony (Noro), the ceremony paying respect to teachers (Gururatana) and intercultural communication (Turkewych).

The reader will note a stylistic difference between the papers from Canada and those from the United States. This is due to the fact that each site coordinator developed a format which suited the location and presentors. The symposium in Toronto lasted two and a half days, and Richard Courtney assembled an impressive group of twelve scholars to present "formal" manuscripts. On the other hand, Charles Combs and Robert Colby oganized a one day meeting featuring four presentations which, comparatively speaking, would be considered informal. In addition, in isolated instances, Canadian scholars use different spelling and methods of notation than American. In each paper, the editor decided to maintain the integrity of the original author and take the chance that the reader will accept these slight differences. Finally, for editorial reasons, the papers are presented in reverse chronological order.

We are grateful to the many who have helped with this project. Most specifically, we wish to thank the CHILDREN'S THEATRE FOUNDATION for its generous support.

We acknowledge the encouragement and assistance of Lin Wright, who as president of CTAA, formed the initial committee for this project, to Ruth Heinig, current president of CTAA and Margaret Lynn, Executive Director of the American Theatre Association, who have done much to facilitate the completion of this publication. We are grateful for the many hours of work contributed by Robert Colby, Charles Combs and Richard Courtney to organize the first two symposia. And we are thankful for the editorial assistance of my friend, Anita Unrich, and my father, C. Robert Kase, who was immensely helpful in the preparation of the final manuscript.

                Judith Kase-Polisini
                January 30, 1984
                Lutz, Florida

# INTRODUCTION

Research in the field of creative drama, a relatively new field of empirical investigation, began about twenty years ago and blossomed in the seventies. A review of research in the United States (Kennedy, 1981 Fordyce, 1975, Klock, 1975), indicates that most studies on the effects of creative drama use research methodologies developed in other fields, and that none to date has been replicated.

Thus far, creative drama research has focused primarily on analyzing methodology, developing strategies, and determining the effects of creative drama on participants physically, socially, intellectually and emotionally. Studies of effects on participants generally concern some form of learning and personal growth.

For the purpose of clarity, a definition of creative drama is needed. The Children's Theatre Association of America has adopted the definition of creative drama as "an improvisational, non-exhibitional, process-centered form of drama in which participants are guided by a leader to imagine, enact, and reflect upon human experiences" (Davis and Behm, 1978). Most Canadians, however, use the term "drama" to refer to what those in the United States call creative drama.

In the papers presented at Toronto, the reader will discover that each presentor finds definite links between the drama process and learning. Otto Weininger, psychologist, opens the discussion exploring the use of pretend play, which he defines as an "as if" mode of behavior (p.5). Creative drama scholars would call this dramatic play as Peter Slade has defined it (1976), including personal play, where the child acts out something with his whole body, and projected play, where the child projects the "drama" into a toy or object. In his review of the literature, Weininger makes a strong case for the argument that pretend play contributes to the cognitive, linguistic and social development of each child. He reports that in early development, pretend play represents a higher level of play than do sensory motor or functional behaviors. He believes that Christie's basic outline

of types of pretend play offers a useful view of
development beginning at about six months with
"early solitary imaginative play...through the-
matic fantasy play in which children act out a
particular story...to sociodramatic play where
they take on the roles of other people..."
(p.6.). Although he agrees that this basic outline of development is fairly clear, the relationship of pretend play to individual character
and specific aspects of development remain more
tentative. However, he points to numerous
studies which appear to support the view that
pretend play is related to creativity, cognitive
and social development. He then reports that
"there seems to be fairly wide agreement on the
basic value of the cooperative imaginative effort
involved in the use of story-or role-enactment as
a form of training which extends the child's perspective on himself and others and is consistently associated in the research literature with
'reducation of egocentricity,' and with improvements in perspective taking and cooperative
social problem solving" (pp.11-12). However, he
cautions that the methods of training must be
carefully worked out in order to effect educational benefit.

Weininger then describes his own recent
pilot studies using training in pretend play. He
found that by encouraging a small group of handicapped and emotionally disturbed children who did
not seem to know how to pretend play to explore
the world of pretend play in a carefully structured environment, the children learned to "feel
safe with play, may take chances, practice their
competencies, and build up their self esteem as
they increase knowledge of themselves and others"
(p.12). His pilot studies indicate some of the
ways in which training in dramatic play may
influence cognitive and social development of
normal as well as handicapped children. In her
response, Sue Martin suggests specific methods of
extending this experiment.

Richard Courtney presents his theory of the
dramatic metaphor and learning, particularly as
it pertains to improvised drama. He views meaning, learning and knowledge as intricately connected and related to the drama process. He
first develops the thesis that drama is a way of

knowing, a way of collecting primary and secondary evidence which contributes to individual
knowledge. Knowledge therefore is the result of
the choices of evidence each individual makes, a
continuing, dynamic process. By improvising
drama, students acquire primary knowledge or
"knowledge learned by dramatic doing...from which
discoursive knowledge derives" (p.46). As Robert
Gardner says in his response, Courtney sees the
drama process as "something which emerges from
our very nature" and that "when we understand the
power of the dramatic form we also understand the
process of learning to a greater extent" (p.66).

Courtney suggests that the curriculum should
be based on two views of knowledge - procedural,
or knowledge based on negotiating certain stages,
steps or sequences to explain phenomena, and personal-practical, or "knowledge-in" gained through
human performance, the knowledge gained by doing
something. He explains that the drama process is
used to accumulate both forms of knowledge. He
then develops a model for "dramatic knowledge"
which includes four types - similarity, contiguity, opposition and differentiation, after
which he draws on the research of Robert Witkin
who in turn bases his theory on the work of
Piaget to suggest how this knowledge can be
sequenced in the curriculum. Courtney seems to
be suggesting that the drama process is in fact a
learning process and if we can understand the
drama process we will understand the learning
process and vice versa. To Gardner, Courtney is
saying that "drama is a map for the self," that
"the great adventure in life is life" (p.65).

John McInnes offers an unusual perspective
of reading as it relates to drama. He suggests
that reading is dramatic. Just as the audience
collaborates with playwright to complete the
imaginative idea, the reader becomes an active
collaborator with the author. He then cautions
that "as a reader/collaborator there are risks
involved in getting together with Maurice Sendak,
Judy Blume, or Marcel Proust" (p.74).

According to McInnes, the reader collaborates by mentally staging the story, taking the
role of director, actor, designer, building into

the story parts of his or her own experience. Thus reading a story is a very active, very personal experience. The child can mentally act or direct with complete safety, knowing that no one else will "see" what is done or how it is done.

McInnes further suggests that success in reading is dependent on the reader's ability to collaborate with the author. Thus it is important to consider drama as it affects learning to read. In this respect, McInnes explains that storying is an essential way of knowing and this ability is developed long before the child learns to read. He states that "children who have had rich experiences in storying bring greater expectations to text than do those who have been passive in the presence of stories" (p.77). He explains that "through play, children develop the 'suppose' element that must be brought to reading" (p.78).

McInnes reports that active classrooms where children are encouraged to dramatize stories they read, develop group consensus about what the story meant, involve themselves in the characters and actions in the stories, reveal feelings which otherwise could not be expressed, make active readers. He also points out the unique educational value derived from reading conventional scripts, silently or aloud. And he suggests that reading dialogue can be an additional classroom challenge because "the implicit information usually explicit in narrative writing demands inference" (p.78). He concludes by stating

"Reading and drama are part of one another. They draw on and extend the same personal resources. They interact with each other. A rich curriculum capitalizes on and develops the inventiveness of minds, the expressiveness of bodies, the sensitivity to language that all children can bring to their explorations of meaning" (p.79).

At a time when accountability appears to be a concern in the field of education, the question of evaluation is critical to those who would infuse creative drama into the school curriculum. Howard Russell argues that if the arts maintain that it is not possible to evaluate the arts as science and math are evaluated, because they are difficult to measure, there will be proportionately less time, attention and money alloted to the arts in public education. For those who subscribe to this rational, Russell invites them to take another look at evaluation and what it can do. He offers a description of two recent model studies which might make evaluation in the arts more acceptable than it has been in the past. Both studies offer examples of educational evaluation methods which meet the highest possible scientific criteria.

First, the Science Council of Canada, conducted by Professor Pierre-Leon Trempe, is part of an evaluation of a science program in a school, in which a school program was described by gathering data at least partly through methods which have been successfully used to evaluate arts programs in American schools (Topping, 1981). Although other technical or quantitive data were collected, it was the qualitative data, or that which was gathered through observation and interviews of teachers and students, which revealed the most critical evidence - that students were studying to pass the tests rather than learning science, a complaint heard frequently about American schools these days. Trempe found that instead of science, the opposite or "anti-science" was being taught. Russell considers this study to be the best example of an evaluation which "documents the nature and extent of the inversion of goals which is caused by the examination system and which in turn seems to plague us in the education of the young in all our disciplines" (p.98). The study reveals how important qualitative analysis can be in educational evaluation. He also points out that such an evaluation method could readily be used to evaluate an arts program. Finally, he observes that the Trempe study was designed to investigate the individual performance of people to "help decide who should pass, who should fail, and who should be allocated to which class in the next term" (p.99).

The second study Russell describes is quantitative in nature and is designed to monitor educational programs, not people. The IEA Second International Mathematic Study offers a model which distinguishes between three "pools" through item analysis. In one pool is placed items to be learned in the intended curriculum, in another, the items learned in the implemented curriculum, and the third, the SIMS pool, rest the items from both other pools plus items not listed in the curriculum but taught anyway. He claims that such an analysis can reveal valuable information for curriculum planners. Russell then argues that there is a need for program monitoring in education today and it is this sort of evaluation which might be most useful to creative drama educators. In his opinion, "what we should expect to find in the data which result from the survey proposed above is that not enough art is taught and that it is taught to too few students" (p.109).

In her response to the paper, Pamela Ritch challenges Russell's rationale that evaluation is needed to justify the arts in the curriculum. Instead, she argues that evaluation is needed in the field of creative drama whether anyone else listens or not (p.112). She offers the reader a perceptive evaluation of the Trempe and SIMS studies in terms of their methodology and their value to creative drama specialists, and then proceeds to offer her own observations as well as some challenges for future research in the field of creative drama.

There has always been a close relation between creative drama and dance. Indeed, as Joyce Wilkinson points out in her response to the paper by Silver and Baird, the psychological benefits of dance and movement delineated by Silver and Baird converge with claims made by drama specialists for more than five decades (see her three illustrations which describe these similarities, (pp.144-146). Silver and Baird review the literature from the fields of anthropology to education to dance therapy to describe the beneficial functions of dance participation as it relates to the learning process. They then offer the thesis that dance assists in learning self-regulation or learning to analyze performance in terms of what works and what does not work (p.129) so that the latter can be eliminated in future efforts to succeed.

Because of the nature of their work, creative drama teachers recognize the special educational needs of gifted and talented children. In
her paper, Sandra Shiner suggests that the literature clearly points to the need for guidance
training to help students realize their full
potential. Many drama specialists would agree
with Shiner that high creatives or creative
intellectuals, such as those scoring high on the
Torrance test, are a population often overlooked
in gifted programs and that these people deserve
the attention afforded the intellectually gifted. Shiner believes that teachers need better
training in guidance and that gifted students in
most need of guidance therapy through the arts
are those described as creative intellectuals or
interpersonally sensitive (p.156). She offers
several approaches using the arts which have been
found to be successful including planned summer
institutes, journal writing, career counseling
via studies of role models or careers found by
reading or seeing plays, seeing and making films,
bibliotherapy, sociodrama and play production.
Shiner concludes her paper with a provocative
list of questions for future researchers.

Bradley Bernstein shares his expertise with
Spolin theatre games as applied to psychotherapeutic situations. He points out that many mentally ill people feel isolated from other people
and that drama can serve as a method of transformation where "each participant can realize him/
herself as an agent, and as a member of a
developing community" (p.182). He emphasizes
Spolin's technique of focusing attention on group
problem solving so that players are not concentrating on individual needs but rather on group
needs. Within the group problem or scene to be
played, each individual is offered the opportunity to explore hypothetical problems before
confronting them in the real world.

Bernstein believes that the "emotional disturbance of psychiatric patients is a function of
their isolation" (p.192) and as a result they
have a low self image. Creative energies, which
have turned inward and "become dark, full of
rage, fear and pain" (p.192) can be released to
view the world and those in it from a positive
point of view. He further suggests that trans-

formation in this sense of community, this living
for others rather than within oneself, has a
definite religious connotion.

Peter McLaren proposes that "drama teachers
and educator-anthropologists... begin to forge
connections between ritual and drama which could
be applied to the creation of improved curriculum
programming..." (p.237). After a thorough survey of the literature, he carefully develops a
general definition of ritual and describes the
functions of ritual in society. He then applies
knowledge of ritual to an analysis of classroom
instruction, specifically describing his own
research with eighth grade Azorean students in a
Metropolitan Toronto Catholic School. He describes two "states" of student behavior. The
first, the streetcorner state, is the free activity of students outside the school when they are
with their peers, and is characterized by lack of
controls, spontanaity, experimentation, catharsis, and playfullness. The second, the student
state, is the behavior students exhibit in
school, when tney give themselves over to the
powerful controls of he teachers. The student
state is characterized by conformity, obedience,
restricted movement, etc. He reports that "students spend approximately 76 minutes of the
school day in the streetcorner state, and 298
minutes in the student state" (p.226). In other
words, the major proportion of school time was
spent in the student state, with teachers exhibiting powerful controls.

McLaren then applies ritual theory to a description of teachers. Readers will recognize
these types as ones found in every school. He
delineates the specific behaviors of the teacher
as entertainer and as prison guard. He then
offers a picture of the more effective teacher,
the teacher as liminal servant. The teacher as
liminal servant essentially uses drama, the "as
if" quality of involvement, as a means of transforming a class into an active congregation where
students can bear "witness to the universal wisdom embodied in the rites of instruction," and
the teacher takes the role of "rabbi or priest of
knowledge" (p.227). He then makes an analogy
between ritual knowledge and Courtney's "dramatic
knowledge."

In his response, Lawrence O'Farrell agrees that "schooling and ritual have much in common and that the elements of ritual can have a major impact on the effectiveness of institutionalized education -- for better or for worse" (p.253). In response to McLaren's attempt to define ritual, he offers his own attempt to explain the place of theatre as one of four modes of symbolic action, which include civil and religious rituals, social interaction and human development and education. He then places creative drama within the human development and education mode. O'Farrell provides practical insight into the nature of creative drama as ritual.

Finally, the multicultural panel offers papers connecting native rituals to drama. Singha explains the historic importance of dance and drama as a unified art form India. After a brief history of the development of classic Indian dance form, Kathak, she explains the relevance of this ancient art form to contemporary needs, including the need for body precision, concentration and self control.

In addition to personal discipline, Noro explains that the Japanese ceremony offers young women in Japan today an opportunity to learn eating manners, sex roles and "performance learning" or imitation of the ritual as it is performed by a model. In addition to the ritual itself, young women learn such skills as sensitivity to the tastes, moods and feelings of others.

Most Americans will read with delight and possibly a little envy the description by Guruatana of the "ceremony paying respect to teachers" in Thailand. Perhaps creative drama scholars can find a way to transfer this idea into a ceremony which could benefit American children and teachers.

Christine Turkewych offers a brief description of education in the multi-cultural Canadian society and then points out that most teachers need to learn intercultural communication skills in order "to promote harmonious interaction" (p.285), including learning how to learn, non-judgmentalness, tolerance for ambiguity, respectfulness, and empathy. She concludes by calling for training of teachers and administrators which will develop the skills needed to educate a multicultural society.

American creative drama scholars are unique in providing numerous empirical studies investigating the relationship between the creative drama process and the learning process, a phenomenon not found abroad. It seems appropriate, therefore, that the next series of papers were dedicated to an inquiry into the nature of dramatic intelligence.

The reader will find that the presentations offered at the Harvard symposium are relatively informal compared to those at the Ontario Institute for Studies in Education. Two of the four presentations are edited transcripts of speeches presented that day.

Howard Gardner leads the Harvard discussions with a brief explanation of developmental psychology. He explains that the developmental approach works towards at least some kind of "end state." He generally prefers the Piaget approach, with some exceptions, one of which is that Piaget's end state is that of a scientist. Gardner is interested in other abilities, especially artistic abilities. After a brief critique of Piaget, Gardner describes an approach developed by researchers at Harvard University's Project Zero over the past ten years - the symbol system approach.

Gardner describes the symbol system approach as a study of development according to domains of knowledge or symbol systems, or skills using symbols, which each person accumulates during the course of development. He believes that it is an appropriate approach to study artists. He explains that the symbol systems approach allows the researcher to describe a variety of literacies related to artistic development.

Gardner then explains his theory of multiple intelligences, or symbol systems, which he believes are involved in human development. They are linguistic, musical, logical-mathemental, spatial, bodily-kinesthetic, interpersonal and intrapersonal (p.303).

Building on this theory, Gardner next suggests that there are several phases or stages of development including a "first draft knowledge" of the basic symbol systems which occurs between the ages of 4-7 or "early flowering," a "literal stage" in middle childhood with attention on technique or the "right way to do things" followed by the adolescent period when a blending or melding of ability occurs.

With this background, Gardner then applies his theory to the development of the actor as an end state. The reader will find his analysis interesting and in some cases provocative. For example, few actors might take issue with Gardner's notion that an actor needs to have interpersonal intelligence, or an ability to understand other people, how they are feeling, how they work, what makes them tick, etc. However, some will probably take issue with Gardner's notion that the actor does not need intrapersonal intelligence, or an ability to have the same kind of sensitivity directed inwards toward the feelings of the actor and what makes him or her tick. And actors who study dance or stage movement might be puzzled by his belief that spatial intelligence is not needed to act.

Gardner then speculates that theatre differs from other art forms in several ways. He believes that one of the major differences between theatre talents and other artist talents has to do with the need to be sensitive to the interactions between people. Artists and musicians and mathematicians can essentially operate without much knowledge of interpersonal relationships of the world outside the self. But theatre people must understand how people interact.

Many actors might disagree with Gardner's contention that "people with a theatrical flair are acting all the time and they are trying out things all the time" (p.308).

Finally, Gardner offers some views about education in general as related to his theory of multiple intelligences. He points out that potentials can be identified early so that people can be educated to develop their potentials.

Dennis Wolf prefers to talk about "dramatic imagination" rather than dramatic intelligence, which incorporates knowledge about theatre and knowledge within the theatre artist such as the playwright's ability to create dialogue, the actor's ability to interpret a role, the designer's ability to realize the meaning of the playwright visually, etc. She describes her work with Project Zero particularly as it applies to the study of symbolic development beyond the ordinary and necessary forms. This involves studying children's poems, songs, and plays created during their make believe play. Over a period of years, it has been possible to compare performances of young children into adolescence and adult life, and thus outline the steps the artist goes through to achieve the artistic end state.

Wolf then discusses the development of "enactive" imagination which she describes as the actor's ability to project a myriad of feelings at any given moment through nonverbal gestures or pantomime. Later she mentions a second kind of enactive imagination for the playwright.

Wolf's description of a "willingness to suspend the here-and-now" in favor of "alternative realities" comes very close to theatre scholars' description of the "willingness to suspend disbelief." She reports that this ability to suspend belief occurs between 12 and 18 months of age when most children learn to pretend. Between the age of two and five, this capacity to pretend performances grows rapidly. She notes that by the age of five, children are able to "absorb intrusions" into their dramas, essentially transforming situations which really happen in the environment into the text of the pretend drama, hanging on to the illusion in spite of interruptions from reality.

Wolf points out that the enactive or acting ability of young children is not fully developed so that a child is unable to act out the whole dramatic moment as a seasoned actor might, using voice and body in subtle ways to describe the moment.  Instead, this ability develops gradually over a period of years.  Her description of six year old Jeannie in dramatic play functioning as player, playmaker and audience points out the complex nature of dramatic imagination, where one child can "engineer" each moment of the drama. In essense, she is saying that very young children recognize and use many languages to express their drama, including speech, intonation, gesture, use of props, etc.

Wolf reports that the ability to provide the actor's unique interpretation of a script in the form of nuances of voice and gesture which add to and/or enhance the playwright's meaning does not occur in improvised socio-dramatic play but occurs only when this talent is "urged into existance" as children perform scripted works in elementary schools.  Both Gardner and Wolf appear to infer that beyond socio-dramatic play, the child should move to formal play production, a theory which would be questioned by many creative drama teachers today.  Both seem unaware of the work of creative drama teachers who guide children beyond dramatic play into improvised playmaking before introducing them to interpreting the scripts of others.

Wolf then offers an extended analysis of metaphors, concertizations and interpretations needed to act in scripts such as "Hamlet", or "Nicholas Nicholby", and then applies this to a description of 10 year olds working on a production of "The Mikado".

When she discusses the linguistic imagination of the playwright, Wolf first differentiates between storytelling and playwrighting as two kinds of language play - dramatic and narrative. The creative drama scholar will note that Wolf's description of dramatic play and replica play come very close to the descriptions of personal and projected play which Peter Slade wrote about in his book, Child Drama, in 1954.

Wolf reports that children engaging in socio-dramatic play or acting out something with their whole bodies, they use present tense dialogue, whereas when they use replica play, they tend to narrate and use past tense when they talk

xxv

about other persons. Thus, by kindergarten, children can distinguish between storytelling and playmaking, or playwrighting and acting.

Wolf believes that elementary school age actors are capable of creating a complete dramatic moment. During this period of development, they are interested in making their portrayals as "realistic" and "right" as possible. By adolescence they are able to make concrete their individual interpretations of the dramatic moment. In describing this development, she cautions that actors and playwrights will continue to refine abilities developed in childhood throught their career.

Virginia Glascow Koste offers another perspective of the infinitely complicated dramatic play of young children, proposing that we develop a new way of thinking about a process which is centered on the mental act of transformation which she calls "meta-thinking."

Jonathan Levy responds by reaffirming that dramatic intelligence is difficult to observe and measure and that the essential part of it is "double version," or simultaneously "doing and being seen doing." He then describes his experience as part of a curriculum development project with the Lincoln Center.

For the reader who choses to read all of the contributions in this book, two points become clear. First, the process of creating drama is a very complicated process, not easily understood or studied. Research in the field is still in its infancy, waiting to develop sound walking legs and a language of thinking which can be accepted by all. Second, there are an infinite number of perspectives or ways of looking at creative drama. Any approach could lead to research which might lend new insights into the nature of creative drama. Each perspective can open up a different way of approaching the study of creative drama.

This publication is offered both as a record of historical events in the history of the Children's Theatre Association of America, and as resource material for those interested in learning more about drama and its relation to education who were unable to attend the symposia.

The reader is invited to study, ponder, wonder, enjoy, question, or argue with the writers as they present their interesting and provocative views.

# REFERENCES

Kennedy, Carol Jean, Child Drama. A selected and annotated bibliography 1974-79 Washington, D.C.: Children's Theatre Association of America, 1981.

Fordyce, Rachel. Children's Theatre and Creative Dramatics. An Annotated Bibliography of Critical Works. Boston: G.K. Hall, 1975.

Klock, Mary E. Creative Drama. A selected and Annotated Bibliography Washington, D.C.: Children's Theatre Association of America, 1975.

Davis, Jed H. and Tom Behm, "Terminology of Drama/Theatre with and for Children: A Redeinition, "Children's Theatre Review, Vol. XXVII, Number 1, 1978, p.10.

Slade, Peter, Child Drama, London: Hodder and Stoughton, 1976.

Topping, Mary, "Artists in Schools Program Evaluation Report," ERIC document #ED213 643. August, 1981.

PART I

DRAMA AND LEARNING

JUST PRETEND:
EXPLORATIONS OF THE USE OF PRETEND PLAY IN
TEACHING HANDICAPPED AND EMOTIONALLY
DISTURBED CHILDREN
by
O. Weininger

To eavesdrop on even the simplest forms of children's cooperative 'pretend' play is to enter a world of delicate and complex imagination and social interaction. A few scraps of 'pretend' dialogue will suggest the basic characteristics of this form of play. First, we note the necessary mutual recognition that literalness will be suspended:

Boy 1: "I've got the map."

Boy 2: "You do?"

Boy 1: "No, just pretend."

Boy 2: "Okay."

Or we may be able to trace a more gradual accommodation of one imagination to another as the play project takes shape--as in this rational 'checking' on the pretend reality which allows the second child to enter the first's play world without disrupting its delicate equilibrium:

Child 1: "I'm looking into this magnifying glass and I see a giant bug."

Child 2: "You can?"

Child 1: "Only for pretend."

Child 2: "Let me see."

Child 1: "You have to look hard."

Child 2: "I'll see it."

Child 1: "Okay."

Child 2: "Oh yeah, I see it. It's really big."

A slightly longer example indicates the often complex interaction of the children's individual contributions to the pretend world they are defining together, the adjustments of individual interests, egos, and senses of what is 'correct' involved in the choosing and enacting of roles:

Girl 1: "Okay, you pretend you call me on the telephone to order a lot of ice cream."

Girl 2: "Who am I?"

Girl 1: "You be the mommy and I'll be the store clerk.

Girl 2: "I'm not playing."

Girl 1: "Let's pretend we go to the movies."

Girl 2: "I like the movies."

Girl 1: "Who would you like to be?"

Girl 2: "I'll pretend to be the big sister."

Girl 1: "I'll pretend to be her friend."

Girl 2: "Okay, let's go."

Girl 1: "You call me on the telephone."

Girl 2: "I'm going to ring your door bell, because I'm already at your house."

Girl 1: "Okay, let's go to the movies."

Girl 2: "You have to wait for me to ring the bell."

Girl 1: "Okay."

The initial defining stages of cooperative 'pretending' suggest something of a nature of that most elaborate form pretend play, socio-dramatic play and the ways in which it may reflect, consolidate, or advance children's development. First of all, to pretend involves the recognition of a basic distinction between fantasy and reality: children let each other know when they are playing and when they are not.

Through this form of play the child learns to perform complex activities within an essentially abstract structure. He learns to transpose rules from one situation to another, to communicate and co-operate in a genuinely reciprocal fashion. He must listen and respond in ways which are appropriate to the pretend game as well as his own imaginative, other, needs. He must take turns and observe the agreed-upon rules of the dramatic role-playing--if one partner departs from the rules, the other may have to correct him and the negligent one usually accepts the correction. At the same time, both are involved in a peculiarly creative partnership which is predicated upon the ability both to express and perceive the subtle clues necessary for the flexible and often rapid development of the play interaction.

Observation and research have taught us a considerable amount about the characteristics of cooperative pretending in childhood. What we are just beginning to do is to investigate fully the relationship of this sort of play to children's cognitive, linguistic, and social development and the efficacy of pretend play as a mode of learning. Over the past couple of years, I have been involved in a series of pilot studies which explore the use of pretend play in the classroom with handicapped and emotionally disturbed children. In the paper I will be discussing some of this work and its implications in relation to certain research on sociodramatic play.

Generally, the developmental position is that the symbolic transformations of literal objects or activities involved in 'pretending' represent a higher level of play than do sensory motor or functional behaviours (Rubin, 1980). The ability to act in what has been called the 'as if' mode of behaviour (Weininger, 1979, Garvey, 1977, Christie, 1982) appears to reflect a change in representational thought which allows the child to substitute one thing for another--a cup for a hat, or a boat, for example (Piaget, 1962, 1966). This process has also been related to the ability to abstract through language; thus

5

Vygotsky (1976) suggested, for example, that the object which is being substituted serves as a 'pivot' which permits the child to shift from the play thing as an 'object of action' to 'things as objects of thought.' Piaget noted that as the child grows older there is an increase in more mature forms of pretend play, ranging from solitary symbolic play with toys or objects to the collective symbolism of sociodramatic play which begins to emerge in the latter part of the third year. Certainly, the flowering of this most complex form of pretend play at about age five, does seem to coincide with a period of major cognitive, linguistic, and social advance for normal children.

Clearly, the most complex forms of pretend play exist in relation to a continuum of pretending or pretend-like actions which begins much earlier. Christie (1982) has recently provided a useful outline of types of pretend play, ranging from early solitary imaginative play--pretending to be sad or asleep or to be a horse or a car, through play which involves object-substitution, through tnematic fantasy play in which children act out a particular story, be it Three Billy Goats Gruff or Star Wars, to sociodramatic play where they take on the roles of other people, attempting to recreate through their own interpretation, real life situations. This outline, of course, leaves out some perhaps related pretend activities--daydreaming, for example, or play with an imaginary companion, and it may also fail to consider possible roots of pretend behaviour much earlier in the child's life.

Thus, for example, as we recognize that one of the commonest early forms of sociodramatic play is the mother-daddy-baby scenario, so we can also observe a real baby of not more than 6 or 8 months of age trying to 'feed mother.' It is almost as if the baby were playing at being the mother. In psychoanalytical terms, we can see this momentary role playing as representing the baby's unconscious effort to return something to the mother, as well as to understand the relationship of giving and taking which exists between two people (Klein, 1975). To call this 'pretending' in the full sense is, of course, to beg the question of intention and also to fly in the face of conventional developmental wisdom which would argue that children have to master the spatial physical development essential to coordination before they can enact symbolic representations (e.g., Fein, 1979). There is no question that the young child of 6 months of age has difficulty coordinating his actions but nevertheless many of us have seen such a young child trying to push something into the mother's mouth, missing at times and hitting her nose, but still trying in his own way to return or give something to the mother. While this action is of course not detached from the real life situation, that of mother-feeding-baby, it still forms for me a rudimentary picture of the earliest origins of pretend play--an experimentation with roles in order to understand the world and one's place in it, which is associated with strong feelings and emotional needs. It is the you-are-form of that pattern of family pretend play which will continue with dolls, or objects which the child treats as people in interaction, from as early as two years of age.

While the child is making his or her earliest experiments with pretending, he or she is also simultaneously involved in sensory motor play--learning how to make use of the object and direct its movement--an exploratory play--finding out what the object is, what it can do or have done to it. Gradually as substitutions are made the play becomes more symbolic and more encompassing of the child's energies and time. The objects that are used in pretend play become less and less similar to things in real life situations and emotionally the child can use the semblance of an object or pantomime gestures in the absence of the physical object to display what he wants or is doing.

Pretend play in the beginning is largely solitary behaviour; at times, parents can participate and even organize it, but usually children under 3 do not share pretend activities with one another. They may play at pretend activities in a parallel way, but there is very little genuinely cooperative behaviour. At about 3 years of age roles and role relationships become shared and a kind of collective symbolism of pretend play emerges. The child will verbally announce

7

the onset of a particular pretend play and the children start to play and talk in an "as if" mode of behaviour. They understand the word pretend by about four years of age (Macnamara, Baker & Olson, 1976) and can also describe their own pretend games (Singer, 1973). Children seem to manage their collective symbolic play through a variety of verbal and non-verbal communications by gesture, by statements, by pointing to objects. By about the age 5 they become involved in very intricate systems of reciprocal roles with ingenuous improvisations of materials and the plots of their play become increasingly elaborated into social role play.

While the basic outline of the emergence of specific types of pretend play is, then, fairly clear, its precise relationships to individual character and specific aspects of development is somewhat more difficult to formulate. There is some evidence that pretend play is related to creativity. Divergent thinking is correlated with pretend play (Hutt and Bhavnani, 1976, Johnson, 1976). Schaefer (1969) reported that adolescents who talked of having imaginary playmates during their childhood achieved higher on creativity tests. This form of play may also be correlated with certain cognitive skills (Johnson, 1976; Rubin and Maioni, 1975). One study indicates that children who engage in high levels of solitary goal directed activity and children who play with objects in a pretend fashion do better when asked to solve problems involving these objects (Moore, Evertson & Brophy, 1974). It also seems clear that a strong preference for pretend play is likely to reflect a more imaginative inner life. Thus, for example, "children who engage in overt pretend behaviour are likely to have an imaginary companion and boys who play this way are likely to daydream and withdraw from social activities" (Fein, 1981a, p. 1104). "Since pretend play is also related to waiting patiently in a boring situation (Singer, 1961), it may be that this form of play reflects a general disposition which can be expressed in either overt behaviour or internal fantasies and daydreams" (Fein, 1981a, p. 1104). What research there is on the subject tends to suggest that the ability to engage in pretend play may reflect "a disposition related to flexibility in a variety of social and non-social situations" (Fein, 1981a, p. 1104).

Generally the research seems to indicate that sociodramatic play is related to positive social development. When children are engaged in pretend play they are likely to be more co-operative, more communicative, and are willing to accept reinforcement from their peers (Charlesworth & Hartup, 1967, Marshall, 1961).

Studies of children's behaviour in freeplay settings report positive correlations between dramatic play and performance on role-taking tasks (Rubin, 1976, Rubin & Maioni, 1975), measures of a general people orientation (Jennings, 1975), cooperation with adults and peers (Singer, 1979), friendliness and popularity with peers (Marshall, 1961, Marshall & Doshi, 1965, Rubin & Maioni, 1975), general adjustment (Bach, 1945) and the use of language during play (Marshall, 1961, Singer, 1979) (Fein, 1981a, p. 1103).

By the same token children who play at a functional level appear as less popular with peers and, interestingly, their scores on a task of spatial and social role taking are lower (Rubin & Maioni, 1975). However the cooperative effort of sociodramatic play does not exclude the expression of aggression (Biblow, 1973, Marshall, 1961). Marshall notes that real hostility is infrequently demonstrated; more usually it is accommodated to the realm of pretend and children who engage in imaginative play tend to demonstrate less aggressive behaviour even when they are not playing or interacting socially (Singer & Singer, 1976). Generally then, "pretend play seems to reflect a pattern of positive social behaviour rather than the absence of negative behaviour" (Fein, 1981a, p. 1104).

The considerable increase in the frequency and complexity of pretend play in the earliest school years clearly coincides with the child's emergence as a social being. Thus Rubin (1976, 1978) and Singer (1973), indicate that pretend play occupies about 10 to 17% of the time in preschool group and it increases to approximately 33% when the children reach kindergarten.

9

Eifermann (1971) sees pretend play as peaking in the first and second grade and with an abrupt decline after this point. It may be, as Piaget suggests, that such a decline reflects the passing of a necessary cognitive stage and that the emerging imaginative and cooperative energies expressed in the initial outpouring are in turn channelled into more conventional forms of creativity and social behaviour. However, the difficulties of assessing the extent and importance of pretend play are also intensified by its very association with the child's emerging sense of his independence from adult control, tutelage, or even observation. Thus, for example, several studies note the fairly small proportion of time apparently devoted to pretend play, as opposed to other forms--Smilansky (1968) for example suggests that only 3% of middle class kindergarten children play in a pretend style. However, as any parent knows, both solitary and social pretend play tend to flourish in the absence of observers, and often in settings where the imagination is stimulated by the unfamiliar or by a determination to avoid being bored by the all too familiar--the rainy day syndrome. Environment seems to be important to social play and may encourage or limit it in a variety of ways. Unhappily, the school classroom where most researchers tend to do their observing, is often the last place any self-respecting child would be caught pretending!

Nonetheless, both the clearly complex association between pretend play and development and the awareness of the crucial effect of environment have encouraged a considerable amount of research on the efficacy of 'training' for pretend play in the classroom. Experiments with such training methods have emphasized their value and their limitations. It appears, for example, that neither toys alone (Feitelson & Ross, 1973) nor extra playing time with peers (Fink, 1976) in themselves encourage pretend play. On the other hand, several studies have found that adult-directed activities such as "a televised adult demonstrating pretend play or an adult verbally teaching pretend themes, providing construction activities or enriched real life experiences, reading fantasy stories, or teaching music does not produce positive effects" (Fein, 1981a, p. 1107).

On several limited measures, training in pretend play has been found to have beneficial effects:

Training may improve performance on tests of conservation (Golomb & Cornelius, 1977), picture sequencing (Saltz & Johnson, 1974), I.Q. (Saltz & Johnson, 1974, Saltz, Dixon & Johnson, 1977), language skills (Lovinger, 1974). A provocative finding is that training enhances impulse control in dull situations (Saltz & Johnson, 1974, Saltz, Dixon & Johnson, 1977), a finding in keeping with correlational studies (Singer, 1961) and the notion that pretense may serve an arousal maintaining function (Fein, 1981b) (Fein, 1981a, p. 1110).

An ability to play in the 'as-if' mode seems to intensify the generally beneficial effects of freedom to explore objects through play on problem solving (Sylva, 1977). An interesting paper by Yawkey and Fox which was presented in 1983 at the Biennial Meeting of the Society for Research and Child Development indicates that classroom emphasis on a program of real-life-based sociodramatic play had a significant effect on the cognitive academic ability of six year olds--resulting in an increase in total readiness scores as well as scores on auditory blending, perception, story comprehension, verbal memory. By the same token, in some cases training may not be effective or it may be more difficult--as found by Nahme-Huang, Singer, Singer & Wheaton (1977)--with emotionally disturbed children, or as Smilansky (1968) noted with children under 4 years of age (Fein, 1981). And it appears that the beneficial effects achieved are not easily transferable to peers (Fink, 1976, Saltz, Dixon & Johnson, 1977). However, there seems to be fairly wide agreement on the basic value of the cooperative imaginative effort involved in the use of story- or role-enactment as a form of training which extends the child's perspective on himself and others (Fein, 1978, Rubin & Pepler, 1979) and is consistently associated in the research literature with "reduction of egocen-

11

tricity (Van den Daele, 1970), and with improvements in perspective taking (Iannotti, 1978, Rose, 1974, Saltz, et al, 1977, Smith & Syddall, 1978) and cooperative social problem solving (Rose, 1974, Shores, Huster & Strain, 1976, Spivack & Shure, 1974, Strain & Wiegernik, 1976) (Fein, 1981a, p. 1110).

Obviously, we need to be very careful in applying methods of 'training' to so delicate and complex an experience as social dramatic play even for normal children. But it does seem to me that the opportunity for such potentially enriching play is part of what the classroom as a truly 'enabling environment' can offer even those children who are not likely to be considered appropriate 'subjects' for 'training' but who may in fact need it most (Nahme-Huang, Singer, Singer & Wheaton, 1977). By exploring the world of 'pretend' to the limit of their abilities, handicapped and emotionally disturbed children may learn to feel safe with play, may take chances, practice their competencies, and build up their self esteem as they increase knowledge of themselves and others. In the studies which I am about to describe we put this conviction to the test of experience, with some interesting results.

Two of our early pilot studies made use of a story-telling method as an encouragement for dramatic play in the classroom. In the first study we worked with a group of six-year and seven-year old multiply-handicapped children, in the second with three- and four-year-old children who were seriously emotionally disturbed.

The children in the first group had at least two handicaps, one of which was below-average cognitive ability and the other usually a physical handicap such as a congenital birth defect-- micro- or hydrocephalus, or Down's syndrome--or other form of brain damage--cerebral palsy, for example. These children had all experienced various other types of schooling-- nursery schools, special schools, or hospital classes-- before entering this multiply-handicapped classroom. They also all came from non-English speaking homes, while the language of the classroom was English. When we started to work with this group in January they had been together in the classroom with the same teacher since September.

12

These children had some speech facility but
there was difficulty in understanding their
language. They tended to use constricted speech
or else remain mute, except for grunts and
occasional perserverative verbalizations. They
were always on the go, often behaving in a
bizarre manner. They were easily upset, unable
to tolerate frustration and apparently had very
little motivation to succeed at a task independently. The children rarely played with each
other and their dependence on the teacher was
stereotyped and perseverative: they asked him
the same questions and showed him the same toys,
over and over. There was a good deal of aggression in this classroom--a lot of hitting, shriek-
ing, and tantrums.

Over a five-week period we gradually
involved these seemingly intractable children in
a rudimentary form of dramatic play based on the
Three Billy Goats Gruff story. Without going
into details of the procedure here, the sequence
was roughly this: the children had the story
read to them, then used small real objects like
goats, a bridge, a hill to play with while the
story was being read out, and finally they
enacted the roles themselves.

This experience of focusing on a sequence of
dramatic play had observable effects on the
children in both specific and general ways. The
children who were hyperactive were now sitting
still for as long as 30 minutes. Language was
increased: the children spoke to each other and
used words from the story--'big,' 'terrible,'
'troll,' 'goat,' 'bridge,' 'over,' 'hills' etc.--
as part of their everyday vocabulary. Their
communication with both peers and teacher
increased. They became more cooperative, even
making attempts to help each other without
aggressiveness. The children's movements were of
course still awkward, but somewhat less bizarre.
Their behaviour generally seemed more purposeful
and meaningful and they were able to concentrate
sufficiently on a project to try to make scrap-
books with drawings related to the Billy Goats
Gruff story.

While these children continued to look to
their teacher to help them start work, they

showed more confidence in trying to do things. They seemed less upset and although at times they cried, sulked, or had temper-tantrums, their thinking processes seemed more connected, not simply a clanging of random ideas. According to the teacher, the children seemed to become generally more responsive, more communicative and more interested in doing things and two months after the experiment they still seemed to have benefitted from the experience.

In our second pilot study we worked with a group of five seriously emotionally disturbed children between the ages of 3 and 4 in a day-treatment centre. These children were involved in essentially the same sequence of Billy Goats Gruff play as the former group, but in this case over a two-month period. The teacher told the story three times a week, usually at the same time and with the children gathered around the same round table. The children not only sat still for the story but sometimes asked that it be repeated. In addition to the same objects used in the first study, we also gave the children plasticene and construction material to help enact the story and finally a felt board on which they mounted cut-out felt figures of the goats and scenery. This somewhat more elaborate sequence also culminated in a total enactment of the play with the children accepting and playing out the dramatic roles.

The behavioural changes that we observed in this group were increased cooperative play, increased attentiveness to the teacher and increased language use and communication. Again, the children were now using the words of the story as part of their own vocabularies. There was an increase in sociodramatic play generally in the classroom--many different social 'pretend' plays began to appear of the mother-father-baby variety. There was also a significant decrease in disruptive behaviour and hyperactivity. The children showed more contact with reality and were even able to form a group. They now played together in ways hardly to be expected of normal 4-year-olds, let alone severely disturbed ones. After three months the teacher reported that the children were still showing the benefits of the experiment in dramatic play.

These two pilot studies serve at least to indicate some of the ways in which dramatic play may influence linguistic, cognitive, and interactional processes even in children we might normally expect would not register significant benefits. There is of course a great deal more that has to be done before we can say with any certainty that this sort of dramatic play does really help such children. As far as I know, there is little or no research which makes long term use of pretend play in working with physically or emotionally handicapped children (Strain & Wiegernik, 1976, Nahme-Huang et al, 1977). This is, in a sense, understandable for such children, particularly the emotionally disturbed, usually have to be helped to learn to play in normal ways at all. The characteristic 'play' of the emotionally disturbed child tends to be rigid and inflexible; he is likely to be unresponsive or unable to make use of even the simplist materials presented to him in the classroom. It would be absurd to expect such a child simply to 'start playing' in the complex, interactive pretend mode, even with help. But our pilot studies suggest that there is a real ability to respond to a simple 'pretend' structure even where we might least expect it. For such children a basic form of pretend play, gradually entered into with the teacher's encouragement, seems to offer opportunities for language use, and for the practice of discriminative listening and recall and rehearsal strategies and a structure within which they can increase and refine their repertoire of fine and gross motor actions. It also allows them to help create and interact within a rudimentary social situation where they can think, act, and talk with each other with a degree of pleasure, confidence, and safety which may be of considerable importance to their fragile self-esteem as well as to the development of specific skills.

In our most recent project we set out to be a bit more systematic in exploring the possible value of pretend play for emotionally disturbed children. This study examines a group of four seriously emotionally disturbed children ranging in age from 4 to 5 years and compares them with a control group of five similarly disturbed children observed at the same time who were taught by a similarly experienced teacher but were not involved in a pretend play project. The children in both groups were diagnosed as seriously emotionally disturbed and functioning within the borderline intellectual range. The entire work was conducted by observation and supplemented in the case of the experimental group by analysis of stories dictated to the teacher by the children in the course of their pretend play project and by discussion with the teacher once a week for approximately one hour to gather her observations and gain a sense of her attitude towards the children. Confirmation of these observations was also obtained through other teachers and therapists at the same institution.

The children in the control group were diagnosed as suffering from such problems as hyperactivity, hyperaggressiveness, and schizophrenia and observation of their behaviour revealed comparable classroom difficulties in the two groups. The children in the experimental group displayed a variety of behavioural difficulties. One little boy had been diagnosed earlier as schizophrenic. His behaviour was erratic and jumpy; he tended to wander about the classroom shaking his hands in front of his face, talking in a kind of gibberish. He would look at things in the classroom, touch them and then move on and was unable to play with toys in anything like a sustained fashion. The second child was hyperactive, flitting from chair to chair, with an extremely short attention span. He seemed unable to accept direction; apparently hearing only fragments of the teacher's instructions, he would go to do something, make mistakes and then get very angry, becoming extremely disruptive and physically and verbally abusive. The third child was perceptually handicapped with a low frustration tolerance, unable to relate to adults or peers; he showed serious temper outbursts and refused to do anything asked of him. His language was difficult to understand; he lisped, stuttered, and repeated what he was saying, and generally showed a high degree of anxiety. The fourth child was a very aggressive child with an exceptionally poor home life where he had been abused both by grandparents and parents. This little boy also had an exceptionally low frustration tolerance and generally showed hyper

16

behaviour. His speech was very difficult to understand; he was non-social, playing by himself, usually by removing toys and dumping them on the floor.

The children were all given a psychological examination and showed serious emotional difficulties along with the apparently borderline intellectual functioning often expected in such cases. On examination they would refuse to answer questions or look blankly at the examiner and generally showed the kind of non-cooperation, hyperactivity, and high distractability characteristic of disturbed children.

Working with their teacher, we were able to observe the baseline of these children's functioning a little more clearly. As expected, they showed an extremely poor level of cognitive skill and were functioning at about the 1 to 2 year-old level cognitively. Their language productions were very limited, generally at the 2 year-old level. These children rarely played with each other, they exhibited a great deal of hostile behaviour. They were easily upset and when frustrated in any way tended to behave aggressively towards their peers, the teacher, or objects in the room. While the children were very dependent upon the teacher they would become very angry and upset when the teacher tried to help them. Their typical behaviour was to cry and scream and have temper outbursts. The children were totally inconsiderate, if not perhaps unconcerned, about the other children in the group and generally showed extremely poor motivation to succeed or accomplish any tasks. Rather they tended to wander around the classroom touching or showing things in a desultory fashion, or to alternate between withdrawn blank inattention and hostile acting out with much screaming and swearing. Generally, their behaviour reflected a very fragile ego structure; that is, it did not appear that they were fully aware of their own behaviour nor were they capable of controlling it by any rational means.

Understandably then the children showed poor reality testing: it was difficult for them to understand what was happening inside them as compared to outer stimuli. They had very little

17

capacity to orient themselves in terms of time or to understand external events: telling them about what was going to happen in a few minutes seemed to be a useless exercise. Their judgments were inappropriate, they had difficulty anticipating dangers or disapproval, they seemed to act as though nothing happened to them from the outside world. As their sense of reality of the world was extremely poor so their sense of self was inadequate. They did not have a sense of uniqueness or a sense of self esteem. Unable to understand their own internal feelings, they had poor regulation and control of their drives and impulses; they were unable to delay or control their feelings, their interpersonal relationships were poor, characterized by anxiety and hostility, and they could not sustain a relationship over even a short period of time.

In psychological terms, the defensive functioning of these children reflected primitive attempts at projection of hostility as a defense against a dependency which is both needed yet feared. In pedagogical terms, their thought processes were inadequate: they could not concentrate or anticipate, their attention span was poor, their language was inadequate and their memory and ability to formulate concepts were immature. While they had difficulty learning routines, they seemed to be able to repeat ideas but with little real impact on their functioning. They seemed unable to achieve any sense of competence either as individuals or as pupils in a kindergarten classroom.

We started to work with these children early in the school year, in October, using a very simple form of pretend play which drew on one of the few interests the children had already demonstrated -- playing with toy cars. We knew that the children were attracted by the cars, that they would move them about--perhaps on their wheels, perhaps on their roofs--but at least we could start from the certainty that the children would push the cars. This activity then gave them an opportunity to enter pretend play on their own terms with some sense of independence and genuine interest and without too much controlling pressure from another person. At the same time we associated this rudimentary play with a controlled and regular group setting at the beginning of each school day. We made use of a small room, approximately 6' x 7', with a one-way mirror for observation, where the children sat around a small table every morning, each with a car which he was able to push as he liked on the table. The children also had a snack of cereal before returning to their larger classroom. By associating their 'normal' noisy and eccentric car-play with both a controlled routine of shared activity and with food, we felt that the children might begin to see self-expression through play as a potentially constructive, not merely hostile or egocentric action, linked to reward, not as was usual to punishment or upset.

The children's morning activity, then, always followed the same routine, which I observed once a week throughout the period of the experiment. The children were brought into the small room, provided with the cars, then the cereal, and helped to push the cars along with table top. After this activity had been going on for one month, we introduced a large piece of bristol board paper so that now the children were running their small cars over bristol board. The children did not seem to be upset by the introduction of something new, but continued to run the cars over the bristol board, eat their cereal and seemed quite contented. They remained in the small room for approximately an hour after which time they were then allowed to go into the large room where there were more toys available and the activities were less structured but still under the direction of the same teacher.

After a week of running the cars across the bristol board, the routine changed so that the food was introduced first and then along with food the teacher talked to the children about their bus trip to the school and tried to help them to talk about their experiences on the bus. After the children finished their snack (which took about 5 minutes), the cars were introduced along with the bristol board. At this point the children were provided with crayons and the teacher demonstrated how the crayons could make a mark along the bristol board, suggesting that the children could make a road on which they could drive the car. This became a more organized aspect of their pretend play. The children eagerly took to this idea. They made crayon marks on the bristol board and pushed their cars along the marks they had made with much scrubbing of the cars on the bristol board, and much noise. It was not difficult to see that the children were involved in a kind of purposeful task of driving their cars along the roads that they made; moreover, as they followed their own path, they were also not looking at each other and watching what the other children were doing.

We were now into the sixth and seventh week of the program and at about this point we began to observe some quite striking changes in the children's behaviour, both as individuals and as a group. First, for example, the child suffering from the perceptual disorder wrote his name, in vertical form and then by himself, changed the vertical to the horizontal. More generally, we observed an increase in cooperative behaviour and peer-interaction. The children began to show more sympathy toward each other. They were also able to share ideas, even to play together in associative cooperative play--for this group a really spectacular advance. Their language skills improved and increased and their auditory responses seemed to have improved: they were retaining more information and were able to feed it back to us in meaningful ways.

The teacher now attempted to respond to and consolidate these emerging advances within the pretend play structure. Since the children were already using the crayons and driving their cars along the marks, she introduced the idea that they were making a map together and encouraged them to talk about where they were driving their cars on this 'map.' The teacher talked about making a long road to a building and asked each child what building he would like to drive his car to. The children usually stated a name, the name of the institution that they were attending, for example, or 'school,' or 'church,' or 'home'--and so gradually the map that the children were making use of had a lot of lines on it and squares and circles representing different buildings. The children were using each other's roads now, driving to each other's buildings and talking about the car going to the school, the house, the church, etc. At about this point the children were not only looking at each other as they played, but saying things to each other the approximately 20 minutes they were involved in this pretend play. The teacher then introduced the idea of saying what they had done before they left the small room for the larger classroom. The children were now encouraged to verablize the pretend play. They said that they were making the car go to the school, that the car was fast; they formulated questions such as 'how does the car go?' and so on. To all of these remarks the teacher responded as she saw fit, participating in their speech, indirectly helping to extend their vocabularies and generally communicating in a dialogue style with them.

At about the eighth week, we added plasticene and popsicle sticks to the play materials, and the children with the teacher's help now made 'stop signs' by sticking a popsicle stick in a blob of plasticene, built 'bridges' for the cars to go over by placing popsicle sticks along blobs of plasticene. The children talked about these additions to the map, then constructed their own stop signs and bridges, and also made walls and people out of the plasticene and popsicle sticks. Interestingly, now that the activity has been going on for 2 months--and remember this was going on every day first thing in the morning-- the children were now not only looking at each other but were talking about what they were doing and even at times laughing. They stayed in the room now for approximately 30 minutes and showed no great desire to run out of the room or behave in the kind of 'hyper' style that had characterized their early forms of 'play' in September.

In the next part of the program we introduced masking tape and pieces of paper of different shapes--circles and squares and triangles--and the children were then encouraged to put these pieces of paper over the holes in the bristol board that they had made by scrubbing their cars along it. They were now able to make new maps, but were being encouraged to use the old form in an effort to provide them with a structure which was safe and also understandable to them. They were also encourged to talk about the kind of shape that they had selected.

21

Gradually, as you can see, what we were trying to do was build up a repertoire for the child in terms of language, as well as expressive feelings, essentially trying to help him formulate a sense of reality about himself and his world and both express and control his impulses and drives. We made use of the intrinsically motivating experience, that is, the use of a little car which permitted him to express aggression in a way which could be converted into constructive aggression. We continued with this mapmaking, car pushing, building with popsicle sticks, putting on pieces of paper for the next month.

When the children returned in January the same routine was followed until the children were able to feel comfortable again in the school setting and to recognize the structure that they had left following the Christmas vacation. The children were eating cereal food, then they were pushing their cars along the map that they had made, they were constructing bridges and stop signs and walls and people and talking about their play with the teacher. When the children became involved in this play, once again, we introduced another concept. We encouraged each child to make up a story about what he was doing. The child told his story after the cars and the maps and the construction material had been put away. We observed that the children's use of words had increased and their capacity to maintain some degree of attention to what they were doing had increased significantly. Following about a week of this activity, the teacher then said that she would write down the stories that they were telling her. Now, into the fourth month, the children continued to use their maps, to build with construction materials and then to tell the story of what they had done when the maps and materials had been removed. The teacher now wrote down what they had told her. What we were attempting to do now was to help them deal with the idea of memory and language usage in a meaningful way; the pretend play had acted as a kind of rehearsal strategy providing them with the opportunity of doing something which they then could talk about. The pretend play activity now lasted for approximately 45 minutes.

Now into February, which was the fifth month of this activity, the children were provided with their own booklets and the teacher suggested that they print their own stories as they told them to the teacher, who continued to write them down herself. By now their stories had progressed from single words to sentences, reflecting the children's more elaborate comprehension of what they were doing. The children were printing their stories in their own kind of pretend print. The teacher printed each of their stories and then when all four children had told and printed their story, the teacher read out each story. Into the sixth month, the teacher then suggested that the child read the story that she had printed and we were very surprised and pleased to find that the children, all four of them, wanted to 'read' and were able to do so! Interestingly, they remembered parts of what they had said and therefore they seemed to read what the teacher had printed--something that pleased them as well. Further, we noticed that while at first their printing consisted of apparently indiscrim-inate marks on the page, gradually these marks took some kind of sentence-like structure, so that the marks were made in a horizontal way across the page, one line under the other. At about the same time, we also noticed that, without any specfic encouragement, two of the children started to print their names. One boy printed his name vertically and then in about another month printed it horizontally. The other child printed his name horizontally and correctly. They asked for the letters of their name when they had some difficulty remembering letters. Another child, the schizophrenic child, began to 'pretend write' in a cursive style and was quickly imitated by the other children. At times their marks seemed more like writing then at other times, but they showed no boredom or hostility at being involved in this task. The children were now reading their names, reading words like "and," "to," the names of other children, the names of favourite characters like E. T. They were interested in what they were doing, and were able to sustain their interest in the pretend play they had developed with their teacher for a period of 60 minutes before going into their larger classroom.

In addition to the specific interests in 'writing' and 'reading' and the considerable improvement in linguistic processes which we have already mentioned, we observed that the children's sense of themselves as individuals seemed much improved as the pretend play project progressed. The withdrawn or angry state we had remarked earlier was noticeably absent. The children seemed more in control of their feelings and impulses and their manifest behaviour was more appropriate to the situation. Their judgment and their awareness of the consequences of behaviour increased markedly. Children who had seemed incapable of sustained activity were able to pay attention, concentrate, and remember. They really wanted to accomplish what they were doing and their interpersonal relationships had improved remarkably. Their anxiety and hostility had decreased greatly; they were talking to each other and were able to sustain a play relationship over the period that they were in the small room. While they still blamed each other for any problems and continued to be quite defensive about what they were doing, they nevertheless were able to interact in more than hostile ways, to look at each other as examples, not merely potential adversaries.

When the children left the small room and went into the larger room, there was a transfer of this kind of activity and its characteristics. They were playing in cooperative ways. Their skills developed in the small room in terms of talking with each other had improved and was maintained in the larger room. They were using more information, information that they had acquired through the pretend play and now were using it in meaningful ways in their other play. Words were more appropriately used. Certainly they still became angry and still swore but nevertheless their language skills had increased remarkably. Their spatial capacity, their fine motor movements, their short term and long term memory had improved. Their aggressiveness had decreased. Their behaviour, now after 7 months of this pretend play appeared more purposeful and meaningful. They looked at the teacher as someone who was a resource to help them play and they allowed others to participate with them.

24

We hope that these developments will be reinforced and consolidated in the children's school experience next year. One of the children in this group will be enrolled in a public school system in a regular kindergarten, another will also be in a kindergarten with a special withdrawal remedial program. A third child--the schizophrenic--has been accepted for a full day program in a day care centre. And the fourth child, who comes from the exceptionally deprived and abusive home, will be attending school at a psychiatric institute where the parents will also be involved in supportive therapy.

Our observations of the children in the control group point up the very real achievements of the experimental children. The control group children still play in an isolated way, show poor ego-function and inappropriate judgment. Changes that one might expect as a result of maturation or the general social experience of the classroom have not occurred in these disturbed children. They have very poor control over their drives, their impulses, and their interpersonal relationships are immature and at times non-existent. These children have difficulty concentrating and their memory and their language skills seem to be at about the same level that they were at the beginning of term. They do not show any motivation for mastery, but rather flit from one thing to another. Essentially then, these children have not shown the kind of growth that the children in the experimental group have. These children are still having difficulty and if one would expect simply time, maturation, and sensitive and experienced care to have taken care of these programs, they have not.

Basically, the primary difference between these two groups was that one was involved in the pretend play I have described, while the other was not. The teachers are of comparable skill and ability and all the children's other activities are similar. No attempt was made to deprive the children in the control group of experiences and if their teacher wanted to ask the researcher any questions about her children, they were welcomed and answered. The crucial difference seems to consist of the regular and sensitive use of a pretend play program that appears to have mediated emotional and then cognitive growth.

There is some evidence that the children in the second pilot group maintained their emotional growth and development over the summer. When these children returned to the center and to the same teacher, they continued to make use of the skills they had acquired earlier in that year. Their play was more elaborate, they continued to be involved in role playing the functions of mothers, fathers, and babies, they continued to use different kinds of materials in their play, they continued to be interested in what was going on around them, asking questions and behaving quite differently than the teacher had expected from her experiences of having children return after their summer vacation.

Certainly this form of pretend play is different from the pretend play described by others (Smilanksy, 1968, Garvey, 1977, Saltz & Johnson, 1974), but it does embody some of the characteristics. The children play with materials, and they are helped to develop a theme. However, there are some dramatic differences. The pretend play described above has a particular beginning in the intrinsic motivated play of the child. The teacher, as a resource person builds upon this adding on the play as the child is ready to accept and use these additions. Some may wish to argue that it is the structure of the play that provided for the observed growth in the children. They may argue that confining the child in a small room and providing a limited number of toys and materials is not play, but tutoring. However, I would argue that since these children did not seem to know how to play, we had to structure a situation which would allow them to do so without further damaging or imposing upon a fragile ego. We limited the materials to not occasion chaotic use of the materials, we provided a framework so the children could feel as 'safe' as they could without the influx of excess anxiety which is as we know so disruptive. By providing this framework, we helped the children play--and their play was pretend play--for they talked about "going to the church," or "to the school" and made all the motions with the car to do so. We helped them by extending their play as I do with normal children (Weininger, 1979) and their pretend play became more elaborate. They made things to go along the road they created. In my way of thinking this is pretend play--it is bringing the unknown dangerous outside world into the safety of the structure and finding out what happens when you recreate the experience.

# REFERENCES

Bach, G. S. Young children's play fantasies. Psychological Monographs, 1945, 59, No. 2, 1-69.

Biblow, E. Imaginative play and the control of aggressive behavior. In J. L. Singer (Ed.), The child's world of make-believe: experimental studies of imaginative play. New York: Academic Press, 1973.

Charlesworth, R. & Hartup, W. W. Positive social reinforcement in the nursery school peer group. Child Development, 1967, 38, 993-1002.

Christie, J. F. Play training strategies. Canadian Journal of Early Childhood Education, 1982, 2(2), 47-52.

Eifermann, R. R. Social play in childhood. In R. E. Herron & B. Sutton-Smith (Eds.), Child's play. New York: Wiley, 1971.

Fein, G. G. Play revisited. In M. Lamb (Ed.), Social and personality development. New York: Holt, Rinehart & Winston, 1978.

Fein, G. G. Play and the acquisition of symbols. In L. Katz (Ed.), Current topics in early childhood. Norwood, N. J.: Ablex, 1979.

Fein, G. G. Pretend play in childhood: An integrative review. Child Development, 1981a, 52, 1095-1118.

Fein, G. G. The physical environment: stimulation or evocation? In R. Lerner & N. Busch (Eds.), Individuals as producers of their own development: a life-span perspective. New York: Academic Press, 1981b.

Feitelson, D. & Ross, G. S. The neglected factor--play. Human Development, 1973, 16, 202-223.

Fink, R. S. Role of imaginative play in
cognitive development. Psychological
Reports, 1976, 39, 895-906.

Garvey, C. Play. Cambridge, Mass.: Harvard
University Press, 1977.

Golomb, C. & Cornelius, C. B. Symbolic play and
its cognitive significance. Developmental
Psychology, 1977, 13, 246-252.

Hutt, C. & Bhavanani, R. Predications from
play. In Jr. Bruner, A. Jolley & K. Sylva
(Eds.), Play: its role in development and
evolution. New York: Basic Books, 1976.

Iannotti, R. J. Effects of role-taking experience on role-taking, empathy altruism and
aggression. Developmental Psychology, 1978,
14, 119-124.

Jennings, K. D. People versus object orientation, social behavior, and intellectual
abilities in preschool children. Developmental Psychology, 1975, 11, 511-519.

Johnson, J. E. Relations of divergent thinking
and intelligence test scores with social and
nonsocial make-believe play of preschool
children. Child Development, 1976, 47,
1200-1203.

Klein, M. Love, guilt and reparation, Volume 1.
London: Hogarth Press, 1975.

Lovinger, S. L. Sociodramatic play and language
development in preschool disadvantaged
children. Psychology in Schools, 1974, 11,
313-320.

Macnamara, J., Baker, E. & Olson, C. L.
Four-year-old's understanding of pretend,
forget, and know: evidence for proposi-
tional operations. Child Development, 1976,
47, 62-70.

Marshall, H. R. Relations between home experiences and children's use of language in
play interaction with peers. Psychological
Monograph, 1961, 75, No. 5.

Marshall, H. R. & Doshi, R.   Aspects of exper-
     ience   revealed   through   doll   play   of
     preschool children.   Journal of Psychology,
     1965, 61, 47-57.

Moore, N. V., Evertson, C. M. & Brophy, J. E.
     Solitary   play:   some   functional   considera-
     tions.   Developmental Psychology, 1974, 10,
     830-834.

Nahme-Huang, L., Singer, D. G., Singer, J. L. &
     Wheaton, A. B.   Imaginative   play   training
     and   perceptual   motor   interventions   with
     emotionally disturbed hospitalized children.
     American   Journal   of   Orthopsychiatry,   1977,
     47, 238-249.

Piaget, J.   Play, dreams and imitation in child-
     hood.   New York:   Norton, 1962.

Piaget, J.   Response to Brian Sutton-Smith.
     Psychological Review, 1966, 73, 111-112.

Rosen, C. E.   The effects of sociodramatic play on
     problem-solving   behavior   among   culturally
     disadvantaged   preschool   children.   Child
     Development, 1974, 45, 920-927.

Rubin, K. H. & Maioni, T. L.   Play reference and
     its   relation   to   egocentricism,   popularity,
     and   classification   skills   in   preschool.
     Merrill-Palmer Quarterly, 1975, 21, 171-179.

Rubin, K. H.   The relationship of social play
     reference to role taking skills in preschool
     children.   Psychological Reports, 1976, 39,
     823-826.

Rubin, K. H.   Fantasy play:   its role in the
     development   of   social   skills   and   social
     cognition.   New   Directions   for   Child
     Development, 1980, 9, 69-84.

Rubin, K. H., Watson, K. S. & Jambor, T. W.   Free
     play behaviors in preschool and kindergarten
     children.   Child   Development,   1978,   49,
     534-536.

Rubin, K. H. & Pepler, D. J. The relationship of child's play to social-cognitive growth and development. In H. Foot, J. Smith & T. Chapman (Eds.) Friendship and childhood relationships. New York: Wiley, 1979.

Saltz, E. & Johnson, J. Training for thematic-fantasy play in culturally disadvantaged children: preliminiary results. Journal of Educational Psychology, 1974, 66, 623-630.

Saltz, E., Dixon, D. & Johnson, Jr. Training disadvantaged preschoolers on various fantasy activities: effects on cognitive functioning and impulse control. Child Development, 1977, 48, 367-380.

Schaefer, C. E. Imaginary companions and creative adolescents. Developmental Psychology, 1969, 1, 747-749.

Shores, R. E., Huster, P. & Strain, P. S. Effects of teacher presence and structured play on child-child interaction among handicapped preshool children. Psychology in the Schools, 1976, 13, 171-175.

Singer, J. L. Imagination and waiting ability in young children. Journal of Personality, 1961, 29, 396-413.

Singer, J. L. (Ed.). The child's world of make-believe: experimental studies of imaginative play. New York: Academic Press, 1973.

Singer, J. L. Affect and imagination in play and fantasy. In C. Izard (Ed.), Emotions in personality and psychopathology. New York: Plenum, 1979.

Singer, J. L. & Singer, D. G. Imaginative play and pretending in early childhood. In A. Davis (Ed.), Child Personality and Psychopathology. New York: Wiley-Interscience, 1976.

Smilanksy, S. The effects of sociodramatic play on disadvantaged children. New York: Wiley, 1968.

Smith, P. K. and Syddall, S. Play and non-play tutoring in preschool children: is it play or tutoring which matters. British Journal of Educational Psychology, 1978, 48, 315-325.

Spivack, G. & Shure, M. B. Social adjustment of young children. San Francisco: Jossey-Bass, 1974.

Strain, P. S. & Wiegernik, R. The effects of sociodramatic activities on social inter-action among behaviorally disordered preschool children. Journal of Special Education, 1976, 10, 71-75.

Sylva, K. Play and learning. In B. Tizard & D. Harvey (Eds.), Biology of Play. London: Heinemann, 1977.

Van den Daele, L. Preschool intervention with social learning. Journal of Negro Education, 1970, 39, 296-304.

Vygotsky, L. S. Play and its role in the mental development of the child. Soviet Psychology, 1967, 5, 6-18.

Weininger, O. Play and education: the basic tool for early childhood learning. Springfield, Illinois: Charles C. Thomas, 1979.

Yawkey, T. D. & Fox, F. D. Sociodramatic play and sex effects on imaginativeness and reading-readiness in young children. Research paper presented at the 1983 Biennial Meeting of the Society for Research in Child Development, Detroit, Michigan, 1983.

Response.  IT IS REAL
by
Sue Ann Martin


"We built a ship upon the stairs all made of the back-bedroom chairs, and filled it full of sofa pillows to go a-sailing on the billows."[1] These images from Robert Louis Stevenson's poem "A Good Play" found in his A Child's Garden of Verses highlight the events that characterize the play of normal children... improvised scenarios, object substitutions, the shared need to try on an adventure and the desire to totally believe in it.  "A good play" for normal children is natural, easy, all absorbing and durable.

Special children, however, caught in the chaos of hyperactivity cannot find the path to "just pretend".  The road is hopelessly cluttered with twigs of broken concentration and blocked by a felled self-image, leaving these children entangled in a briar patch of confusion and hostility.  Their play path must be cleared of distractions both physical and psychological if they are ever to travel down the yellow brick road to that developmental outpost called "just pretend".

Weininger's procedures with four emotionally disturbed four and five year olds not only cleared the pathway to social play it also planted the seeds for future cognitive growth. His "one-step-at-a-time" approach gave direction to their emotional traffic jam.  This was accomplished by continually focusing down their area of attention from the room to the table in the room to the cardboard on the table to the road lines on the cardboard.

The entire selection of toy cars proved very useful to the success of Weininger's entire experiment.  First, since the cars were objects in which the children already were interested, motivation was not a problem.  Secondly, the manual movement of the cars provided a vehicle for the release of the children's hyperactivity. Thirdly, the cars were a natural invitation to their auditory involvement.  Furthermore, because the children shared a common interest in the cars

these objects actually socialized the group ---
enabling them to share the cardboard and eventually share the roads! This was quite an astonishing development for four hostile children who up until then rarely played with each other.

Weininger, by controlling the environment and clearing away distractions, focusing attention on a specific object of pleasure and demanding involvement with others via sharing roadways led each child to the opportunity to discover social play. The complexity of that play was then made more and more elaborate with each step. Popsicle sticks were used, towers were built and story lines developed. The once "withdrawn" and angry children now shared ideas, conversation and even laughter! This new use of language gave them a way to not only express their inner feelings but also interact as individuals with others. This sense of themselves was a vital step in their ability to progress. As Howard Gardner states in The Arts and Human Development, "With the advent of language use, the child becomes better able to conceive of himself and to regard himself as a separate entity having both typical and unique experiences, an entity that acts, feels, perceives, and enters into relationships with others."[2]

If this research had had the luxury of being extended for a few more months, the children could have marched down the road to a broad spectrum of learning situations via playing with a variety of art forms. In an effort to exercise the sensory system, the children could have made an audio tape of their own mimicked sounds of car engines and horns, they could have explored a real car for all of its tactile properties including the smoothness of the glass windows, the coldness of the chrome, the rough texture of the carpeting, the soft surface of the fabric on the seats, the pliability of the rubber mats and the raised texture of the license plate letters and numbers.

Creative movement could have been explored via floor patterns of traffic with each child becoming a car and moving to the music of Chitty Chitty Bang Bang. Roleplaying could have then been developed from simple scenarios including such characters as gasoline station attendants, mechanics, drivers, passengers, traffic policemen and pedestrians. The Little House, a story by Virginia Burton about a small house in the country that is taken over by the hustle and bustle of the city as conjestion builds up all around it, could have provided story playing opportunities around an environmental problem harassing the real world in which the children live. Through such a broad spectrum of play, children are led naturally to learning. As Joseph Chilton Pearce states, "While the child plays on the surface, the great work goes on beneath. Regulatory feedback, conceptual construction, and synthesis, all mechanics of learning, are nonconscious procedures."[3].

There is no doubt that these four children experienced play and derived the benefits of learning that skip hand in hand with play down the lanes of childhood. However, Weininger feels somewhat uneasy about those who might say these children experienced tutoring not playing. "Tutor" is derived from the Latin past participle, "tuire" which means "to watch" or "to protect". Surely this is what Weininger and his staff did. They watched and protected these children while they were on their pilgrimage to play. The Weininger group tutored. The child group played.

Is it not fortunate for these four special children and for the community in which they live that they had a Weininger group to watch and to protect them...to act as guardian and to see that they did walk down that road to "just pretend"? And isn't it unfortunate that all special children are not equally afforded? In fact, all children, special and normal, need a tutor to watch and protect their birthright to play. Many events and situations can steal this right including mental disabilities, physical handicaps, emotional imbalances, economic hardships, family stresses, overworked teachers and unaware parents who have lost their childhood skill to play.

As stated by Weininger, "Environment seems to be important to social play and may encourage

or limit it in a variety of ways."[4] Every
teacher and every parent should know how to
create a play environment that, in the face of
any of life's disadvantages, can protect each
child's play right. Free workshops and services
should be made available to not only teachers but
also parents so that they can learn to recognize
all the faces of play and respond to them. The
tremendous benefit of play to our children and
our world --- including enriched imaginations,
healthy self-images, a heightened awareness of
the environment, an appreciation of culture and
the ability to interact with others --- is not a
matter of make believe. It is real.

\*REFERENCES

1. Robert Louis Stevenson, "A Good Play", <u>A Child's Garden of Verses</u> (New York): Platt and Munk, 1961), p. 16.

2. Howard Gardner, <u>The Arts and Human Development</u> (New York: John Wiley and Sons, 1973), p. 140.

3. Joseph Chilton Pearce, <u>Magical Child: Rediscovering nature's plan for our children</u> (New York: E.P. Dutton, 1977), p. 143.

4. O(tto) Weininger, "Just Pretend: Explorations of the use of pretend play in teaching handicapped and emotionally disturbed children (Toronto: Ontario Institute for Studies in Education, 1983), p. 9.

# BIBLIOGRAPHY

Gardner, Howard. The Arts and Human Develop-
    ment. New York: John Wiley and Sons, 1973.

Pearce, Joseph Chilton. Magical Child New
    York: E.P. Dutton, 1977

Stevenson, Robert Louis. "A Good Play". A
    Child's Garden of Verses. New York: Platt
    and Munk, 1961.

Weininger, O(tto). "Just Pretend: Explorations
    of the use of pretend play in teaching handi-
    capped and emotionally disturbed children."
    Mimeographed. Toronto: Ontario Institute for
    Studies in Education, 1983.

# THE DRAMATIC METAPHOR AND LEARNING
by
Richard Courtney

## INTRODUCTION

We all know that Shakespeare said that "All
the world's a stage." The idea that life is like
a theatre (the theatrical metaphor, or the
Theatrum Mundi) was ancient in Shakespeare's
time: it may have been used by Pythagoras and it
was, indeed, the last thing said by Augustus
Caesar. Shakespeare made this metaphor uniquely
his own yet, at the end of his life, he changed
it significantly.

> We are such stuff
> As dreams are made on; and our little life
> Is rounded with a sleep.

Thus said Prospero in The Tempest.[1] With one
giant rhetorical sweep, Shakespeare's last great
poetic vision changed "the theatre metaphor" into
"the dramatic metaphor." For Prospero, life was
not simply like a theatre: it was a play. Human
existence was a dramatic illusion that melts and
dissolves.

I wish to show that the dramatic metaphor
fits well with modern views of life and education; as a result, sociodramatic play, creative
drama, improvisation and role playing are vital
parts of all education processes. I shall not
discuss theatre as I have done so elsewhere.[2]
I shall limit myself to those implications of the
dramatic metaphor which show that we create
meaning. Our inner mental processes make sense
out of the world - create meaning - whereby we
learn. This learning becomes the knowledge with
which we work. Thus the dramatic metaphor indicates that meaning, learning and knowledge are
intricately connected. They can only be separated in abstraction; in practical reality they
are intertwined.

Looked at another way, what we are dealing
with is imagining. Imaginative thought works
with possibility - internally. Thinking about

possibility is thinking in the imaginative mode. But how do we express this imagining in the external world? Specifically, by dramatic action. The child at play or the student in creative drama is practising with possibility, experimenting with fiction. Each is engaged (as Northrop Frye and others have said) in "the great lie." The dramatic world is not actual, it is fictional. It is created out of the possibilities we imagine and then enact. We are, indeed, the stuff our dreams are made on.

When very young children imagine in their heads they must act: the drama is overt. It is with maturation that we do so only "in the mind's eye," covertly. Early dramatic action, being embodied, is the basis for the later covert drama that takes place "in the mind's eye." Early imagining and action provide the ground for later meaning, learning, and knowing.

On this view, the dramatic metaphor has many implications for education. I shall look at these implications in the light of modern scholarship, and in two ways. First, I will consider drama as a way of knowing, discussing the nature and sources of knowledge, how knowledge occurs, the types and structure of knowledge, together with some relevant research studies in curriculum. Second, I will consider dramatic action from two perspectives: as fiction and as metaphor.

KNOWING

## The Nature of Knowledge

What knowledge does drama provide? This is a complex educational issue and I must oversimplify matters in order to deal with them in a common-sense way.

Thinkers disagree about the nature of knowledge: for Plato it was objective, "out there" independent of mind; yet for Locke and the British empiricists all was given by the senses and so knowledge was mental; while some sociologists claim that knowledge is created by society, existentialists insist that there is only <u>felt</u>-knowledge. It is no wonder that Dewey said that teachers should not be dogmatic about knowledge; rather he said, they should assist the student to gain his own knowledge - which might well be different from theirs. We need to follow Dewey's wise advice.

Simply stated, knowledge is having the right to be sure.[3] When children play in sand, they <u>learn</u> its consistency; when later they play with it they <u>know</u> its consistency - they are sure about it. How does this happen? When children play in sand they think about it and act with it, simultaneously. But simple thought and action do not necessarily produce meaning, learning and knowledge. To result in knowledge, thought and action must be centered on the dramatic metaphor: thinking must be "as if" while action must be "trying out." Both must be imaginative: thought must conceive of possibilities and action must dramatize them. By trying out various fictional possibilities, children learn which work and which do not. Those which work create meaning for the children; they have importance and significance <u>for them</u>. When thought and action create meaning, students can relate them to a context and understand their effectiveness: they learn. Yet it is only when children fit these dramatic meanings into a pattern or structure that we can say they have knowledge.

Given this common-sense approach to the issue, let us now examine in more detail some important aspects of knowledge

## The Sources of Dramatic Knowledge

Knowledge is based on evidence. The evidence from which knowledge derives is of two kinds: direct and indirect.[4]

Direct evidence consists of sense data. In his play a child encounters, say, a table. From its sense data (its shape, its colour, and so forth) he infers that it is a table. (Later, any object with such properties fits the existing pattern and is also known as a table.)

There are two kinds of indirect evidence. First is simple description which provides the

41

child with indirect evidence from other people, books, television, and the like; additionally it can derive from such fictional sources as socio-dramatic play. For example, most Canadian children have no direct evidence about elephants; but they do obtain indirect evidence from the simple descriptions provided by their parents, peers, books, television, or dramatic play. This can always be proved or not proved by experience.

The second type of indirect evidence is abstract and cannot be proved by experience. Ideas like "2 + 2 = 4" or "beginning/middle/end" for play construction are abstract descriptions; that is, they are <u>a priori</u> generalizations created out of experience.

Direct and indirect evidence are merely the materials from which we create meaning and, thereby, knowledge. But how are these created?

## How Knowing Occurs

We come to work with evidence because the human mind is active. Knowing occurs through volition.

We review the evidence and see its possibilities for action. But possibility is the imaginative mode. We choose from amongst the possibilities and, if our choice is accurate, we begin to learn: with increasing accuracy of choices we learn well and come to know. The point here is clear: out of the possibilities we make an interpretation, and every interpretation involves, at some level, a decision; essentially <u>we come to know the result of our choices</u>.

Yet knowing is not entirely personal. What we come to know is related to objective reality.[5] Knowing is not entirely subjective nor entirely objective: rather, it lies in the <u>relationship</u> between inner and outer. When the child at play uses imaginative thought and dramatic action to make choices from the evidence, he or she relates the inner world to the environment. Knowledge, in other words, is not an object but <u>a process, a relationship, a dramatic dynamic</u>. The child at play makes this dynamic dramatic in two ways: (1) he or she

42

thinks out possibilities through empathy and identification; and (2) he or she acts out possibilities through impersonation - he or she tries things out by "putting himself in someone else's shoes." But it is the <u>qualities of the dynamic</u> - empathy, identification, and impersonation - that are specifically what characterize any activity as dramatic.[6] In other words, knowing is essentially dramatic.

## Types of Knowledge

What types of knowledge do we work with? Elsewhere I have distinguished between two types of dramatic knowledge: "Knowledge IN" and "Knowledge ABOUT."[7]

Knowledge IN is primary knowledge. We obtain this while we are playing, improvising or acting. "Learning by doing" is too simplistic a statement; "learning by dramatic doing" is much nearer the mark. (Nor is this limited to obvious drama where the dramatic qualities are overt; it also includes all covert dramatic knowing through other media.) Dramatic action provides a "whole" form of knowing, a kind of embodied knowing, where the Self <u>is</u> the dramatic metaphor. It provides an <u>apprehension</u> that is simultaneously cognitive, affective and aesthetic. Partially it is what existentialists have called <u>felt-knowledge</u> but, more accurately, it has been called intuitive knowledge[8] and personal knowledge.[9]

Knowledge ABOUT is secondary knowledge. We usually obtain if <u>after</u> we have acted when we observe, reflect, talk or write about the action. It provides a <u>comprehension</u> which is analytic, re-cognitive, and/or linguistic in character. It is a kind of discursive knowledge.

When we act we ground knowledge. Discursive knowledge can arise only out of acting. In creative drama or improvisation lessons students come to know directly while they are improvising. When they discuss it afterwards, the knowing that occurs is not quite the same. Something changes. The actor's knowledge is different from the talker's knowledge. It is no wonder, therefore, that Robert W. Witkin comes to question the

inevitable discussion that follows most practical
drama classes.[10]

## The Structure of Knowledge

Students in play or improvisation adapt what
they learn to their previous knowledge. That is,
they take their new knowledge and fit it to their
existing knowledge structure. They do so by
choice. They actively order their conception of
reality. They create an organizational structure, an interpretative framework, in order to
impose order on their experience of the world.
They literally shape their own perceptions; their
dramatic actions are always an experiment.

Their organizational structure is not fixed.
It is a changing and self-created pattern: a
fluid and developing process that occurs between
the student and the world. The focus of this
changing structure is the meaning for the
student. Students search for coherence in such a
way that significant meanings become the framework of their own knowledge structure. This
happens in (at least) three ways: (1) internally
they use perception to create thought patterns by
anticipating, confirming and reconstructing; (2)
externally they adapt to the environment by
empathizing and dramatizing; and (3) collectively
they join with others to create social and cultural patterns.

Let us look at this another way by asking:
what happens when drama gives the student a new
experience, and this leads to new learning and,
thus, to new knowledge? Two events occur: (1)
the student both discovers and constructs a new
representation; and (2) the student both
explores and maintains that construction, fitting
it to previous patterns. The drama leads the
student, first, to conceive of a new idea and
this becomes a new order, pattern, metaphor or
model. This is what is known as the "Ahha!"
moment of discovery - the intuitive insight that
gives the student a gestalt of meaning, primarily
in the right hemisphere of the brain. But,
second, the student then fits this intuitive
insight into an existing mental structure. He or
she does so step by step, over time, in a logical

and analytical way. This occurs primarily in the left hemisphere of the brain.

I must point out that this way of discussing knowledge structures is not exactly new. Modern scholars have described it in a variety of ways. George Kelly has said that each individual actively creates a "personal construct," a bi-polar pattern that each person tries to fit to reality; other modern examples of such bi-polar structures include Jean Piaget's play and imitation, Michael Polanyi's innovation and fixed rules, Jerome Bruner's intuition and intellect, and modern neurology's two hemispheres of the brain.[11] Yet not all modern explanations of knowledge structures are bi-polar: for example, Stephen C. Pepper has said that there are four world constructions, or "root metaphors," to which individuals fit new knowledge. Such explanations are not mutually exclusive. Rather they represent some of the lenses by which modern scholars examine the phenomenon of knowledge structures.

If we turn to the literature on educational drama, we discover that it is full of examples of the working of knowledge structures. The first example is a famous one: Peter Slade's classic technique where the teacher tells a story leaving blanks for the children to fill in, something like the following:

> Once upon a time there was a little girl and her name was _____? All right, her name was Mary. It was a fine summer day and Mary was walking down the path. Suddenly she came across a _____? O.K., she came across a rabbit. What did she say to him?

And so on and so forth. With the story told through once, the children then act it out with the teacher re-telling the story using all the children's inventions. From such an example, we do not know what particular knowledge events discover and construct new representations; these will vary enormously from child to child, and from culture to culture. But the fitting of the new knowledge to an existing structure is clearly seen because the teacher is expecting the children to learn sequencing.

Most spontaneous improvisations in classrooms are group activities where each student is at a different level of working out meaning. At any one time, some students are discovering meaning while others are maintaining it. This was the case in our second example: the group of thirteen year olds who improvised a coal mining scene of the nineteenth century in social studies, as described in Lynn McGregor's <u>Learning Through Drama</u>.[12] For most of the time the students were maintaining meaning - about conditions down a mine, about the family life of miners, and so forth - and fitting this to their existing structures. Yet, for some, there was some knowledge that they discovered and constructed. This centered on the miner kissing his wife goodbye as he left for work in the morning. To these students (as for all adolescents at one time or another) the act of kissing within the dramatic play was a discovery - something new - which had yet to be fitted to their knowledge structures.

Interestingly, descriptions of play, creative drama, improvisation and role play in the literature of dramatic education have not generally been analyzed in this way. Yet all can be considered in terms of the discovery and maintenance of knowledge. This is because dramatic action is an instrument of adaptation: it formulates and maintains constructions of reality based upon significant meaning.

<u>Summary</u>

In brief, we can say that: knowledge is the right to be sure; the sources of knowledge are direct and indirect evidence; students choose what to know within a dramatic dynamic; acting provides us with primary knowledge from which discursive knowledge derives; and that when students discover new knowledge they fit this into their existing mental structure.

## Metaphor and Knowledge in Curriculum Research

Interestingly, in the last ten years or so educational researchers have begun to refocus their perspectives on education by using metaphors derived from the arts and the humanities. Such metaphors have included aesthetics and art criticism,[13] literary criticism,[14] journalism,[15] music,[16] theatre,[17] and drama.[18] With all but drama, scholars have been engaged in what Milburn calls "discipline-stripping," namely, the use of concepts and methods in the arts discipline to provide a new perspective on education. In contrast, I hold that the dramatic metaphor is the essential under-pinning for meaning, learning and knowledge.

The pervasive nature of the dramatic metaphor can be seen if we examine modern views of knowledge held by curriculum researchers. I will deal with two: (1) procedural knowledge; and (2) personal-practical knowledge. Both are in the mainstream of American pragmatism with an epistemology allied to that of John Dewey and Joseph J. Schwab.

Procedural knowledge is a term used by Kenneth A. Leithwood and others. This is the kind of knowledge that permits curriculum planners "to gain control over an otherwise muddy sea of complexities." Thus it is critical rather than comprehensive, and works by three criteria: generalizability, accessibility, and effectiveness. Complex phenomena contain within them stages of development (steps, or sequences) and it is the successful negotiation of these stages that constitutes procedural knowledge.

These stages of procedural knowledge can be achieved in two ways. First, the curriculum planner can <u>understand</u> the model and, thereby, achieve a curriculum design that will be effective at all levels of implementation. Second, the planner can <u>perform the role</u> of the model and, thereby, achieve procedural knowledge at a particular level of curriculum design and implementation.

It is clear that procedural knowledge can be extrapolated to most, if not all, types of human performance. But if procedural knowledge hinges upon models, together with the necessary roles to activate such models, then the human knowledge and action that results is, precisely, dramatic in the sense that I have been using it.

Personal-Practical knowledge, in the sense used by F. Michael Connelly and others, is somewhat different. Although it, too, has similarities with Dewey and Schwab, it has close connections with Michael Polanyi's Personal Knowledge. The concept of personal-practical knowledge is an attempt to understand the minded practical life of teachers, and the researchers concerned have stated their aims as follows:

> Our special interest in the practical is with the personal. We want to understand and conceptualize the nature, origin and expression of a practitioner's metaphors, images, rules and principles which we envision as components of his personal-practical knowledge.[19]

To do so, they examine the rhythms, rituals and habitual actions of school life. Specifically, therefore, they are concerned with what I have called Knowledge IN -- the practical knowledge gained within a particular type of human performance. Yet their approach could equally be extrapolated to the personal-practical knowledge of hockey players, secretaries, mechanics and, indeed, any group going about its practical tasks. Apart from its use of rituals, research in personal-practical knowledge has not approached what I would regard as the key to an understanding of such knowledge; namely, the essentially dramatic quality of the practitioner's metaphors, images, rules and principles. Without placing the dramatic dynamic at the centre of our study of knowledge, we risk not accounting for human volition.


DRAMATIC ACTION


Fiction

Dramatic action creates dramatic fiction. It transforms the actual into what is "real-for-me,"

48

into a world of created meaning. It transforms an obdurate environment into a fiction with which I can deal.

Children at play create "let's pretend" but, as Slade points out, "pretence" is not the right word for it. Play is a very serious business as we can see from the children's concentration; it is the natural way in which they learn. When students improvise they bracket mundane life and live for a time in a fictional world. There they act as if all occurs in the present: even if they are improvising about an event in history, they act as if all takes place in the present now - as if it was a living event. It is similar with the covert drama of role play: when we rehearse a job interview in our heads, it takes place in the present although the event is in the future. Essentially dramatic action creates a fictional present out of both past and future. Through drama we learn to adjust to time.

Dramatic fiction is so powerful that it is a matter of constant comment in the literature. In particular it provides a motivation for learning in all subject areas and is a potent force for the transfer of learning.[20] This is because drama enables students to face life experiences at a functional and symbolic level. Not only do they "try out" possible futures and "act out" problems of the past, but they engage in problem-solving in a deep personal way through the fictional present.

Dramatic fiction carries both manifest and latent content. Manifest content is the subject of the fiction: the story or tale that is told through the drama. The latent content, however, is made up of the themes that underlie the story. For example, in the improvisation about nine-teenth century miners that we have discussed above, the manifest content was the story of mining life in the period; the latent content, however, included the significance of kissing. We should also note that modern structuralists have shown that there are certain common latent themes in all such fiction - such as death-and-resurrection, the hero, the journey, and so forth.[21] In terms of knowledge, when children play or students improvise they learn both

manifest and latent content: they gain historical knowledge if the story is from history but,
at the same time, they gain knowledge of the deep
themes that are inherent in human existence.

Yet, as I have shown elsewhere,[22] manifest
and latent content are elements of the extrinsic
knowledge secured through enacting dramatic fiction. In addition, drama provides both intrinsic
and aesthetic knowledge. The focus of the
dramatic metaphor is the actor. We are all, as
Shakespeare said, "merely players," and our play
and improvisation give meaning to our Self.
Through dramatic action we gain intrinsic knowledge about our Self. Abner Cohen tells us[23]
that the Self is continuously in the making
between, on the one hand, contractual roles that
involve only a part of the personality and, on
the other hand, the totality of the Self. When
the child is playing or improvising he or she is
putting the whole Self into a group activity; he
or she is the symbol of the Self. And, as Cohen
further remarks:

> Selfhood is achieved by a person when he
> interacts with other persons with the
> totality of his self....Symbolic action is by
> definition action involving the totality of
> the self. Symbols vary in their potency.
> The more potent the symbol, the more total
> the involvement of the self. Nearly all
> social action has both symbolic and contrac-
> tual elements, but some activities are more
> symbolic and less contractual than others...
> The contractual element is subversive of
> selfhood; the symbolic element is recreative
> of selfhood. It is in the symbolic act that
> we continually create and recreate our self-
> hood.[24]

As drama is the symbolic act par excellence, it
is a key factor in the obtaining of intrinsic
knowledge. The same applies to aesthetic knowledge. We have seen above that choice is an
essential part of dramatic thought and action:
unless choice is involved, drama cannot exist.
But choice is also at the nub of aesthetic knowledge whether the activity is making, liking or
appreciating. As I have shown elsewhere,[25]

aesthetic criteria placed in a specific context are learned through dramatic action.

Finally, we should note that dramatic fiction provides a unique reality. There is always at least a double meaning: the actor is himself and yet another; the objects used in creative drama are both actual and representational; and the dramatic world and the actual world co-exist simultaneously. Not only does this lead students to a growing awareness of reality and illusion but also it leads them to symbolic knowledge -- the most human element of human beings.

## Metaphor

Dramatic action also creates the dramatic metaphor. The universality of dramatic action makes the metaphor also universal.

Max Black has suggested the way in which metaphors work.[26] For the dramatic metaphor ("Life _is_ drama"), life is the primary subject and drama is the secondary subject, yet both are viewed as identical, synonymous and simultaneous. Metaphors work, Black says, by the implicit relationships embodied in the secondary subject being projected onto the primary subject: drama and life are presented as essentially the same but life is provided with the characteristics of drama. Although fixed in form, the dramatic metaphor can allow for a great deal of internal ambiguity and (like a work of art) can accommodate a wide variety of individual and subtle interpretations. All this exists because the dramatic act is performed.

Metaphor is created prior to metonymy. Although an absolute distinction between metaphor and metonymy cannot be maintained, they do have some differences. "He has a green thumb" is metonymy but "he is as cold as ice" is metaphor. In metaphor there is an arbitrary relationship between two contrasted subjects. In metonymy the two elements are related as part to a whole.

However, as Anthony Wilden shows, one can slide into another. Taking the relationship of two dogs as an example, Wilden shows that "nip" and "bite" are metonymical when the dogs begin to communicate (nip is part of play and bite is part of war) but can become metaphorical (nip and play become metaphors for bite and war). Now it is fair to say that the words of Shakespeare which began this discussion - "We are such stuff/As dreams are made on" - are metaphorical but they also have metonymical implications.

This being the case, the typology of Floyd Merrell can be of great use to us in trying to grasp the meaning, learning and knowledge that result from the dramatic metaphor. This typology is specifically not logical and precise; rather it is paralogical with many graduations ranging from biologically embedded knowledge to tacit and finally to conscious knowledge (see Figure 1). In this typology, Similarity and Opposition are Gestalt wholes while Contiguity and Differentiation are parts of a whole. The dramatic act provides knowledge that is primarily whole. The actor focuses on the Gestalt of his activity while relatively unaware of the particulars: while acting, he creates Knowledge IN - he knows how, not explicitly that.

Dramatic action deals with the relations between wholes in broad categorical frameworks. Opposition is not required in metaphor yet it is a necessary precondition for dramatic action: the actor is more concerned with likeness than distinction. The child at play contradicts contiguity because he emphasizes wholes not parts: yet this same child complements differentiation when he distinguishes between the parts that make up the whole. The dramatic fiction is made of elements that are nonlinear: the two sides of the metaphor are seen as continuous.

Dramatic action creates similarities, the axiological basis for meaning, learning and knowledge. Thus the dramatic metaphor underlies what others have called scientific paradigms,[27] root metaphors or world hypotheses,[28] world views,[29] and forms of life.[30] Around the human drama, opposition bifurcates the universe so that systems can arise in hierarchies which attempt to organize cosmic chaos. Around the human drama, contiguity and metonymy relate concepts cognitively and so arises the universe of discourse. Metonymy is pure imagery: a crown for a king, a sail for a ship - these contiguous images are imcomplete wholes revealed by the drama yet, at the same time, they allow us to live with paradox. Drama is always ambiguous but the mundane existence of ordinary life resists ambiguity. Always there is tension between the structure, symmetry and harmony of the differentiation and classificatory pigeon-holes of ordinary life, and the ambiguity, paradox, analogue, and similarity of dramatic life.

It is these conditions of learning and knowledge in drama that can lead John McLeod to suggest the following educational actions: (1) the whole nature of metaphor within the development of arts curriculum needs to be addressed; (2) examples should be grounded firmly within an explicit and apparent context; (3) the dialectic between structure and transformation, together with the metaphorical relationship between the two, needs to be exposed; and (4) more emphasis needs to be placed on the tacit domain of knowledge as well as on that which is explicit.

I would go further. I would suggest that the phrase "drama across the curriculum" be re-worded to "the dramatic curriculum." By basing education on the dramatic metaphor, I am saying that meaning, learning and knowledge rest fundamentally on similarity, analogue, the nonlinear and the continuous. But, at the same time, similarity cannot exist without contiguity, opposition and differentiation. In drama, metonymy is placed in the context of metaphor.

When we discuss this issue in terms of teaching, however, we need to be more practical. If the dramatic knowledge is of four types - similarity (the fundamental type), contiguity, opposition, and differentiation - how as teachers do we sequence these types developmentally from grade to grade?

Perhaps the clearest answer to this question comes from the research of Robert W. Witkin[31] when, using the framework of Piaget, he shows there is a difference in the aesthetic development of pre-adolescents and adolescents (see Figure 2). For pre-adolescents he says that there are four qualities of aesthetic knowledge:

(1) Harmonies, corresponding to multiplication; (2) Semblances, corresponding to addition; (3) Discords, corresponding to division; and (4) Contrasts, corresponding to subtraction. The higher-level operations of adolescence order these four qualities of knowledge into: (1) Syntheses; (2) Identities; (3) Dialectics; and (4) Polarities. As these four qualities of knowledge, in their different stages, correspond exactly to the typology of Merrell (Figure 1), we have here an example where research and theory come together to be of value to the drama teacher in the classroom.

## CONCLUSION

I have attempted to show that drama, as internal and external action, as identification and impersonation, is at the very heart of meaning, learning and knowing through some aspects of research in curriculum, fiction and metaphor. Should this be acknowledged, we will have changed education irrevocably. This is already beginning: increasing numbers of teachers acknowledge that drama is a way of knowing and learning; simulation is used in the space program to a remarkable degree; and Seymour Papert has shown that the youngest children become highly creative with computers if imaginative drama is used. As we approach the twenty-first century perhaps the dramatic metaphor will be acknowledged as the primary root metaphor. If so, learning may become unending re-creation.

Figure 1

TYPOLOGY: QUALITIES OF KNOWLEDGE

(after Floyd Merrell)

THE DRAMATIC METAPHOR

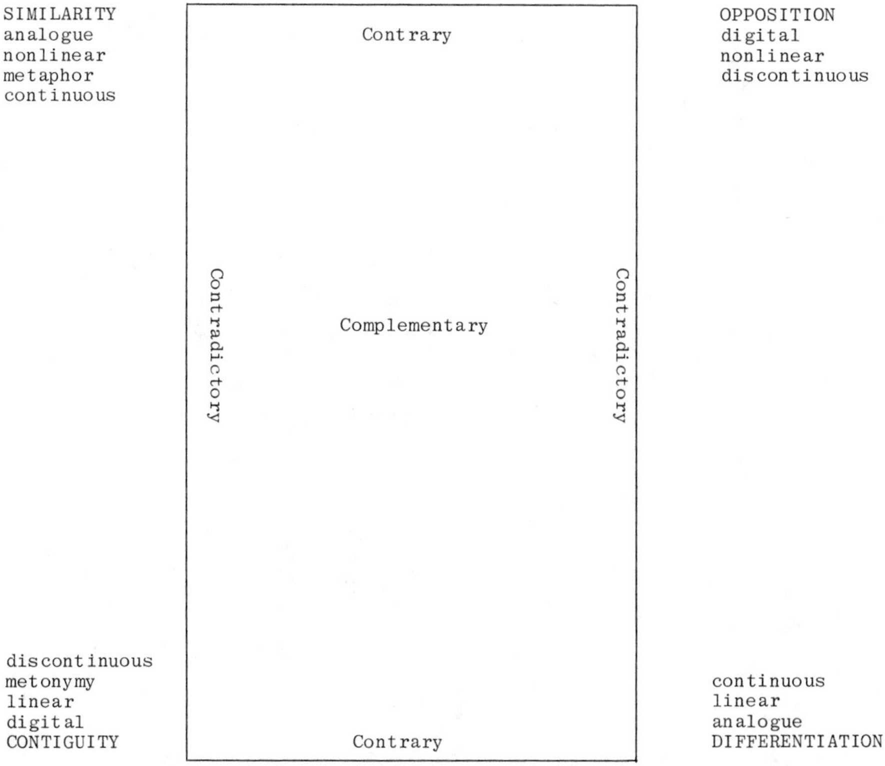

SIMILARITY
analogue
nonlinear
metaphor
continuous

OPPOSITION
digital
nonlinear
discontinuous

Contrary

Contradictory

Complementary

Contradictory

discontinuous
metonymy
linear
digital
CONTIGUITY

Contrary

continuous
linear
analogue
DIFFERENTIATION

Figure 2

QUALITIES OF KNOWLEDGE IN DEVELOPMENTAL STAGES

(after Robert W. Witkin)

| Merrell's Typology | SIMILARITY | CONTIGUITY | OPPOSITION | DIFFERENTIATION |
|---|---|---|---|---|
| Pre-adolescent Operations | HARMONIES wholes | SEMBLANCES tension of parts | DISCORDS conflict of parts | CONTRASTS individualizing of parts |
| Piaget's | multiplication | addition | division | subtraction |
| Adolescent Operations | SYNTHESES totality of individual wholes are absorbed into a synthesis | IDENTITIES various semblances are ordered as identities within wholes | DIALECTICS discords in various wholes are seen as dialectics | POLARITIES contrasts in various wholes are seen as polarities |

# FOOTNOTES

1. William Shakespeare. The Tempest, IV, 1: 156-58.

2. See my, "Human Performance."

3. A. J. Ayer. The Problem of Knowledge: 31-35.

4. Bertrand Russell. The Problems of Philosophy: Chapter 5.

5. This is essentially Kierkegaard's position. See, Louis P. Pojman. "Kierkegaard's Theory of Subjectivity and Education," in Curtis and Mays (eds.) Phenomenology and Education: 1-12.

6. See my, The Dramatic Curriculum: 30.

7. Ibid.: 72-73.

8. "Knowledge has two forms: it is either intuitive knowledge or logical knowledge; knowledge obtained through the imagination or knowledge obtained through the intellect; knowledge of the individual or knowledge of the universal; of individual things or of the relations between them: it is, in fact, productive either of images or of concepts." Benedetto Croce. Aesthetic: 1.

9. Michael Polanyi. Personal Knowledge.

10. Robert W. Witkin. The Intelligence of Feeling. 84-85.

11. Robert E. Ornstein. The Psychology of Consciousness.

12. Lynn McGregor et al. Learning Through Drama: 59.

13. Elliot W. Eisner, "Educational Connoisseurship." Idem, "The Perceptive Eye." Idem, The Educational Imagination.

14. E. F. Kelly, "Curriculum Evaluation." D.
    Jenkins and B. O'Toole, "Curriculum
    Evaluation, Literary Criticism, and the
    Paracurriculum," in, G. M. Willis (ed.),
    Qualitative Evaluation. G. M. Willis,
    "Curriculum Criticism and Literary
    Criticism."

15. T. Barone, "Education as Aesthetic Experi-
    ence." B. MacDonald, "The Portrayal of
    Persons."

16. Elliot W. Eisner, "The Art and the Craft of
    Teaching."

17. M. R. Grumet, "Curriculum as Theater." R.
    Oram, "In Defense of Curriculum
    Criticism."

18. See my, The Dramatic Curriculum. N. J.
    Gehrke and S. Bravmann, "The Applica-
    tion of Dramatistic Criticism to
    Curriculum Evaluation." Geoffrey
    Milburn, "Derivation and Application of
    a Dramatic Metaphor for the Assessment
    of Teaching."

19. F. Michael Connelly and D. Jean Clandinin,
    "Personal Practical Knowledge at Bay
    Street School": 1-2.

20. See my, Re-Play: Chapters 2 and 3.

21. Robert Gardner, "The Dramatic Script and
    Procedural Knowledge."

22. See my, "Goals in Drama Teaching."

23. Abner Cohen, "Symbolic Action and the Struc-
    ture of the Self," in Ioan Lewis (ed.)
    Symbols and Sentiments: 117-28.

24. Ibid.: 123.

25. See my, Re-Play: 179-86.

26. Max Black, "More about Metaphor," in Andrew
    Ortony (ed.) Metaphor and Thought.

27. Thomas S. Kuhn.  The Structure of Scientific Revolutions.

28. Stephen C. Pepper.  World Hypotheses.

29. Lucien Goldmann.  Pour une sociologie du roman.

30. Ludwig Wittgenstein.  Philosophical Investigations.

31. Witkin.  The Intelligence of Feeling:  178-79.

# BIBLIOGRAPHY

Ayer, A. J. The Problem of Knowledge. Harmondsworth: Penguin, 1956.

Barone, T. "Education as Aesthetic Experience: 'Art in Germ'," Educational Leadership, 40, 4 (1983): 21-26.

Best, David. Expression in Movement and the Arts. London: Lepus, 1974.

Bolton, Gavin. Towards a Theory of Drama in Education. London: Longmans, 1980.

Bruner, Jerome S. On Knowing: Essays for the Left Hand. Cambridge, Mass.: Harvard University Press, 1962.

Burger, Peter L., and Thomas Luckman. The Social Construction of Reality. New York: Doubleday, 1966.

Burke, Kenneth. Language as Symbolic Action. Berkeley, Cal.: University of California Press, 1965.

Burton, E. J. Teaching English Through Self-Expression. London: Evans, 1949.

Connelly, F. Michael, and D. Jean Clandinin. "Personal Practical Knowledge at Bay Street School," unpublished paper, n.d.

Courtney, Richard. "Goals in Drama Teaching," Drama Contact, 1,1 (May 1977): 5-8.

———— . The Dramatic Curriculum. London, Ont.: University of Western Ontario; London, England: Heinemann; New York: Drama Book Specialists, 1981.

———— . Re-Play: Studies of Human Drama in Education. Toronto: Ontario Institute for Studies in Education Press, 1982.

———— . "Human Performance: Meaning and Knowledge," Journal, National Association for Drama in Education (Australia): forthcoming.

———— , and Gertrude Schattner (eds.) <u>Drama in Therapy</u>, 2 vols. New York: Drama Book Specialists, 1982.

Croce, Benedetto. <u>Aesthetic: As Science of Expression and General Linguistic</u>, trans. Douglas Ainslie. London: Peter Owen, repr. 1967.

Curtis, Bernard, and Wolfe Mays (eds.) <u>Phenomenology and Education: Self-Consciousness and its Development</u>. London: Methuen, 1978.

Dewey, John. <u>The Schools of Tomorrow</u>. New York: Dutton, 1915.

Eisner, Elliot W. "Educational Connoisseurship and Educational Criticism: The Forms and Function in Educational Criticism," unpublished paper, n.d.

———— . "The Perceptive Eye: Towards the Reformation of Educational Evaluation" unpublished paper presented at A.E.R.A., 1975.

———— . <u>The Educational Imagination: On the Design and Evaluation of School Programs</u>. New York: Macmillan, 1979.

———— . "The Art and Craft of Teaching," <u>Educational Leadership</u>, 40, 4 (1983): 4-13.

Gardner, Robert. "The Dramatic Script and Procedural Knowledge: A Key to the Understanding of Dramatic Structure and a Foundation for the Development of Effective Curriculum Design in Dramatic Instruction at the Tertiary Level, unpublished Ed.D. dissertation, University of Toronto, 1983.

Gehrke, N. J., and S. Bravmann, "The Application of Dramatistic Criticism to Curriculum Evaluation," unpublished paper presented at A.E.R.A., 1981.

Goldmann, Lucien. <u>Pour une sociologie du roman</u>. Paris: Galimard, 1964.

Grumet, M. R. "Curriculum as Theater: Merely Players," Curriculum Inquiry, 8, 1 (Spring 1978): 37-64.

Hadfield, J. A. Dreams and Nightmares. Harmonds worth: Penguin, 1954.

Heathcote, Dorothy. "Improvisation," English in Education, 1, 3 (Autumn 1967): 27-30.

Kelly, E. F. "Curriculum Evaluation and Literary Criticism: Comments on the Analogy," Curriculum Inquiry, 1975, 5: 87-106.

Kelly, George A. The Psychology of Personal Constructs, 2 vols. New York: Norton, 1955.

Kuhn, Thomas S. The Structure of Scientific Revolutions. Chicago: University of Chicago Press, 1970.

Lakoff, George, and Mark Johnson. Metaphors We Live By. Chicago: University of Chicago Press, 1980.

Landy, Robert J. Handbook of Educational Drama and Theatre. Westport, Conn.: Greenwood, 1982.

Leithwood, Kenneth A. "Graduate Curriculum Studies with a Focus on Curriculum Processes," unpublished paper presented in Caracas, Venezuela, 1981.

Lewis, Ioan (ed.) Symbols and Sentiments: Cross-Cultural Studies in Symbolism. London: Academic Press, 1977: 117-28.

Lyman, Stamford M., and Marvin B. Scott. The Drama of Social Reality. New York: Oxford University Press, 1975.

MacDonald, B. "The Portrayal of Persons as Evaluation Data," unpublished paper, 1976.

McGregor, Lynn, et alia. Learning Through Drama. London: Heinemann, 1977.

McLeod, John. "Metaphor and Metonymy in the Arts," unpublished paper, Drama Resource Centre, Melbourne, 1982.

Merrell, Floyd. "Of Metaphor and Metonymy," Semiotica, 31, 3/4 (1980): 289-307.

Milburn, Geoffrey. "Derivation and Application of a Dramatic Metaphor for the Assessment of Teaching," unpublished Ed.D. dissertation, University of Toronto, 1982.

———— · "On Discipline-Stripping: Difficulties in the Application of Humanistic Metaphors to Educational Phenomena," unpublished paper presented to Canadian Society for the Study of Education, 1983.

Oram, R. "In Defense of Curriculum Criticism," Cambridge Journal of Education, 1983, 13(1): 7-13.

Ornstein, Robert E. The Psychology of Consciousness. Harmondsworth: Penguin, 1975.

Ortony, Andrew (ed.) Metaphor and Thought. Cambridge: Cambridge University Press, 1979.

Papert, Seymour. Mindstorms: Children, Computers and Powerful Ideas. New York: Basic Books, 1980.

Pepper, Stephen C. World Hypotheses. Berkeley, Cal.: University of California Press, 1942.

Piaget, Jean. Play, Dreams and Imitation in Childhood. London: Routledge, 1962.

Polanyi, Michael. Personal Knowledge: Towards a Post-Critical Philosophy. New York: Harper and Row, 1964.

Russell, Bertrand. The Problems of Philosophy. London: Oxford University Press, repr. 1968.

Schwab, Joseph J. "The Practical: A Language for Curriculum," The School Review, 78, 1 (November 1969): 1-31.

Schwab, Joseph J.  "The Practical:  Arts of the
    Eclectic,"  The School Review, 79, 4 (August
    1971): 493-542.

Schwab, Joseph J.  "The Practical 3:  Translation
    into Curriculum,"  The School Review, 81, 4
    (August 1973): 501-22.

Slade, Peter. Child Drama.  London:  University
    of London Press, 1954.

Way, Brian.  Development Through Drama.  London:
    Longmans, 1968.

Wilden, Anthony.  System and Structure.  London:
    Tavistock, 1972.

Willis, G. M.  "Curriculum Criticism and Literary
    Criticism,"  Journal of Curriculum Studies,
    1975, 7: 3-17.

Willis, G. M.  (ed.)  Qualitative Evaluation:
    Concepts and Cases in Curriculum Criticism.
    Berkeley, Cal.: McCutchan, 1978.

Witkin, Robert W.  The Intelligence of Feeling.
    London:  Heinemann, 1974.

Wittgenstein, Ludwig.  Philosophical Investi-
    gations.  New York:  Macmillan, 1958.

Response. DRAMA: A MAP FOR THE SELF
by
Robert Gardner


Sometimes scholarship approaches the domain of poetry. Statements by an especially erudite scholar can become so compact, so condensed that they require the type of critical analysis one might normally invest in the field of literature. Marshall McLuhan typified that type of scholar. Professor Courtney's paper, The Dramatic Metaphor and Learning, displays that same type of density and impact.

I approach Courtney's ideas from the perspective of a teacher of media writing and as a practitioner in the worlds of film and television. My work, always, has a practical bias. I live in an environment - both as an editor of other people's work and as a writer - where theory is rapidly translated into a visible reality. Theory which can be substantiated in fact is tremendously valuable to me. That's why I find Courtney's work so intriguing.

When I read Courtney's paper I find ideas and tools which assist me to grapple with the notion of drama in education. He is saying, I believe, that the great adventure in life is life: from the womb to the grave. We emerge from what Eric Neumann called "urobic incest", or oneness with the mother, to be bombarded by literally millions of sensory impressions.[1] From this mass of impressions we hammer out our islands of reality, or what we take to be reality. In this sense, our perception of the outside world is a cultural artefact.[2] The self, too, may be thought of as a cultural artefact.

Courtney reminds us that we are all map makers and that our magnetic north derives from our biochemical makeup and what Levi-Strauss called the structuring capacity of the mind.[3] We desperately need structures - in language, in art, and in social interchange.


In Drama and Therapy, edited by Courtney and Schattner, there were discussions about ego

65

strength. Until the ego has the courage to venture out into a world which has disintegrative tendencies mounted against it, there can be no learning. With Robert Lifton, Courtney would also argue that without "imaginings" there can be no absorption of raw sensory experience into the structure which we call knowledge.[4] The self must be involved in what Propp called "moves".[5] The moves are opposed - not through maliciousness, necessarily - but through entropy, inertia, and sheer uncaring. There is a tendency, always, for the move to be beaten back. That is why resources have to be so carefully mounted; that is why the move must be imaginatively examined prior to action in the external world. Without the mind acting like a flashlight probing into the unknown we would be afraid to venture out. If we refused to venture out we simply would not learn.

Professor Courtney's model is of an organism attempting to gain a sense of individuality, gaining confidence to adventure, and then absorbing and categorizing a set of experiences into a structure which ensures some measure of predictability. Our search, right from the beginning, is to find repeatable and transferable structures. We are always looking for what will work. Predictability brings us some sense of peace.

I believe that Courtney is attempting to sensitize us to the essential fiction of the separation between the outer and the inner. There is a slushing action going on all the time, back and forth. The inner confusion of impressions, images, and projected scenarios belies the outward mask of role performance and what appears to be the contunuity of the personality. That's why our identities and our personae are so fragile. They are, in fact, convenient guises which serve the needs of the moment.

Courtney does not use the dramatic paradigm as a way, simply, of looking at learning. Rather, the dramatic process is something which emerges from our very nature. When we understand the power of the dramatic form we also understand the process of learning to a greater extent. When he talks about the ego strength of the child he is also talking about "the self as hero" looking out on the world with some anticipation of success. When he talks about the mental capacity to imagine and to test alternatives, he is mirroring the narrative flow which persists in the whole range of story telling forms, from the myth and fable to the novel and the drama. When he refers to the absorption of new information or experience into a way of looking at life, he is dealing with the move to a new status which, as Frye has pointed out, is one of the persistent characteristics of dramatic content and structure.[6] The successful journey builds the confidence, and the hero can move on, once more, to yet another plain. The heights achieved become ground zero for the next ascent.

Courtney has underlined the importance of the imaginary "trying out" process. This is the habit of mind which allows us to mentally predict what a particular situation might entail and what we might say or do in a new environment. Actual journeys begin in an inner testing arena. The imagination creates a possible map which serves most of us well enough as we proceed to muddle through.

The imaginary move leads to actual interaction with the external world. But the interaction, as it occurs in time, only provides us with raw sensory experience. That raw data is assimilated, rationalized, and placed within our knowledge structure. We select pieces of the external experience to fit within our mental map. In such a process even failure can be rationalized into success. Indeed, if we are to proceed through life we must remain the hero of our own story. A failure to imagine - or to image - associated with a failure to rationalize would impede maturation. Indeed, the ego strength would not be present to power the series of moves which are necessary to keep the tendency towards growth ongoing.[7]

A structure, however, may only be useful if we can share it with others. A shared view of the world and a shared vision of reality is tremendously comforting simply because it tends to validate our experience. We feel that our construct of the world is not completely an illusion. Individual structures may be somewhat arbitrary, but - in the main - they will be structures which we share with the mass of so-called normal humankind. Men like R. D. Laing might even call it "shared illness".

Courtney is also indicating that drama, itself, is a comforting pattern in which we find that we are members of a tribe rather than a single aberration lost in wildly varied and infinitely different sensory impressions. Experience with drama and dramatic play provides a bridge between inner and outer which strengthens the sense of self. Thus when Peter Slade fits the words of children into a narrative he is permitting them to participate in a shared structure. They are, teacher and students, dealing with a reflection of the journey they are either passing through or have passed through. We are transfixed by the dramatic form in much the same way as we are transfixed by images of ourselves or accounts which mention us.

I am not as certain that drama delivers actual knowledge. In fact, it is my belief that drama misrepresents the life journey and that it is - very frequently - an embodiment of lies, although they may be - as Wilde said - beautiful lies. We are far more interested in the comic form than the tragic form. In any event, the successful hero is a stand-in for us (or more properly, me) while the unsuccessful tragic hero is rather like a sacrificial victim whose spectacular lack of success strengthens the onlooker.[8]

The main value of drama, in my mind, is its capacity to strengthen the ego: the necessary prelude to the journey which is the crucible where true learning can begin.

There is another major implication in what Professor Courtney has said: if we can construct a life map which has broad replicability we can also dismantle it, or at least analyze it. Structural knowledge offers us an insight into how that analysis might be put in place. We can get inside drama and understand why it acts as a magnet to our attention. If we understand that attractive power we can invest it in the classroom and in the lecture hall to link information delivery with the natural processes for assimilation.

Essentially, Courtney is saying something which is not widely appreciated. He is saying that dramatic structures and processes can be visible manifestations of how the human mind tends to work. He is saying that fantasy, play, improvisation and scripted drama are all hints of what is going on inside the human mind. He is also saying something else. He is urging us to recognize that the knowledge and skills exist NOW to bring the impact of these perceptions into education. Courtney is not talking only about dramatic education, he is also talking about the broad range of teaching and the way in which we regard the flow of information. He is saying that once we understand the dramatic process and why it bridges the span between the inner and outer world then we will all be more effective teachers. The only journey that transfixes us, he is saying, is the journey of the self.

## FOOTNOTES

[1] Erich Neumann, The Origins and History of Unconsciousness, trans. R.F.C. Hull, New Jersey: Princeton University Press, 1954, p. 45.

[2] Ernst Cassirer, The Philosophy of Symbolic Forms, Volume 2: Mythical Thought, trans. Ralph Manheim, London: Yale University Press, 1945, p. 34.

[3] Claude Levi-Strauss, quoted in Jonathan Culler's Structuralist Poetics, London: Routledge and Kegan Paul, 1975, p. 41.

[4] Robert Jay Lifton, The Life of the Self, New York: Simon and Schuster, 1976, p. 20.

[5] Vladimir Propp, Morphology of the Folktale, trans. Laurence Scott, Austin: University of Texas Press, 1968, p. 20.

[6] Northrop Frye, Anatomy of Criticism, Princeton: Princeton University Press, 1973, p. 166-167.

[7] Lifton, p. 50.

[8] Frye, p. 214.

SELECTED BIBLIOGRAPHY

Agyris, C., and Schon, D. A., "Evaluation
    Theories of Action". The Planning of Change.
    W. G. Bennis, editor. New York: Holt,
    Rinehart and Winston, 1968.

Barthes, Roland, Trans. Richard Miller, S/Z. New
    York: Hill and Wang, 1974.

Becker, Ernst, The Denial of Death. London:
    Collier Macmillan, 1975.

Bettelheim, Bruno, The Uses of Enchantment. New
    York: Vintage Books, 1977.

Bluestone, George, Novels into Film. Los
    Angeles: University of California Press,
    1966.

Bruner, Jerome S., On Knowing. Cambridge: The
    Belknap Press of Harvard University Press,
    1962.

Bruner, Jerome S., The Process of Education.
    Cambridge, Mass.: Harvard University Press,
    1963.

Cassirer, Ernst, Language and Myth. Trans. by
    Susanne K. Langer. Toronto: General Publish-
    ing Company Limited, 1953.

Courtney, Richard, Play, Drama and Thought. (The
    Intellectual Background to Drama in Educa-
    tion). New York: Drama Book Specialists,
    3rd ed., 1974.

Courtney, Richard, "The Discipline of Drama". A
    paper adapted from a lecture first delivered
    to the Department of Drama, Queen's Univer-
    sity, Kingston, Ontario, January 22, 1976.
    Queen's Quarterly, 84, 2 (Summer 1977):
    231-43.

Courtney, Richard, The Dramatic Curriculum.
    London, Ont.: University of Western Ontario,
    1980.

Frye, Northrop, The Secular Scripture: A study of the Structure of Romance. London: Harvard University Press, 1966.

Frye, Northrop, The Stubborn Structure. London: Methuen and Company Limited, 1970.

Gardner, Robert, "The Adaptation of Works of Literary Merit into the Film and Television Forms". Unpublished M.A. Thesis, McMaster University, 1969.

Gillis, Lynette, Implications for Children's Educational Television from Story Grammar Research. Toronto: OECA, 1980.

Laing, R. D., The Politics of Experience. New York: Pantheon Books, 1967.

Laing, R. D., Sanity, Madness and the Family. New York: Basic Books, 1971.

Levi-Strauss, Claude, Myth and Meaning. Toronto: University of Toronto Press, 1978.

Lifton, Robert J., The Life of The Mind. New York: Simon and Schuster, 1976.

May, Rollo, The Meaning of Anxiety. New York: Washington Square Press, 1979.

Piaget, Jean, Structuralism. Trans. Chaninah Maschler. New York: Harper Collophon Books, 1970.

Propp, Vladimir, Morphology of the Folktale. Trans. by Laurence Scott. Austin: University of Texas Press, 1968.

Robinson, F. G., ICPGMU: A Framework for the Preparation of Curriculum Guidelines and Related Instructional Materials. Toronto: Ontario Institute for Studies in Education, 1979, Mimeographed.

Selye, Hans, The Stress of Life. New York: McGraw-Hill Book Co., 1976.

THE DRAMA OF READING
by
John McInnes


New understandings of reading have brought about considerable change in reading instruction in the last decade. The central concept behind such change is a simple one. The child's search for meaning drives the language learning processes. The reader's purpose is to find out what his or her world is about, what people mean. Margaret Donaldson, in Children's Minds explains, "The primary thing is now held to be the grasp of meaning--the ability to 'make sense' of things, and above all, to make sense of what people do, which of course includes what people say." (Donaldson 1978). The focus on the child's search for meaning has caused educators and researchers to look for the links among the child's many learning activities, conversation, play, spontaneous drama, representation in many media, writing. Seeing the links, educators make better curriculum decisions. Students experience heightened learning opportunities, and deeper satisfaction of their need to understand.

Reading has special links with drama. The act of reading is in itself dramatic. It allows the reader to participate in other lives, to engage in enactments, in his or her mind, of stories shaped and enhanced by personal experience and imagining. James Britton comments "Basically we never cease to long for more lives than the one we have; in the role of spectator we can participate in an infinite number." (Britton, 1968). In reading, the child draws selectively and reflectively on experiences in his or her life and projects from that personal base into the lives of people in stories. The reader exerts control in shaping to his or her satisfaction a unique version of the text.

In reading, the child experiences dramatic encounters with authors. The reader forms a relationship with each author, submitting to that person's influence while at the same time maintaining the validity of his or her own perceptions and knowledge. The reader orchestrates a collaboration which has the potential, at any time, for tension release, joy, sorrow, argument, compromise. The excitement of reading is in part the drama of entering into the reader/author relationship.

"Any but the most naive kind of reading puts us into implicit relation with an author. A novelist (or a playwright) may be directing our attention mainly to the action and exper- ience of his characters, and part of our job is to enter imaginatively into them. But he is at the same time conveying his own evalua- tion of what is done and felt, presenting it...as heroic, pathetic, contemptible, charming, funny...and implicitly inviting us to share his attitudes. Our task as readers is not complete unless we tacitly evaluate his evaluation, endorsing it fully, rejecting it, but more probably feeling some less clear-cut attitude based on discriminations achieved or groped after." (Harding, 1971).

As a reader/collaborator there are risks involved in getting together with Maurice Sendak, Judy Blume, or Marcel Proust. There is the risk of embarrassment, the fear of not being quite experienced enough for the task. There is the excitement of mind meeting mind in an endeavor where each brings special knowledge, skill and experience. Of course there is the safety valve. The reader can dismiss a particular author, no matter how brilliant, in favour of another with whom he or she can work more easily and inti- mately. The reader sometimes slows the reading as a book comes to a conclusion in order to prolong the relationship. There is the feeling of loss, of regret in finishing the collabora- tion. There is often a lurking wish that the relationship had gone better, had been more productive. There is always anticipation of forming new relationships with new authors and renewing collaboration efforts with those who have become old friends. Reading is a personal investment.

The reader's success in reading is based on various experiences of collaboration in other settings. The reader deliberately takes risks. The challenge of reading is in knowing that it will demand growth and change in the light of new shared experience that goes beyond the dimensions of the actual events of the reader's life. "Responding adequately to a great work means becoming something different from your previous self." (Harding, 1971).

Reading is an active process. There is no higher degree of activity than when the reader employs all his or her resources to mentally stage a story. Michael Benton suggests that the reader, "recreates something that approximates to the original conception of the author. In this sense he is the performer, the interpreter of text. Granted he does not have the expressive outlet of a stage, of an audience, but, instead he builds a mental stage and fills it with people, scenes, and events that the text offers him...and with other images generated by his own individual inclinations and limitation." (Benton, 1979).

In the process of reading narrative the reader takes on a variety of roles. In the mental staging of text the reader becomes director. Since a new and unique version of the author's text is being developed director's decisions come rapidly. The reader controls the lighting of the scene, calls for brilliant light or murky darkness. The reader paces the action in ways that seem appropriate, often lengthening the reading time by slowing down the process to match the time element and structure of the text. Aidan Warlow comments, "The delicately paced account of Mary's encounter with the robin in Chapter 7 of The Secret Garden may force the child to reduce the speed of his reading to match the tentative movements and hushed expectancy of the situation. And the opening page of Ted Hughes' The Iron Man cannot be read rapidly even when one tries; the sentence structure forces us to pause and 'vocalize' as we read - as when we read poetry." (Warlow, 1977).

The reader/director cuts scenes, and even rearranges them in the process of reflecting and rereading. He or she heightens the traits of certain characters and plays down others. The reader/director is in control of the shaping of a unique version of the text in ways that he or she cannot experience in watching television or film. The technology of the book makes it possible for the reader to bring his or her own creativity of interpretation into play from paragraph to paragraph, scene to scene. As director, the reader, with nodding consultation with the author, brings the text to life in his or her head. The version remembered is the version personally directed.

Engaging in a book, the reader at times takes on the role of actor. He or she may take the opportunity of becoming a part of the story as it is constructed. He or she may project into, or for a brief time live the part of a character, or characters in the story. The reader may build into the mental enactment of the story bits of his or her own experience. These are melded into interpretation in subconscious ways. The reader may come away from the story with a feeling of having actually interacted in the lives of the characters in the book. Since each reader brings a set of unique experiences to the text the internal enactments of stories are highly personal.

The child reader can try on, or act out roles as he or she wishes in complete safety. The range of characters to be played is endless. Through readings, the child extends the knowledge of what it might be like to be in danger, under threat, in crisis. Yet the reader is protected through distance in place and time, through the remoteness of a fantastic setting, through humour. Catherine Storr comments "...a first class writer like Rosemary Sutcliff...can treat desperate situations and complete realism. She never minimizes danger, but in her stories the passage of time serves the same function as the proscenium arch, or the spotlight in the theatre, it enables the audience to believe in what is happening on stage while retaining the consciousness of immunity from danger." (Storr, 1971).

Children need to learn to use reading fully in their school years. Educators need to consider what aspects of the school program develop readers fully. In taking the view that reading is a constructive process serving unique purposes for individual readers, teachers need to review the school activities that might develop readers more completely. The consideration of drama as it affects reading and learning to read is essential.

Storying is an essential way of knowing. Storying is learned in play. Dimensions of story telling are explored before the child begins to read. At the root of prediction as a reading strategy is story sense, or knowledge and how stories go. Teachers offer children many opportunities to tell anecdotes, to retell familiar stories. They offer them occasions of playing out stories, their own or someone else's. In informal and spontaneous enactments children see the options of character and plot. They discover that they can manipulate their people and events in exciting and revealing ways. Children confirm their knowledge about how stories go in non-print experiences and in their own writing. Children who have had rich experiences in storying bring greater expectations to text than do those who have been passive in the presence of stories.

The reader learns flexibility in moving from predictions to confirmation of story directions. The reader learns flexibility through reading and writing but this ability to hold tentative has been nurtured in play and dramatic speculation.

Two four year old boys playing with blocks in a junior kindergarten were harrassed by another boy who continually knocked down whatever structure they built. They were angry and frustrated but continued their activity. The disturbing element finally lay flat out on all their blocks preventing them from continuing. At that point one of the children said to his friend, "Hey, Joe, this guy has had a terrible accident we got to get him to the hospital."

They moved around and sat down at the victim's head, as if he were an ambulance. They "drove" him to the hospital. Sirens wailed and there was considerable talk about the accident. When they arrived at the hospital the victim had become a full participant in the play. He lay stiff as a board so that they could carry him into emergency.

Through play children develop the "suppose" element that must be brought to reading. They elaborate the "suppose" in their puppet plays, their impromptu dramatizations, their story telling and writing.

Children learn the give and take of collaboration in their planning and carrying out many school tasks. They invest most in collaboration when they initiate ideas and work to build representations of experience in a variety of ways. Inventive dramatic experiences allow them to test, modify, reshape in collaborative ways that are more manageable than cooperative writing tasks. The fluidity, the give and take of collaborative play, and collaborative production is instructive to the role of collaborator with author when reading begins.

Dramatic responses to text display elements of comprehension not often revealed in paper and pencil tasks. Children in groups can share their individual comprehension of stories read, and work through some group consensus of what the story meant. The live involvement in responding actively to stories often displays the depth of feeling children have attained in reading. Sometimes feelings cannot be articulated in words in a reporting manner. They can be discerned when children engage in reworking or replaying part or all of a story. Active classrooms develop active readers.

The reading of plays deserves special attention in school. The conventions of script need to be understood. The implicit information usually explicit in narrative writing demands inference. An oral reading of script can be a satisfying experience for a group of children. In most cases the memorization of script is too demanding and time consuming for what it is worth. Silent reading and enjoyment of plays should be encouraged in the same manner as silent reading of stories, poems and informational text. Of course there is a strong likelihood that reading plays will result in improvised extensions of what the author has written.

The conditions of reading instruction must respect the fact that what the child intends to do with text is to create a whole, complete version of text, shaped to his or her satisfaction. Susanne Langer says: "Whatever our integrated organic response may be, it is a response not to cumulative little stimuli - a precariously sustained progress of memories, association, unconscious wishes, emotions - but, a response to a strongly articulated virtual experience, one dominant stimulus." (Langer, 1953).

Reading instruction must not distract the reader from the intention of creating the whole interpretation. It must not, through questioning, drilling, interrupting, and explaining, interfere with the attempt to deal in a holistic way, with text, whether it be a short story, a poem, or a novel. The production in the reader's mind should be complete unless he or she determines to terminate it at some point along the way.

Reading and drama are part of one another. They draw on and extend the same personal resources. They interact with each other. A rich curriculum capitalizes on and develops the inventiveness of minds, the expressiveness of bodies, the sensitivity to language that all children can bring to their explorations of meaning.

## THE DRAMA OF READING

a poetic summary of a presentation

John McInnes

The reader opens the book
where the wild things are
blubber
remembrance of things past
and the drama begins.

The reader opens the book
and people begin to move
through different dramas
on mental stages
of the reader's choice
lit to order
lightened

brightened
bathed in brilliance
dimmed
faded to black
at the reader's cue.

The reader reads
and sets and props
emerge from the page
tastefully arranged
placed, replaced
always appropriate
to the unfolding scene.

The reader listens
to the accompanying sounds
music
heartbeats pounding
brought up and out
perfectly tuned
meticulously timed
complete.

The reader directs
asks each actor
to move
to talk
to react
consistently please
to satisfy the conditions
of the text.

The reader/director
records impressions
of this well directed version
of the work
activated and ordered
with such personal energy
and commitment
unforgettable.

The reader reads and acts
gets in and out
of parts
at will
feeling what it is like
to win
to live
to be strengthened
to be humiliated

to cry
projecting recklessly
into other times and places
and emerging
safe but different
from a previous self.

The reader collaborates
excited by selected minds
Maurice Sendak
Judy Blume
Marcel Proust
thousands to choose from.

The reader feels
the tension of collaboration
the risk of embarrassment
the fear of not being experienced
enough
to share the joint undertaking
of bringing new meaning
to the page.

The reader senses the drama
of this personal interaction
mind meeting mind
each offering special knowledge
language
and the strong intention
to mean.

The reader works
to sustain the relationship
with the author/partner
respecting what is special
about that person's contribution
expecting respect
composing together
as if under contract.

The reader feels power
knowing at any time
the unseen collaborator
may be dismissed
banished
in favour of easier voices
that promises to become
instantly intimate
one night stands
easily forgotten.

The reader collaborates
filled with the knowledge
that having engaged a mind
for hours, days and weeks
there will be loss
perhaps regret
when the book ends.

The reader comprehends
peopling worlds
within distinct perimeters
within particular constraints
events, behaviours, feelings
bound into a cohesive whole
captured in meanings
personally defined.

How shall we teach
the reader what to do
when the reader
opens the book?

## Bilbliography

Benton, Michael. "Children's response to stories." Children's Literature in Education, 10 (2) 1979, pp. 68-85.

Britton, James. "The nature of the reader's satisfaction." The Cool Web, Margaret Meek, Aidan Warlow, Giselda Barton (Eds.) The Bodley Head, London, 1977, pp. 106-111.

Donaldson, Margaret. Children's Minds. Fontana/Collins, Glasgow, 1978, p. 38.

Harding, D. W. 'The bond with the author,' Use of English, 22(4), Summer 1971.

Langer, Susanne. Feeling and Form. London: Routledge and Kegan Paul, 1953, p. 266.

Storr, Catherine. "Things that go bump in the night." The Sunday Times Magazine, March 7, 1971.

Warlow, Aidan. "What the reader has to to." The Cool Web, Margaret Meek, Aidan Warlow, Griselda Barton (Eds.). The Bodley Head, London, pp. 91-96.

A RESPONSE TO THE DRAMA OF READING BY JOHN McINNES
by
David W. Booth


In his paper, John McInnes has described the drama of reading, and, as he states, the very act of reading is dramatic: the reader constantly creates an imaginary theatre of the mind from what is being read, staging the story from personal experience and imagination, taking on roles and interacting in the lives of the characters, safely, protected by time and place. However, as an act of learning, reading is basically a private experience, and drama generally a shared one. But, as McInnes says, reading and drama are closely linked in the teaching/learning processes: they are part of one another, interacting with each other, developing the same personal resources in the reader/participant and encouraging collaboration. This response paper is concerned chiefly with examining activities that promote thinking/feeling strengths in students whether they are interacting with print or with people.

The search for meaning does link drama and reading in several ways, and it is necessary to re-think this relationship in order to fashion strategies that promote heightened learning opportunities and deeper satisfaction. (Bolton, 1979). Human beings are essentially creatures who have the power to experience meanings, and being human exist in a pattern of meanings (Phenix, 1969). General education is the process of helping human beings to find essential meanings in life, through intellectual development and through processes that imply feeling, conscience and inspiration. These meanings accrue through personal experiences, and reading and dramatic interaction allow children to understand the experiences of others, enlarging their own spheres of meaning. The transmission of meaning is therefore of prime consideration in language teaching. Finding meaning and developing language potential is bound up with the child's attempts to make sense of life's situations by being involved in them in an active sense, and by drawing inferences from them. (Donaldson, 1978).

The reading experience is a personal one and a private one: readers understand what the words say to them, translate the experience they have read about into their own context, and have feelings and attitudes about the experience and the text. It is common for teachers to discuss the knowledge relevant to a text, but not much time has been devoted to those qualities that the reader brings to the text - feelings, experiences, attitudes, values and beliefs. "No amount of hindsight will help us to understand what we can't yet 'live through'. There is a sense of growing involvement with the experience and the past incident slips momentarily into the present". (Dixon, 1975, p. 117).

In drama, it is possible to move from the particular experience to a more general understanding of the nature of what is being explored. Drama can then be used to understand the nature of themes and abstract concepts; it can aid students in finding levels of meaning. If the source being explored is print, then the drama investigation will concern finding implicit truths rather than simply telling events from memory. "Weak drama as is weak reading, is concerned with the word rather than the meaning." (Moffett, 1983, p. 42). Drama is concerned with cognitive/affective learning, a realization on the learners' part that they are growing, moving forward and gaining new understanding. In the interchange between drama and text, the child meets a wide range of cultural symbols. The drama must help the child in finding levels of meaning in those symbols. Drama makes explicit much of what is implicit. The teacher must relate the print to the lives of the students for significant learning to occur. Drama can allow the reader's own subjective world to come into play, where subjective experience is released, helping the student in the understanding and application of the meaning in a text. Students who will develop language abilities must have activities placed in a meaningful context that is unified and vital. Drama in education is a whole representation of thought, providing language learning with whole meanings from each student. (Courtney, 1978).

An individual develops a feeling for story, for narrative, as much through kinetic activity and association as through more intellectualized approaches, and drama seems to be the most promising vehicle at hand to allow such direct engagement. (Duke, 1975). It is from reading drama draws a large part of its content, and drama can be an effective strategy for promoting reading for meaning. Certain dramatic activities will prepare the students for the story; others can be used while the student is reading and still others can be used after reading. Training in reading must focus on the systematic examination of the ideas of the author, and facilitate the exchange between the reader and the print. It seems advisable for a teacher to utilize as many instructional techniques as possible in developing understanding of the reading process. Through drama, teachers can contribute to the possible responses the students can have, helping them to acquire the means of more fully understanding what they read and what they mean. Participating in dramatizing events, problems, situations and stories is an appropriate way of providing active involvement and experience that reading seems to require.

Drama can add interest and vitality to a reading program. (Stewig, 1983). Story as a source for drama has a place in education. The teacher must understand the search for meaning under the text as paramount in teaching. The students need to interact with the textual ideas and their own thoughts in order to bring about meaning. Many stories which children will encounter are well-suited to drama. Whether it is a folk or a fairy tale, a basal reader, a trade book or made-up in an experience-approach program, stories can be the basis for drama (Rosen, 1973). The teacher must consider the story carefully for dramatic possibilities - an issue, a concept, a situation or a problem to be solved. The story can be told or read by the teacher or read silently by the students before or after its use as motivation for the drama. The students can enact incidents from the story, extend the action of the story, or elaborate upon the details of the story. The teacher must constantly help the students go back and forth between the stories and their own improvised responses (Fines and Verrier, 1974). A person can translate print into meaning by bringing to it the understanding that it is a code to be cracked, and that to make sense of that text requires the application of one's own experience (Heathcote, 1978). In order to bring drama into a text, students have to think about the meaning and the implications of words. Using the words of others as cues for their own responses allows the students to test the implications of their statements. Through drama, questions can be raised about the text that will stimulate the class to read more selectively and insightfully. By choosing situations from stories and poems as a beginning point for drama, the teacher can give the pupils the power of literature, with all of its encompassing levels of meaning. The teacher can draw on the vast resources of the story - its situations, characters, problems, relationships, mood, atmosphere, texture and concepts, as a way of stimulating and enriching the students' dramatic explorations.

Moffett (1983) defines the difference between enactment and improvisation, and relates the terms to print. All improvisation is based on a story idea, which is the least elaborated, most summarized statement of character and event that will give the participants the feelings of having enough to work with - the minimal situation. The difference between enactment and improvisation is a matter of degree only, since there are always some given information or suggested ideas that are the starting point for drama. In improvising, one makes up more of the story as one goes along and when enacting, one has more details specified in advance. Therefore dramatic activity breaks down into two main kinds - inventing one's own dramas and enacting the stories of others. Both are improvisational: the difference is in whether the student creates the situation and actions, or uses the details of word and movement that flesh out the borrowed story. Enacting occurs when the student relives what has happened, but turns it into an event that happens as it is spoken about (Dixon, 1975). Enactment helps the students to live through and experience again, helping them to gain more control, more intellectual grasp. In order for students to dramatize text, they have to think about the meaning of it and follow those implications. Enacting a selection from literature translates that text into voice, movement and speech. The language of the children may even be different because the story langauge may be incorporated into the drama. The students become involved - physically and immediately - in the text they are dramatizing and may go back to the printed page for additional insights or to settle arguments. They may find additional, practical reasons for wanting to re-read. Sometimes children have numerous ideas for dramatizing a story, and sometimes they can carry out these ideas on their own, as the teacher guides and organizes the drama. Often the teacher must help the children in selecting their materials, in seeing the possibilities for drama, and in structuring the drama. The teacher may role-play when necessary, or perhaps serve as a narrator whenever the drama needs to be refocused (Beall-Heinig and Stillwell, 1982).

There are limitations to enactment. For some students, enactment may be an important therapeutic or social experience. Since decision and action are not required, the students are free "to savour feeling and to focus on form" (O'Neill, 1976, p. 14). However, the students may not actually experience drama, just imitate the emotion. As well, the impulse to get the sequence of events in the story right may take away the emphasis on the inner meaning of the narrative. It is even possible that traditional enactment may dilute the initial experience of the literature rather than enrich the student's understanding. In Down the Rabbit Hole, Winnifred Lear recalls her experience in school, as a pupil, in an enactment class:

For literature we read Hiawatha, The Heroes and the Talisman, and wrote scenes from them which we acted in the form-room with a toasting fork as Pallas Athen's spear and an upturned waste basket for the tribal fire. The idea, as I discovered when I did teaching practice years later, was that the child, by participation, enters more fully into the spirit of the book studies. It had the opposite effect on me. Left to myself, I gorged deliciously on Hiawatha sailing away into the sunset, Richard Coeur de Lion and Saladin competing in the word-play the Medusa's snakey looks and the three Grey Sisters passing round their communal eye as the stranger approached, but the thing was spoiled for me once I had seen Doris Birchall in a fit of giggles and a couple of faded curtains being Queen Berengaria, or Jenny Denton as noble Andromedia chained to the rock, emitting mouse-like squeaks for help, tied up with a piece of string to the handle of the art cupboard (p. 119).

It is not the process of enactment that is the problem; rather, it is the lack of exploration of the meanings of the story - the themes, concepts and issues - that weakens the process. Though stories may be the inspiration for the planning, it is not stories the students re-enact; they simply live through some events as best they may, using what they already understand to 'inform' the situation, and give them hold on it. And this, in turn, leads them to need further information, gleaned through the "living-through". (Heathcote, 1978). Drama is not stories retold in action; rather drama is human beings confronted by situations which change them, because of what they must face in dealing with those challenges. Since a story presents a completed narrative, the teacher must use the implications of the story, shifting the thinking of the students from events to the themes and concepts within the story so that the students will bring a new understanding to the original story.

Dramatization can provide motivation for children to do research on the period in which the drama is set, using encyclopaedia, history books and biographies. When students start asking for and using dictionaries, art books, texts of all kinds, then drama has created a need for information. "The code has been cracked, and the learners have found they have power over material written rather than its having power over them." (Wagner, 1976, p. 135).

There are few scripts for children to read aloud. There are plays written by adults for other adults to present to children, but the writers of children's literature generally choose other genres for their writing. Using drama in education, teachers have found sound educational goals for working with children on oral reading activities. One excellent source lies in using good dialogue (found in novels, poems and picture books) written by authors of children's literature. Children can work in pairs or small groups, reading the dialogue silently and then aloud. The teacher can have the children change roles, change the setting, present new tensions, change the time period and help the children dramatize the selection so that the children can bring new meanings to their interpretation of the print. Scripts can be created from the improvised drama and then transcribed from tapes or from memory by those who were involved in the drama. These scripts can then be read aloud by other groups. Although reading aloud is not necessary for proficient reading comprehension, it can be a learning process if drama is the goal of the oral reading. It can help the children transfer the print to the voice, allowing them to hear what the voices in the selection are saying, helping them to be free to manipulate print and to train their eyes and ears in exploring the rhythms of language. Reading aloud can externalize the reading comprehension and give reason for demonstrating the comprehension. It can give the students a chance to take in new language styles and patterns and make them their own. Oral reading also helps silent readers to hear dialogue. However, the children should read when there is a contextual reason for doing so: drama presents such embedded opportunities. The students can chant and sing, read proclamations and letters, present research from documents and reference materials, summarize each group's findings - all within role, within the dramatic context. They can read aloud poems that reflect the drama, excerpts that present comparisons and analogies, and journal comments to share feelings.

In summary, drama and reading are related in four ways:

1. drama presents learning experiences that increase the students' personal meanings, thus altering the information they bring to the page.

2. children who have rich experience in storying bring greater expectation to print. As McInnes states, dramatic speculation nurtures the ability to hold tentative, and develops the "suppose" element that must be brought to reading.

3. drama increases silent reading power as pupils explore the situations, characters and problems in their stories and poems and then reveal their private comprehension in-role. Through interaction, these personal meanings are expanded, adapted, clarified and altered until the story itself becomes clearer to those involved as the attitudes of each participant are revealed to the group.

4. drama is an excellent technique for developing in children the skills of oral interpretation. While in-role, they can read aloud poems, songs, dialogue, and excerpts from novels and stories; while reflecting about the drama experience, they can share poems and journal writings.

McInnes is concerned with helping children comprehend in the fullest sense, so that they can

witness and know
events, behaviours, feelings
bound into a cohesive whole
captured in meanings
personally defined.

(A Poetic Summary, p. 79)


Drama can be a way of helping children make meaning through sharing individual understanding, and then reshaping and modifying these ideas and values through group collaboration and consensus, within the dramatic art form.

REFERENCES

Bolton, Gavin. Towards a Theory of Drama in Education. London: Longman, 1979.

Courtney, Richard. The Dramatic Curriculum. Faculty of Education, University of Western Ontario, London, Ontario, 1980.

Courtney, Richard. Play, Drama and Thought. London: Cassette; New York: Drama Book Specialists, 1974.

Cowen, John E. Teaching Reading Through the Arts. International Reading Association, 1983.

Dixon, John. Growth Through English. National Association for the Teaching of English, 1975.

Donaldson, Margaret. Children's Minds. Fontana/ Collins, Glascow, 1978.

Duke, Charles. Creative Dramatics and English Teaching. National Council of Teachers of English, 1975.

Finis, John & Verrier, Roy. The Drama of History. London: New University Press, 1974.

Heathcote, Dorothy. "Cracking the Code" in The English Quarterly, Volume XI, No. 1, Toronto: Canadian Council of Teachers of English, 1978.

Heinig, R. B. & L. Stillwell. Creative Drama for the Classroom Teachers. New Jersey: Prentice-Hall, 1982.

Lear, Winnifred, Down the Rabbit Hole. MacMillan, 1975.

Moffett, James. A Student-Centered Language Arts Curriculum. New York: Houghton, Mifflin, 1982.

O'Neill, C. et al, Drama Guidelines. London: Heinemann, 1976.

Phenix, P. H. Realms of Meaning. New York: McGraw Hill, 1964.

Rosen, C., & Rosen, H.  The Language of Primary
    School Children.  Penguin International, 1973.

Stewig, John.  Informal Drama in the Elementary
    Language    Program.    Colubmia    University,
    Teachers College Press, 1983.

Wagner, Betty J., Dorothy Heathcote.  Drama as a
    Learning    Medium.    National    Education
    Association, 1976.

# PROGRAM EVALUATION IN THE ARTS
by
H. Howard Russell

## Introduction

It may be true that school programs, or curricula, which are evaluated, are also valued, and as a consequence are likely to continue to exist or perhaps even attract more time, more students, more money, or more attention. Also, it may be true that programs which are not evaluated, are not valued, and as a consequence may encounter a cut in the amount of allotted time, number of students, budget, or other. A third statement which seems to be even more likely to be true is that it is much more difficult to "measure" or evaluate programs in the arts than it is in mathematics, science, reading, or other school subjects. The consequences of these three statements are not difficult to figure out, even for a mathematician or an educational researcher. They suggest that there will not be as much evaluation in the arts as in science and mathematics, and that in turn there will be less time, less money, less attention, and fewer students in the arts programs. If this scenario fits a part of the world which you see, and if the rationale which supports that scenario is in any sense like the rationale I have presented, then you have an incentive to take another look at evaluation in the arts, and that is precisely what I want you to do. I want you to see one or two features of recent evaluation studies which I hope will make evaluation, and evaluation in the arts more palletable than it has been in the past. What I propose to do then is to consider some particular studies which illustrate these points and then we can see how they apply to the arts.

The first study I wish to consider illustrates very clearly how we can fool ourselves with common external examinations. The fact that the study was conducted in connection with science means that we can enjoy the thoughts that subjects which appear to rely on precision and standards are not immune from the human capacity to distort things beyond recognition.[1] The fact that the Science Council of Canada sponsored

95

the study and that it was conducted by a competent researcher from the University of Quebec, Professor Pierre-Leon Trempe, means that it was carefully planned according to the highest standards known to the scientific community at this point in time. The second study I wish to consider also bears the stamp of approval of a significant segment of the academic community, in this case mathematicians. The study is the Second International Mathematics Study[2] of the IEA and it illustrates how a large scale international study can be conducted so that the kinds of distortions identified in the Trempe study are not likely to occur. In fact the SIMS data may even be sufficiently complete that they could detect the kind of distortion which Trempe was able to detect. In any event there are a number of ways of looking at data which SIMS employs which I believe may interest you. They highlight issues such as the differences among the three well known curricula, namely the intended curriculum, the implemented curriculum, and the attained curriculum. They also highlight programming features such as coverage, retention or participation, pace and yield. On the basis of the SIMS Study, and the Trempe (SCC) Study it is reasonable to suggest that evaluation in the arts may proceed in a basically different way from most currently employed studies. It is also possible to render some harsh judgments about external examinations as well as some positive judgments about observation data in education evaluation. If I do my analysis well I hope to be able to show you how to conduct an evaluation study in the arts which capitalizes on the most up-to-date methods available.

## Evaluation and Alienation

The first study I have chosen to describe is perhaps the most significant study which I have read in recent years. It is a part of an evaluation of a science program, and because of that I must ask you to trust me for a few minutes so that I can make the case before making the connection to our topic, evaluation in the arts. Professor Trempe of University of Quebec was given the task of describing a science program in a school by means of gathering data in the school, in particular observation data. This was a part of a larger enterprise of the Science Council of Canada. The school which was chosen met some overall design requirements and the staff offered to cooperate. There was the research study of the "official" programme description and the careful connection of the textbooks to the programme, and there was the usual rich description of the teachers and the students which showed them to be more or less normal people.

The study began to take on special significance when Professor Trempe entered the classrooms and recorded his observations. Almost immediately he noticed that the instructors offered "odds" for each question, or topic, corresponding to the likelihood it would be on the provincial examinations. The mere mention of the odds seemed to be of interest on its own, but the fact that it could be associated with quite different treatment both by the teacher and by the students was of fundamental importance. Items with low odds were done quickly and with limited detail whereas items with high odds were covered slowly and with great detail. As far as the students were concerned the difference was almost as simple as keeping notes or not. To put it bluntly both students and teachers were working exclusively on passing the provincial tests.

At this point in the description it is possible to conclude that "God is in his Heaven" and that is the way we want it. The difficulty becomes more compelling as Trempe reviews the purposes of the science program and then matches such purposes with what is happening in the classroom. An underlying purpose of science classes is to help youngsters understand science processes and to accumulate science knowledge sufficiently to permit them to make effective use of both parts of science in their work lives and in their private lives. It would seem then, that in the classes Trempe visited there is evidence that the students are going to accumulate knowledge about test items which are on an "anticipated list". But what it is that they learn about these items is even more meaningfully revealed by Trempe. He spent a considerable amount of time questioning students, and his notes indicate that in nearly all cases the

students were not interested at all in understanding the principle which was the central
feature of the test item, but rather they were
interested in the precise "trick" needed for
answering correctly the specific question. This
showed up time and time again when Trempe tried
to explain scientific principles to students who
raised their hands about questions during the
class period. They only wanted a neat "trick"
which they could record so that it could be
memorized later. They did not have time, nor did
they have any apparent interest in learning
"science."

Prof. Trempe has made a serious analysis of
his data and he is confident that the case
reveals not only an inversion of science teaching, i.e. the teaching of anti-science, rather
than science but also the alienation of a large
group of teachers and students. The inversion of
purposes takes place because the central purposes
of science are not learned by the students at
all. At least the evidence suggests that the
students are not interested in these purposes.
What the students learn is an efficient way to
maximize their scores on provincial tests and it
seems unlikely to matter which subject is used as
the vehicle. They still learn how to pass tests
without learning the substance of the tests.

I realize that the above scenario is not new
to you. I do believe however that the Trempe
Study is the best example I know which documents
the nature and the extent of the inversion of
goals which is caused by the examination system
and which in turn seems to plague us in the
education of the young in all disciplines. The
fact that this Trempe Study involved science
education and that the most revealing part of the
study came from qualitative data and non quantitative analysis is significant. I hope you will
agree with me that such data and such analyses
can be used in the domain of the arts with
results possibly similar to those of Trempe. The
consequence of such studies must be a strong commitment to take another look at evaluation. Not
only is it likely true that common external
examinations can have the effects documented by
Trempe but also it is true that non quantitative

data and non quantitative analysis may be necessary to explicate the issues.

## IEA Second International Mathematics Study

Since I have used the first part of my time period to make a case for non quantitative data and non quantitative analyses I should point out in this part of my presentation that although the features of IEA SIMS which I shall concentrate on now have a quantitative component to them it is nevertheless true that IEA SIMS is founded on a wide variety of non quantitative data and non quantitative analysis. What is perhaps more important to note at the beginning of the next part of my presentation is that none of the testing which is done in connection with SIMS should lead to, nor tend to lead to, the kind of teaching to the test documented by Trempe. The rationale is simple but profound. In the SIMS evaluation the focus of attention is on program monitoring, as opposed to people monitoring. Let me digress a minute to clarify the difference. In the Trempe study the purpose of the provincial tests was to monitor people, i.e. to help decide who should pass, who should fail, and who should be allocated to which class in the next term. The tests probably perform the people monitoring function reasonably well, in spite of the disastrous consequences for the science program. In other words the weakest students fail and the better students proceed further towards their higher level social role, and hence the test has performed a screening function or a people monitoring function.

Program monitoring, on the other hand, has as its purpose, meaningful comparisons among parts of the program. How well is one part learned compared with another part? Are institutional procedures associated with particular positive or negative outcomes which can be replicated? Is what we claim to cover what we actually cover? Is what we cover what students actually learn? Could we cover things differently and improve our overall yield? Is our pace appropriate to student capability? Is there content diversity in the program or do all children get the same substance? These questions are different from the usual evaluation questions, and focusing on

99

them can lead to program change which may lead to outcome change. But throughout the program monitoring enterprise there is no need for people monitoring and there should be no tolerance of people monitoring. People monitoring seems to be the root cause of the scenario revealed by Trempe, and because program monitoring does not need to involve, nor even tolerate people monitoring, it is possible then to conduct program monitoring a la SIMS without suffering the consequence described by Trempe.

In order to "do" program monitoring we need some new tools, or perhaps old tools which have fallen into disuse. We need to distinguish between what the central government suggests or mandates or "intends" to be taught and what the teacher actually "implements" in the classroom. Also we need to be able to distinguish between these two curricula and a third curriculum which is the substance actually learned by the student. Within SIMS we became accustomed to the concepts intended curriculum, implemented curriculum and attained curriculum. This seemed to occur naturally because in the First International Mathematics Study there was great criticism about the lack of curriculum content data, and there was considerable confusion about the implemented and the intended curricula. In that first study the curriculum data consisted largely of official documents and intended curricula, while the arguments were more concerned with the match between the test used in the study and the common content across countries.

It was customary in large scale studies of that era to use a common test devised by the participating countries, but the decision procedures leading to rejection of unsuitable items were such that not many items survived, and hence the test covered a very restricted domain. Many arguments arose as a consequence of the elimination of important mathematics topics, but that was a natural consequence of the items selection.

In order to eliminate such problems as restricted content domain in the SIMS (the second study) there was an early decision made to adopt a comprehensive domain rather than a restricted domain. Such a domain could be narrowed or restricted for particular purposes as the occasion required, but it would represent a broad basic definition of mathematics content. With a commitment to distinguishing among intended, implemented, and attained curricula, and a further commitment to build a comprehensive domain, i.e. as long as two countries considered a topic important it would be included, the item development enterprise began in 1976 and it was completed in 1980. At the same time the various supporting instruments were developed, i.e. teacher opportunity-to-learn questionnaires and student attitude questionaires, etc. and these in turn lead to some new concepts.

FIGURE 1

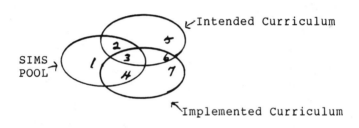

Evaluation in the Arts

We should study Figure 1 for a moment because it can help us see some of the things which have gone wrong in the past, and which went wrong in the first mathematics study. Figure 1 is based on the idea that we have a comprehensive array of mathematics test items, or what may be called an item pool. The items in the pool correspond to the points in the spaces labelled "1", "2", "3", and "4", in Figure 1. For instance, the item "What is the number of which 15% = 6? is in the algebra part of the pool and it is in most "intended curricula" and most "taught curricula" for the participating countries. Thus the item in question is in space labelled "3", in most classrooms.

In order to find an item in space "2" we need to locate one which the central government guide-lines mandate for teaching, but which - for whatever reason - is not actually taught. Many government officials believed there would be no items in space "2" but the empirical data gathered to date shows them to be wrong. There are indeed items in space "2".

Space "4" is equally awkward for government officials to explain. Why should there be items which teachers teach, although they are not on the intended curriculum? If such items are in the content domain of textbooks, or standardized tests, that may account for it. Suffice it to state that space "4" is rarely empty. It is true also that spaces 5, 6 and 7 are rarely empty but it has been a part of the commitment to compre-hensiveness of the SIMS pool from the beginning which has kept these external spaces (5, 6, and 7) to a minimum.

The introduction of the term coverage index is useful at this point because coverage tells how much of the content is taught to the stu-dents. The index is $C_T = \dfrac{n3 + n4}{n_1 + n_2 + n_3 + n_4}$. Perhaps you would be interested to know that the standard deviation of C+ is an indication of one type of program diversity. Yes, it is true that mathe-maticians must contend with diversity in the content of mathematics as it is taught in the

schools. Thus we have new symbols which have
given us greatly increased capacity to document
the nature of mathematics content. I hope this
bit of insight about the problems in the mathematics curriculum will offer you some comfort in
your thinking about the arts. Diversity is not
unique to the arts.

One last point about the SIMS enterprise
which may help us in the arts is the symbolism we
use in order to describe national (or provincial)
curricula.

FIGURE II

| | | SIMS POOL ITEMS | | | | | | | | |
|---|---|---|---|---|---|---|---|---|---|---|---|
| | | 1 | 2 | 3 | 4 | 5 | 6 | 7 | 8 | 9 | 10 |
| | a | 1 | 1 | 1 | 1 | 1 | 1 | 1 | 1 | 1 | 1 |
| | b | 1 | 1 | 1 | 1 | 1 | 1 | 1 | 1 | 1 | 1 |
| Teachers | c | 1 | 1 | 1 | 0 | 0 | 0 | 0 | 0 | 0 | 0 |
| | d | 1 | 1 | 1 | 0 | 0 | 0 | 0 | 0 | 0 | 0 |
| | e | 1 | 1 | 1 | 0 | 0 | 0 | 0 | 0 | 0 | 0 |

We use diagrams like Figure II in which the row
data come from individual teachers and the column
data come from individual items. In Figure II
the first teacher (row a) has apparently taught
all the items. The same is true for the second
teacher. Each of the other teachers has taught
only the first three items and no more. Thus
$C_T$ for each of the first two teachers is 1.00
and for each of the last three $C_T = 0.3$. These
computations do not tell us as much as Figure II
itself, because this one figure tells who taught
what for all teachers in this small hypothetical
country. The Figure II also tells us that the
better students are getting a superior program by
being with the first two teachers while all the
other students are getting a watered-down version
of the course.

One of the comments which has arisen in the
IEA SIMS work is that summary tests cannot be
made which will make fair comparisons possible
across countries, or even across schools. This
comment is based on the analyses of coverage
indices, and once this type of unfairness is
clarified, even quantified, there is no more need

103

to pursue the possibility of developing an acceptable summary test.

A study by Courtney and Park provides an opportunity now to make a connection between the research methods I have been promoting in science and mathematics and those used, or potentially useful in the arts. The study "Learning Through The Arts"[3] is a recent study of significant scope and magnitude. The part of the study which is of particular interest now is the conclusion that drama education is such that "Perception of the self in relation to others and sensitivity to others is developed" (p. 114). I can understand that this is a very important conclusion and I have no difficulty believing that it is a valid conclusion.

I wish to pursue the issue of how we know this conclusion is true, and how we can convince skeptics that it is true. Courtney and Park have gathered data from teachers, and such data focus on teacher perceptions, and these data lead to the conclusion that the students' sensitivity to others is developed through drama. The words that the teachers choose to describe this development lend credibitility to the conclusion, but the skeptic can insist that the teachers are merely seeing what they want to see and neglecting to see what they prefer not to see. Such a criticism is natural for the skeptic and I believe it is worthy of some attention in our present deliberation.

I realize that arts educators and researchers in the field have been skeptical of preordinate research, research which is designed to prove something which is specified beforehand. I believe they have been skeptical for good reasons, but I do not believe that the reasons they give are the right ones. Perhaps I can reveal what I mean by making a suggestion on the specific drama outcome in focus above. I believe there is general consensus on what is meant by sensitivity to others, but in spite of that I have not seen an operational definition or a working definition. I recommend that we try to find some working definitions and test them in the same situations from which the teacher perception data were so clear. One working definition I know comes from an OISE doctoral student, Z. Marini, who has developed a test of social sensitivity which is based on cartoon type presentations of social situations. Children are clearly separated into the categories "more sensitive" and "less sensitive" by each item and by the test. The face validity of the test is perfectly obvious. I believe that we should try to use instruments like this to test the impact of drama classes on youngsters and I feel quite confident that the resulting data will be positive. I believe that past attempts at such preordinate research have foundered because the instruments were not adequate to the task. Now there are better instruments available, and where instruments are still inadequate to the task it may be more appropriate to try to develop adequate instruments than to blame the design of the research.

The part of this line of thought which is most exciting to me is the consequence of contemplating a relatively complete array of instruments. I do not mean instruments for each and every possible consequence of programs in the arts, but rather a small number of instruments which cover in some way each of the main types of consequences of arts programs. The social sensitivity factor is just one illustration of an instrument that is newly developed, but is likely to go unnoticed in schools because it does not yield data which can be used on student report cards or in student promotions. We just do not want to fail youngsters because of a lack of social sensitivity. However, if we introduce a school program or a national program with social sensitivity as a possible outcome then it becomes exceedingly important to have data (a sample variety is all that is needed) which indicate the levels of performance of students (groups of students, not individuals) on this particular variable. I realize that one instrument does not indicate much about the total domain but it does indicate to me that it will be useful for arts educators and researchers to think again about possible parallels between the mathematics science domain and the arts domain.

If you wish to change arts education programs, and if you are afraid that arts education

is getting less than its fair share of attention
in the schools of today, then I believe that you
will want to plan to get a comprehensive account
of what the current program of the schools is,
not only the intended curriculum but also the
implemented and the attained. Until you have
such an account and until you can reproduce such
accounts on a regular basis it is going to be
difficult to engage in meaningful debate about
what should be changed. From my position as an
outsider, I cannot anticipate what we are going
to find in the arts area. I know some of my
students believe there is a serious discrepancy
between the "intended" curriculum--in Ontario
this is our Provincial Guidelines--and the
implemented curriculum. I would not be surprised
if the phenomena we encountered in the Trempe
study shows up somewhere in the arts. Examinations have been around a long time and their toll
on programs may be well know to teachers but it
is far from well documented in research at this
point in time. Of course it is possible that
examinations in some settings actually foster the
attainment of the objectives set for our programs. It is also possible that the stated
objectives of a program, such as the science
program, are not really the objectives which the
community wants the schools to pursue. It is
possible that the community, indeed the entire
society, is just as indifferent to the essence of
science as were the students who talked to Trempe.
Under such circumstances it may well be true that
the democratically derived objectives of the
school would be to "beat the provincial test".

I do not have answers to the above questions
but I do know how to get you to the point where
you can be expected to engage in meaningful debate
about them. First you must recognize that there
are two distinct types of testing going on these
days, one is for the purpose of people monitoring
and it requires testing every pupil with all
tests. The other type is for the purpose of
program monitoring and it requires only anonymous
sample surveys for data gathering. It is the
latter type of testing or evaluating which in my
view you need to consider more carefully in the
arts area. In order to conduct such a monitoring
program it is necessary to build a comprehensive
array of instruments or tests or test items which

constitute the best representation of the domain that is possible within the limitations of time and money which prevail. This pool of items or instruments may seem to be the type of pool which evaluators have been discussing for about twenty years, but it is not as clear as it should be, just what is the nature of such a pool.

The central problem with pools is that there are two basic varieties and the distinction between the two is rarely given the extent of attention that is required. One type of pool is used for evaluations which monitor people. The other type of pool is used for evaluations which monitor programs. Unfortuntely some pools currently in operation are used for evaluations which serve both purposes.

The need to keep the two types of monitoring separate has never been clearly established, and as a consequence the weaknesses of the people-monitoring-type uses are likely to erode the value of such pools. The careful documentation of the Trempe Study goes a long way towards making the case against people monitoring pools. It shows that an inversion of purposes can take place if the students and the teachers, and the community want the students to maximize their marks regardless of what they learn. The same incentive is there in the case of a pool which is used for people monitoring, and although no documentation is available yet to show how the inversion or the distortion takes place, it does seem reasonable to predict that it will take place.

Program Monitoring

If we return to our main purpose now, we can see that our primary need is for program monitoring capability and furthermore, there is no real need to risk the inversion problem or the invalidation of data problem which results from using the data for the people monitoring purpose. We can afford to use the pool exclusively for program monitoring. This choice leads to one or two consequences I wish to mention and I wish to emphasize in light of the widespread confusion about the purposes of evaluation.

The pool can include a diverse array of items/instruments, and these items can be heterogeneous in the psychometric sense. Most existing pools have items of a standard type and the items are screened or homogenized so that they discriminate in the same way from one item to the next, i.e., they have family resemblance. Item homogeneity is required for people monitoring but not for program monitoring.

The next point about the pools is that whereas people monitoring suggests secrecy and security of the items, program monitoring, on the other hand, has no such requirement. In fact, pools which are placed in the public domain, or open, are revealing their essential purpose to be program monitoring. Pools which are secure or secret may, on the other hand, be revealing their essential purpose to be people monitoring.

One of the most clearly evident features of evaluation programs is their use of sample surveys as opposed to "every-pupil" surveys. The random sample survey with anonymity guaranteed, has become a standard mechanism for evaluations which are of the program monitoring variety. People cannot be compared and that is clear, because different people are answering different questions, and anonymity is seen to be assured. Every-pupil surveys are the main instrument for people monitoring enterprises and they have a long tradition of use, and a long history of erosion of the validity of the resulting data, in part, based on the consideration made public by Trempe.

If you build a pool with program monitoring in mind, and if you take your time -- it must be of the order of years -- then you should be in a position to conduct a large-scale survey, or small-scale surveys, in the next few years. Such surveys should give you the best indication of the scope of the arts programs in your schools. It should give you the best indication ever, about what the arts mean in the classroom. It should give you some indication as to whether or not there is a characteristic arts program, or perhaps there is just too much diversity among schools and among countries for there to be anything like a characteristic program.

The question "what art is taught to which students" is the central question in the proposed surveys, and it leads to answers to other questions such as how close is the implemented curriculum to the intended curricula, and how close are each of these curricula to the attained curriculum? Discrepancies are almost certain to emerge and these give rise to potential changes in the curriculum. For instance, if a large segment of the intended curriculum is not actually implemented, then what should be done?

If the suppositions which I used in the opening paragraph are in any sense realistic, then what we should expect to find in the data which result from the survey proposed above is that not enough art is taught and that it is taught to too few students. If that is the case, and if it is also true that there is general consensus on the point, then a long-term plan for the expansion of educational service in the domain of the arts should be prepared. I cannot anticipate what such a plan would look like but I can suggest that the proposed survey data will be most helpful in identifying the starting points. I believe I should not speculate any more than that.

I have now done what I set out to do. I have told you about a few research projects concerned with program evaluation and I believe I have highlighted the points in these studies which have relevance for evaluation in the arts. I chose the Trempe study first because it deals with one of the most important problems in student evaluation, namely the inversion of purposes of the curriculum and the invalidation of evaluation data. The mechanism by which this was revealed was a type of observation study which I believe is likely to flourish in evaluation in the arts. The second study, SIMS, made use of the sample survey method of gathering data and I hope it opened up the possibilities for new types of items and instruments in the arts which more truly focus attention on the objectives of the arts than has been possible with traditional test items which fit neatly into the every-pupil survey studies which have characterized evaluations in the past. I wish you well in your future evaluation efforts.

Footnotes:

[1]Trempe, Pierre-Leon. Lavoisier: Science
Teaching at an ecole polyvalente, in Science
Education in Canadian Schools, Vol. III -
Case studies of science teaching. John Olson
and Thomas Russell (eds.). Ottawa: Science
Council of Canada, 1983.

[2]Travers, K. T. The second international mathematics study: an overview, in Comparative
studies of mathematics curricula change and
stability 1960-1980. German: University of
Bielefeld, 1980.

[3]Courtney, Richard and Paul Park. Learning
through the arts: the arts in primary and
junior education in Ontario - roles and relationships in the general program of study.
Toronto: Project funded by the Ministry of
Education, Ontario, 1980.

Response To: "PROGRAM EVALUATION AND THE ARTS."
by
Pamela Ritch


Howard Russell's provocative paper, "Program Evaluation and the Arts," makes a valuable contribution to research and evaluation in the arts, particularly with respect to creative drama/ theatre education by suggesting new avenues by which we can meaningfully describe ourselves and our work to others in the field as well as the general public. I am grateful to have this opportunity to give a selective response. I will comment upon those aspects of the paper that had most relevance to me, and any areas that are neglected are due to either space limitations, personal ignorance of all the implications of the particular topic, or a somewhat superficial judgment on my part as to the potential relevance for others in the field, based upon my own biases and experiences.

Mr. Russell's premise that the evaluation tail wags the curriculum dog would be agreed with, provided these were more rational times. Existing as we do in the U.S. in economic chaos these days, with arts programs receiving a disproportionate share of the budget cuts in education, this premise becomes distorted in the looking glass of 1983 academic reality. It is my perception that the decision as to which programs receive more support depends in large measure on administrative perceptions of vulnerability (who will not protest loudly if they're cut?) and the current academic fad, such as "back to basics." Thus, many school systems find science cut alongside physical education and the arts (but not the football team or the marching band--a phenomenon I'll discuss later). So you see, while I appreciate the new program evaluation strategies given to us through Mr. Russell by way of the Trempe study and the SIMS study, I do not put much faith in the notion that because we conduct good, rigorous programmatic evaluation, arts programs will be supported, added, or restored. So rather than raise false expectations from evaluation, I will simply assert that we in the arts MUST undertake programmic evaluation for its own value in enabling us to talk to ourselves. If anyone else is listening, and I intend that they should, fine.

The Trempe study was provocative not only because it was a case-study-like report, but because of the insights yielded. The methodology of the Trempe study is also controversial: is it more evaluative, or is it analytical? Trempe's methodology, that is, observing classes and becoming quite involved in the life of the school, appears to be quite intrusive. So we must question: does he report what is, or the reaction to his presence? And how do we know? And how do we know that Trempe knows?

The documented observation, in the tradition of Frued (N-1) presented anecdotally in the report, is still a relatively new avenue of qualitative research for the arts. Certainly the cost in time for such a human-intensive effort is one reason that it is not a widespread technique.[2] While some dissertations in creative drama have examined a particular teacher in detail, such as Dorothy Heathcote or Geraldine B. Siks, we have, to my knowledge, seen only one indepth study of a creative drama program in the Trempe tradition (Perks' unpublished master's thesis on the Keith County Day School, Rockford, Illinois).[3] I think the descriptive, anecdotal case study-like methodology could yield very important information to those of us who believe every school system should have a creative drama program. It would also communicate valuable insights between specialists in the field, since many do not have access to creative drama programs per se, but work and teach in relative isolation.

The notion of the intended/taught/attained curricula as three different curricula is not new, and in fact is often called the "hidden curriculum", but this marks the first time I've thought about it in relation to drama teaching. The fallout from the Trempe study (that teachers actually wound up teaching to the national exams, and the students wanted to learn only tricks that would get them through the exam, get the unit, or grade, a phenomena Trempe labeled "anti-science" or the inverted curriculum) brought to mind parallels in drama. Barbara Salisbury, in her recent dissertation on Geraldine Siks,[4] observed that students

112

did better in what she termed "pay-off" activities, that is, activities that were presented to an audience. It would be interesting to see if teachers of creative drama taught to pay-off activities instead of what might be the intended curriculum, and for what purposes. Some in our field would maintain that audience-oriented activities are not properly part of creative/ developmental drama work, which is oriented towards individual growth and not performance, and might even label these activities anti-drama to the extent they discourage individual exploration and encourage a less creative scripted performance. Others would maintain that developmental drama should lead to theatre performance eventually (and just when in the sequences of learning activities is also debated). I would guess that the field would be about evenly split on the issue, depending on whether the practitioner subscribes to the more-American school of thought, or the more-English school (and even the definition of those notions has no consensus).

At the secondary level, I would suspect (and this was confirmed by high school teachers I asked) that in many high school speech and theatre classes, the curriculum has more to do with winning the play/speech contest than with what the English/speech/ theatre department originally intended. The American infatuation with contests, the ironic obsession with ranking and sorting people in our democracy, is one reason why the speech team, marching band, and football team survive when programs that are first cousins, such as theatre, orchestra, and gymnastics, are cut. It would be more provocative to do a case study, or work with the sample survey in the manner of the SIMS study to find out.

The possibility that this may be done isn't too remote. The State of Illinois has a state-endorsed arts plan in place in a number of school districts. The Children's Theatre Association of America, together with the Secondary School Theatre Association is writing a national drama-theatre curriculum K-12. Either has possibilities for programmatic evaluation through case study work.

In both cases (drama education and the Trempe study), values laden decisions are made up-front and conflicts are evident. Trempe promotes hands-on experiences and "everydayness" to lead to "scientific literacy," and uses that value to critique what he felt to be anti-science. However, parents and administrators value this "anti-science" approach with respect to student advancement. Low scores on the national science tests would violate the values of students, administrators and parents. Wrote Norm Stenzel, of the Illinois State Board of Education, regarding this matter: "The case study will not outrage the community and I doubt that it will change much at the school. An issue embedded here is, whose values will serve as the basis of judgment of a program? When Trempe selected "alienation" as an analog for the conditions he was observing he made a value laden choice. The test of his data would be 1) to determine if an independent observer "could see what he saw" and 2) determining if some alternative template was a more complete explanation (better fit) than "alienation". (While "alienation" has a negative connotation some more neutrally phrased template such as a "production model" could also provide insight into the nature of the setting and transactions therein.)"

The issue of whether or not performance is or should be a part of creative drama is also a values-laden issue. The point is, however, that neither empirical nor evaluative studies, nor extended public debate is likely to resolve the situation, nor gain added support for drama education. It is likely that in both cases, the values conflicts embedded in the practices are unreconcilable.[5]

The use of the SIMS pool methodology promises to be equally potent. The SIMS pool would tell us if students are exposed to certain drama objectives, and if so, how and what are people doing and the relationship to learning as classes, not as individuals. Most evaluation in drama has focused to date on developing instruments to measure individual responses,[6] growth and retention of materials, etc. Again, no programmatic evaluation in the arts has taken place using the methodology of the SIMS study that I know of, but the prospect is fascinating.

We have, however, much internal housekeeping to do. Within our own field of drama/theatre, we need to reach a consensus on variables, sequencing within primary and secondary drama/theatre curriculum, and develop a sense nationally of what is to be taught and why. When that is done, we can then take samples to detect the presence or absence of certain characteristics, look for trends between programs, counties, and/or states, and assign meaning to those trends following the SIMS model. Another possibility is to begin to depict what the elementary classroom teacher who teaches generalized aesthetic skills (i.e. activities involving aesthetic appreciation, sensory awareness, and others not tied to any one art form is doing) using Broudy's dimensions of aesthetic experience.[7] And yet another avenue is to incorporate Schroyer's critical moment studies, where a videotape could be stopped at pre-determined moments and the participant asked "What are you doing at this moment?" A taxonomy or topology of answers could yield variables that could later be checked using the SIMS model for their absence/presence across programs, and thus give us a better picture of what is occurring by class.

I am indebted to Mr. Russell for giving us new insights and models to follow to build our confidence in the power of qualitative programmatic evaluation in the arts. I am confident that qualitative studies in creative drama incorporating the concepts and methodology of both Trempe (anecdotal, case study-like work) and SIMS (sample survey method), together with critical-moment studies, will enable us to better communicate to ourselves and the public what we actually do, what we intend to do, what is attained by our students, and finally, what it all means.

# Endnotes

1.  Norm Stenzel, Illinois State Board of Education. Letter to Pamela Ritch, 15 October 1983.

2.  Ibid.

3.  Wendy Perks, Keith County Day School: an Experiment in Education Through Drama, unpublished M.A. Thesis Project, University of Washington, Seattle, 1975.

4.  Barbara T. Salisbury, A Descriptive Analysis of the Teaching/Learning Behaviors in Creative Drama in an Elementary Classroom Taught By A Drama Specialist, (unpublished) Ph.D. dissertation. University of Washington, 1982.

5.  Stenzel

6.  See Helane S. Rosenburg, Patricia Pinciotti, and Jeffrey K. Smith, "On Quantifying Dramatic Behavior," in Children's Theatre Review Research Issue (Spring, 1983): 3-8 for a concise summary of instruments.

7.  Harry S. Broudy, Enlightened Cherishing: An Essay on Aesthetic Education (Urbana: U. Illinois Press, 1972): 28-44.

# PSYCHOLOGICAL BENEFITS OF DANCE AND MOVEMENT
by
## Judith A. Silver and William C. Baird

Dance is a cultural art form which has been important to almost every society throughout history. As far back as the early cave dwellers who drew pictures of their dancers on their walls, people have danced their joys and their sorrows (Kennedy and Silver, 1974; Kraus, 1969). In Europe during the Renaissance, when country dance was considered "pagan, vulgar, obscene, lascivious, ugly" (Lange, 1977, p. 2), the common people still clung to their social communal dances. Even when the Christian Church repeatedly banned the performance of folk dances, folk plays and processionals, still people persisted (Emmerson, 1972; Nicoll, 1963). For them, the dances fulfilled important functions and no institutionalized religious bans could move them.

What are the functions that dance fulfills? How do participants benefit? These questions will provide the thrust for the first section of this paper. In this part, we will review some of the anthropological, dance education and dance therapy literature related to the functions and benefits of dance participation. In the second section of the paper, we will sketch a psychological approach to dance suggesting possible underlying mechanisms relevant to children's development and learning.

## FUNCTIONS OF DANCE AS SEEN BY ANTHROPOLOGISTS

Early anthropologists such as Frazer (1911) and Hambly (1927) were concerned with the manifest functions of primitive dance, that is, the sacred ritual functions of dance. These included such things as making the crops grow, giving strength and speed to their warriors, initiating new members into the tribe, sanctioning the joining of a man and a woman in marriage, and alleviating sickness.

More recently, anthropologists like Brown (1976) have also looked at what they call the "latent functions" of dance. In Brown's study of the natives of the Taos Pueblo, he discussed those dance functions which were only observable to someone standing 'outside' the event - the dancer's feeling of integration within the community through participation in this mimetic group activity, improved self-esteem because the activity is highly valued by the tribe, and enjoyment of the physical exertion. He hypothesized that participation in communal dance acted as a "restatement of traditional values of cooperation and collectivisim" with an "emphasis on group rather than on individual" (p. 238).

Many anthropologists have emphasized that it is important to look at the context of the dance event (Kurath, 1960; Royce, 1977), since in every culture the functions of the dance are somewhat different. For instance, do men and women dance different dances? Do they use the same or different movements? Do the dances lose their potency if outsiders like tourists watch the dance? Do the dances have a different meaning for participants when done as part of a wedding or a funeral or a preparation for war? Thus, while dance in and of itself may serve certain functions, the context in which it is performed can radically change the import of the dance for the participants.

Alan Lomax (1968) has drawn our attention to the fact that dance movements are intimately related to our physical movements in everyday life. After analyzing films of natives from 22 different cultures doing both work and dance activities, Lomax concluded that "movement style in dance is a crystallization of the most frequent and crucial patterns of everyday activity" (p. 226). Just as in songs where people sing of concerns so elemental that they sing together as one, in unison, so do people dance the motions and rhythms of their culture in mimetic harmony. Culture is thus synthesized not only in people's language, work and family role structures, but also in their dance. And the dance in turn reinforces a sense of cooperation and unity through common activity.

BENEFITS OF DANCE AS SEEN BY DANCE EDUCATORS AND
DANCE THERAPISTS

In contrast to anthropologists who have
discussed the function of dancing which is an
integral part of a culture, dance therapists and
educators have looked at the function of dance
for those participants who have previously had
very little experience with this art form. They
take people who are limited in their competence
for rhythmical body movement, and they teach them
new ways of moving.

H'Doubler (1940), one of the early dance
educators, saw dance as a creative art activity
which taught dancers how to control their bodies
and gave them a physical outlet for the discharge
of nervous tension.

Dance educators such as Melamed (1977),
Duggan, Schottman and Rutledge (1948), Jensen and
Jensen (1973) and Weikart (1982), have advanced
the use of folk dances for all age groups to
improve physical fitness, to widen people's
appreciation of other cultures, to enhance participants' self and body concepts, to provide an
enjoyable social and recreational activity, and
to improve social interactional competence.

Weikart has stressed the importance of first
of all learning to move comfortably on one's own;
then and only then, can children (or adults)
learn to enjoy moving with others, adapting to
another person's movement and learning interactional syncrony. She has pointed out the fact
that many children have trouble making the cognitive connection between what was done (modelled)
by the teacher and what they should do. For young
children, this is often related to a misunder-
standing of the movement language used. Weikart
suggests that through the use of dance games,
children can be taught different body parts
(knees, elbows, shoulder, head), different movement forms (hop, skip, walk, slide) and different
movement qualities (soft, abrupt, smooth, explosive, graceful). They thus learn about variations in space, form and time, and what these
feel and look like. For those having trouble
with rhythm (she found in her study that half of
grade 3 children could not walk to a simple beat),

she emphasizes the use of direct tactile stimulation. For example, children patting their thighs to the beat of the music or teachers patting a child's shoulders to the rhythm, is more effective than relying upon a solely auditory method, such as the teacher clapping out the beat.

At about the same time that educators began to seriously discuss the usefulness of dance for students, psychotherapists also began to consider the benefits of dance participation for patients. People like Marion Chace (1953) were invited into hospital settings to work with autistic, schizophrenic and other deeply disturbed children - children who could not be reached with purely verbal approaches. Chace found that dance could be used to establish and maintain contact with these patients, that dance helped to promote group interaction and to reduce the children's feelings of isolation.

Other therapists such as Bender and Boas (1941), Bainbridge, Duddington, Collingdon and Gardner (1953) and Fine, Daly and Fine (1961) combined dance with psychodrama, music and mime. Generally, they also found that patients developed better concentration, improved interpersonal functioning and more positive feelings about themselves.

Lindkvist (1981) views movement in therapy with autistic children from the perspective of dramatic action. She uses the standard method of meeting the child on his/her own terms by using the child's movement vocabulary as a starting point. From there, she develops movement skills through mirroring and exaggeration of the child's movements. Dance/ drama, according to Lindkvist,

> can be used as a means of communication, for developing relationships, increasing body awareness, and for minimizing stereotypes [i.e., autistic behaviours] if that is considered desirable. It can give satisfaction to the doer, and encourage verbalization as well as group awareness and a sense of sharing a creative experience. It can also increase confidence. (p. 109)

Kaslow (1969) discusses similar benefits of dance therapy in her review of the literature, particularly release of tension, communication with others and expression of emotion. Using dance themes and dance-drama, participants learn to express their concerns physically, to begin with on an individual one-to-one basis, then in groups using techniques such as circle and line dances. They learn to interact physically with others in an accepting supportive environment. And they learn to relax their muscles and to discharge unnecessary tension. Participants' self concepts are enhanced through self assertion and mastery experiences and by developing their abilities to be "in cooperative harmony with others".

Over the past two decades, variations of dance techniques have been used therapeutically with children who were normal, emotionally disturbed, deaf, psychotic, retarded, learning disabled and autistic; with adults who were normal, neurotic, psychotic and depressed. All types of patients have demonstrated improvements, mostly in body image and self-esteem, interpersonal functioning and anxiety level. Many of these studies are reviewed elsewhere (Kaslow, 1969; Silver, 1981).

One of the most recent developments in dance therapy has been the introduction of folk and ethnic dance forms in both educational and institutional settings. Elaine and Bernard Feder (1981), in their recent book on the expressive arts therapies, advocate the use of folk dance to expand participants' movement range and vocabulary, to promote self awareness, to teach interactional syncrony with others, and to encourage socialization.

In my recently completed doctoral dissertation (Silver, 1981), I looked at the effects of both folk dance and fitness classes on the self concepts, body concepts, social distancing and ethnic distancing of participants as compared with academic controls. I will limit my discussion here to those results related to self and body concepts. To begin with, however, allow me to describe what a folk dance class consists of.

At a typical international folk dance session, participants learn dances done in various formations including closed circles, open circles, couples, trios and lines. Members may hold hands in a circle, clasp shoulders, link arms, have arms around each others' waists, or hold each others' belts. Thus members learn to meld their actions with those of the rest of the line or circle, to cooperate in order to create a unified movement. They are in constant physical contact with others whom they do not necessarily know but whom they learn to trust in a non-verbal manner by touching and dancing with them. It is acceptable to touch; no one will misunderstand. This seems to be a non-threatening way to make 'contact' with others.

Folk dancing is a very social situation. Participants are invited to introduce themselves. Depending upon the interest and age range of the dancers, sessions may include 'mixers' which aid the social interaction process. While in this friendly social situation, they learn new physical skills - how to move rhythmically with others, how to master particular steps and sequences. They learn that it feels good to exert themselves and that gradually their physical condition may improve because of it, allowing them to feel better about their physical abilities, their bodies, themselves, and about the other participants who share this experience with them. During some types of dances, spontaneous behaviours such as shouting, singing, stamping and swinging arms are encouraged.

The plan of each session follows a basic pattern: simple running and walking dances to begin, as warm-up and to provide immediate success experiences for even those having the most trouble. This may be followed by one or two 'mixers' which enable the dancers to greet each other and again get used to being in close physical contact with others. In the middle of the session, new, somewhat more challenging material is introduced to provide new learning experiences and some excitement which the whole group can share. Finally, there is some review of simple material taught earlier in the session to reinforce prior learning and to renew the spirits of those who have had problems with the more challenging material. The class is finished off with a couple of slow, simple, circle dances which bring everyone back to the circle again, working together, moving together, creating a warm group feeling on which to end the session. The last dance will often become regularized (one of the class favorites) and participants may gradually learn the words (if any) of the song and sing along.

The participants in this study were tested at the beginning of the first class, at the end of the last class (12 weeks later) and then one month later. Most were university students (83%); others were staff, teachers or alumni. Self and body concepts were measured in two ways. Firstly, participants rated themselves using bipolar adjective scales (Osgood, Suci and Tannenbaum, 1957) such as passive-active, awkward-graceful, good-bad, slow-fast, powerful-powerless, and so forth. Secondly, they completed open-ended questions as to whether they had gained personally and interpersonally as a result of taking the class. Participants in both folk dance and fitness classes demonstrated strong and sustained improvement in both self and body concepts when compared with the controls (e.g., self concept post test $F(2,71)=15.56$, p is less than .001 on the adjective scales) and their comments underlined this improvement. But whereas the exercise classes seemed to help participants as far as their physical mastery abilities were concerned, the folk dance classes also developed dancers' social interactional skills. Let me read you a few quotes to illustrate this.

I feel more relaxed among people maybe because I centre or internalize my dancing experience. I can communicate on several levels (emotional, mental) much better. Still to improve.

I do feel less embarrassed in physical contact with the opposite sex, a problem which was probably linked with some residual guilt feelings about sex which I had refused to admit I had.

I'm more aware of how I interact with others (at times my awkwardness, at time my naturalness) and being aware helps me to change.

I took folk dancing because I enjoy it, because in addition to the exercise/physical activity, it provided me with a relaxing entertaining few hours/wk. as well as a social setting, an environment conducive to meeting people...dance gives me a way of expressing myself which other physical activities would not. Terrific! My way of "getting high".

Many other studies have been conducted in the past two decades using a variety of dance therapy techniques which have demonstrated significant improvement in the self concepts of both children and adults as a result of participating in ongoing dance classes. Furthermore, such dance therapists as Jane Manning, Barbara Mettler (in Wallock, 1977) and Blanche Evan (1959) have called for a recognition of dance therapy as a method, not just in the treatment, but also in the prevention of psychological disturbance.

To summarize, according to anthropologists, dance educators, and dance therapists, dance can serve many beneficial functions for participants. These benefits include improved physical competence and mastery of movement skills, energy discharge, enhanced self confidence, and better social interactional skills.

Theoretically, how do dance therapists account for these wonderful changes in their clients? Both Kaslow (1969) and Feder and Feder (1981) in their literature reviews, have asserted that dance therapy is still at the stage of a 'technique in search of a theory'. Based upon their clinical experiences, practitioners have developed techniques which result in particular therapeutic outcomes, such as using folk dance to develop socialization skills (Feder and Feder, 1981). The theoretical underpinnings, however, are typically poorly enunciated.

For the next section of this paper, therefore, we would like to suggest some psychological concepts gleaned from the child development and learning literature which may help to explain why dance participation learning seems to serve the functions that it does.


SOME PSYCHOLOGICAL CONCEPTS AND THEIR APPLICATION TO DANCE

A few years ago, Gregory Bateson (1979) gave the following account of an example of animal learning. A dolphin was let into a training pool for a series of sessions during which he would be rewarded for any novel behaviours he might exhibit. For the first 14 sessions, the dolphin's behaviour was relatively placid, and it was only toward the end of each session that the trainer would notice any behaviours which were out of the ordinary and worthy of reward. At the beginning of the fifteenth session, however, the dophin appeared somewhat agitated or aroused upon entering the pool, and within a short period of time vigorously executed a series of six novel behaviours for which he was promptly rewarded. Bateson explained that the dolphin had not learned a specific skill, but had learned something about the context in which the learning had taken place. Specifically, the dophin had learned that it was novel behaviours that his trainer was expecting and rewarding. This contextual learning Bateson (1972) coined "deutero-learning", indicating that it was a second-order achievement, that is, reflexive knowledge about the learning process itself, what we can call learning about learning.

Deutero-learning develops to a high degree in human beings, resulting in self-reflexive knowledge about one's own psychological processes. Such knowledge has been labelled "metacognition" in the psychological literature (Flavell, 1981). It is understood as consisting of the internalized controls which people use to self-regulate their mental performances in any context. For example, a dancer having trouble learning a dance sequence can step 'outside' him/herself to ask 'why am I having difficulty?' Having had previous experience with dance learning, (s)he may be able to reason that (s)he has rehearsed too long and that fatigue is beginning to interfere with performance. Metacognitive knowledge is not simply a by-product of learning in any skill domain, but rather is crucially involved in the successful acquisition of any skill. In a recent paper, Brown (1981) urges a revised theory of children's learning emphasizing the processes by which specific skills are generalized to new contexts.

Novices often fail to perform efficiently not only because they may lack certain skills, but because they are deficient in terms of self-conscious participation and intelligent self-regulation of their actions. (p. 97)

As a consequence, children often exhibit "production deficiencies" in their performances - they fail to apply knowledge or strategies they have already acquired to help them in a new learning situation (Brown, 1981). It is important for children to become able to monitor and self-regulate their learning experiences. To do this, children must learn what to pay attention to in any situation. They must also learn how to evaluate the general conditions associated with any performance - mental, social and physical.

Any activity has two possible learning consequences - acquiring specific skills (skill learning) and acquiring general knowledge about skillful perfomance (learning about learning). While there is much useful literature on the development of children's motor abilities, there is a complete lack of research on the influence which movement experiences may have on the acquisition of general self-regulative know- ledge. For example, it is surprising that the important research programme begun at Harvard (Gardner, 1973) investigating the influence of art experiences on children's development, while studying children's painting, music, language, play, fantasy and creative writing, has com- pletely ignored their rhythmic and expressive movement activities. By contrast, we propose that movement activities, especially dance, offer a learning context of unusual promise for teach- ing general self-regulative skills. Because there is no existing developmental research testing such a hypothesis, we can only support this suggestion by describing what might charac- terize an effective learning context according to developmental theory, and by demonstrating how movement activities incorporate those characteristics in an integrative way.

Children acquire and internalize skills through the processes of imitation. Current child developmental theory clearly opposes the notion that imitation is no more than repeated behaviour, opposes the idea that it connotes a passive orientation on the part of the learner. Rather, imitation is the process by which a child <u>actively</u> reconstructs a model's goal-directed behaviour. Researchers of infant development (Yando et al., 1978; Uzgiris, 1981; Kaye, 1982) who used naturalistic observational studies, have concluded that imitative behaviour emerges soon after birth, and fulfills two evolutionary functions: the satisfaction of "1/ affective, attachment-related motives and 2/ competence, effectance-related motives" (Yando et al., 1978). Both of these motives must be satisfied for an activity to be effective as a learning context. As Kenneth Kaye (1982) explains, this requires the presentation of two different types of performance model. Firstly, a model is needed whose performance is "just beyond the learner's competence" in order to encourage progressive achievement. Secondly, a model is required whose performance is "familiar" and composed of already-learned, but enjoyable actions, to encourage affilitation and emotional expressivity. By intertwining mastery experiences with affiliative and emotional experiences, an activity can be sustained because it avoids the negative outcomes of recurring frustration or boredom.

However, it is not enough for an activity to be merely motivating. Any activity must offer clear lessons about attentional or attributional proccesses if it is to promote change in general psychological functioning.

## Attentional Self-Regulation

Being able to control one's attention is essential to any form of achievement. Csikzentmihali (1978) points out that such control is commonly known as "concentration", and explains that

Since any scientific, artistic or other creative effort depends on acquiring, recombining, or producing information, and since this process requires attention that is in limited supply, concentration must be the inevitable prerequisite of creative work. (p. 345)

Concentration refers to a performer's successful maintenance of an optimal level of arousal and optimal information flow during mental functioning. We do not, however, have direct access to our attentional processes. Rather we become aware of their efficacy through the subjective state of mind or "mood" that they produce (Hamilton, 1981). Optimal attentional processing produces the experience of intrinsic enjoyment which Csikzentmihali (1978) calls "flow", while sub-optimal processing produces boredom or frustration and anxiety. The person who is successful at self-monitoring is the person who is able to use the mood (s)he is feeling as feedback about the effectiveness with which his/her attentional processes are being used. If (s)he cannot adapt in such a way, the continuing experience of boredom or anxiety, and the neurotic forms of compensation for such moods, may lead to psychopathology (Hamilton, 1981; Csikzentmihali, 1978).

Our culture tends to accept emotional moods as epiphenominal to, rather than intimately connected with, our habitual activities. Indeed, it is only recently that research has been done on the hypothesis that emotional mood directly affects cognitive functioning. Bower (1981) showed that people learned more about situations, and remembered them in greater detail, when these incidents were congruent with their mood at the time. With reference to dance, for example, people would remember better an exuberant joyous dance if they were in a joyful mood when they were learning it. The ability to interpret the implications of one's habitual moods is an ability that has to be learned.

Another form of attentional self-regulation is the control over one's arousal level. Hamilton (1981) points out that there are three forms of arousal control: cognitive, behavioural and

128

biological. Behavioural control is the most effective means for young children to modulate their arousal level. Of particular relevance to dance and movement is the influence of body rhythms on arousal. In a recent paper, Shaffer (1982) offered convincing evidence of an internal timing mechanism which controls the temporal performance of all skillful movement. Ashton (1976) had earlier postulated such a mechanism, arguing that the rhythmic quality associated with any physical activity originates from within the brain and not from the extrinsic qualities of the activity itself. Specifically, the internal timing mechanism originates in the physiological rhythms of the midbrain (Ashton, 1976). This fact is important because it explains the link between rhythmic movement and arousal. Ashton reported that rhythmic stimulation of any kind has a calming influence on infants. The effect is the same whether they are sucking, being rocked, or being sung to, as long as this is done with a regular rhythm. Ashton argues, further-more, that the calming influence of rhythmic stimulation continues into adulthood. For example, repetitive auditory stimulation induces sleep in adults (Ashton, 1976). Rhythmic move-ment, it seems, has a built-in control over arousal level. One cannot attend to, or repro-duce, a rhythm without falling into a state of calm, optimal arousal. Participation in rhythmic activities, therefore, presents a very effective context in which to teach chidren the benefits of managing arousal level.

## Attributional Self-Regulation

Young children have great difficulty in know-ing to which factors they should attribute the causes of their successes or failures when they attempt to perform a task. As a consequence, they are inconsistent in evaluating their own performances. Consistency in evaluation is necessary for the development of "perceived self-efficacy" (Bandura, 1981), that is, a self concept solidly grounded on accurate self-appraisal skills. As Bandura explains, these skills can only develop to the extent to which a child is capable of attributing performance outcomes to a variety of factors:

...the difficulty of the task, the amount of effort they expend, the amount of external aid they receive, the situational circumstances under which they perform, and the temporal pattern of their successes and failures. (p. 205)

Therefore, children require structured learning situations which will help them to direct their attention to specific sources of influence on their performance. They can thus learn about the many factors which affect their performance. Movement activities are versatile enough to be structured in a variety of ways conducive to the acquisition of self-appraisal skills. For example, the difficulty of a dance sequence can be closely regulated. A dance teacher can begin by teaching very simple movements, like hopping on one leg. (S)he can then add another simple movement to it - jumping from one leg to the other. And when the children have mastered this, (s)he might add clapping, and so forth. Thus dance and other rhythmic movement activities can provide an excellent forum for children's learning about their attributional processes.

Another important requirement for improved self-efficacy is the ability to discern the relative contribution of ability and non-ability factors in performance. Bandura (1981) describes how people with low self-esteem have a bias in crediting successful performance to circumstance rather than to their own capabilities. He suggests that they need to attempt challenging tasks which require minimal external aid. What better task could fit this requirement than rhythmic body movement, an activity in which a person has only his/her own body to rely upon (no external aids). Moreover, this is an activity which contains clear and unambiguous criteria for evaluating performance achievement. Lending further support to this notion, Bohrnstedt and Felson (1983) demonstrated that children's self-esteem can improve only if there is very little discrepancy between actual and perceived performance achievement. For an ambiguous ability like 'popularity', children tended to overrate or underrate their actual performance, depending upon their previously established level of self-esteem. However, for an unambiguous ability such as 'athletic ability', children were better able to accurately rate their actual performance. As a consequence, successful achievement in athletics was found to improve self-esteem. Movement activities, therefore, provide children with clear and consistent criteria by which to evaluate their actual performances, and thus to consolidate positive self-esteem.

A further major influence on perceived self-efficacy is the information generated by social comparison processes. Dance provides a rich context for social comparison. The learner has at his/her disposal a number of models to observe while being a participant at the same time. The teacher, as expert, provides the ideal standards of achievement. These will be helpful for the learner to the extent that the teacher 1) can establish sub-goals appropriate to the learner's abilities (for example, break down dance sequences into sub-units or steps), and 2) can provide relevant "cognitive modeling"; that is, verbal communication accurately describing the level of difficulty of challenging tasks and the relevant achievement level for attempted performances. From their peers, on the other hand, children acquire appropriate norms by which to evaluate their own performances. Bandura (1981) points out that children are initially ignorant of the fact that similar others provide the best criteria for accurate self-appraisal. Therefore, they need to be guided in selecting appropriate models for internalizing achievement norms. Dance classes are often conducted using circle formations which direct children's attention to each other as models (normative) as well as to the teacher (ideal). The dance teacher may stress performance of movement sequences in a highly interactive way, so that children must watch each other, must meld their movements to those of the whole group. Thus they learn to look to each other for achievement norms.

If a learning context is successful in providing the modeling experiences described above, then it will nurture two types of conditions which will sustain progressive development in self-efficacy. Firstly, appropriate sub-goals and achievement norms guarantee that a learner will experience enough successes to consolidate

131

self-esteem and to help overcome periodic failure experiences (Bandura, 1981). Secondly, when peers can share successful achievements in a cooperative task, interpersonal attraction between the participants is heightened (Levin, Snyder and Mendez-Caratini, 1982). As a result, a learner who is experiencing temporary failure may persevere with a difficult task in order to maintain affiliative contact with a peer group with which (s)he closely identifies.

Thus far, I have described how participation in movement activities can offer clear and consistent lessons in attentional and attributional self-regulation. These lessons will not be learned unless a child is motivated enough to attempt challenging tasks, and is persistent enough to experience a wide variety of performance outcomes. To return to a previous point - an activity will be motivating if it offers some tasks which satisfy emotional, affiliative-related motives and some which satisfy mastery motives. This account, however, lacks a temporal dimension. It does not explain how and when these tasks can be most effectively presented to produce learning.

Let us again return to the example of infant learning. A contemporary expert on infant development, Colwyn Trevarthen, has described how neonates are able to imitate facial expressions and body gestures before they can imitate actions performed using objects (Trevarthen, 1982). Furthermore, if a mother does not respond to these attempts at imitation, the infant will show signs of avoidance, distress, and eventually psychopathology. Trevarthen concludes that infants have a primordial desire to share internal states of mind, what he calls "shared intersubjectivity". He further speculates that this motive for "cooperative understanding" is the primary regulator of all subsequent mental development.

Two leading child psychiatrists, Alexander Thomas and Stella Chess (1980) echo this argument that attachment and affiliative motives are primary to learning. Based upon the evidence of years of clinical work, they conclude that any adequate theory of child development and learning must be "homeodynamic" - it must account for the simultaneous continuity and change in children's experience. Continuity is guaranteed if a child receives adequate social support, and change occurs if a child is secure enough to individuate (to engage his/her abilities in new challenges). Clearly, a teacher of dance and movement must take advantage of the social aspects of these activities to establish a generative context for learning.

A second important point about the temporal presentation of learning activities is that attentional self-regulation should be taught before attributional self-regulation. In a comprehensive review of the development of social comparison processes, Ruble (1983) found that children do not spontaneously use information obtained from social comparisons to evaluate their own performance before seven or eight years of age. She hypothesized that before this age, children are using all of their cognitive resources to establish what the norms of behaviour are by observing others' performances. Once these are learned, then they can be applied to their own performances. For younger children, therefore, a teacher should concentrate on the somatic and emotional experiences of dance and movement, as well as encouraging group participation, to develop the observational skills necessary to internalize behavioural norms.

This suggestion is supported by the work of Griffin and Keogh (1982), who have studied the development of "movement confidence" in children. Movement confidence is the sense of self-efficacy felt specifically about movement tasks and challenges. They explain that movement confidence has two components: "movement competence" and "movement sense". The former refers to achievement outcomes, while the latter refers to the pleasurability of the sensory experiences accompanying any movement activity. They suggest that movement sense, rather than the feeling of achievement, is the primary motivation in younger children for attempting new movement tasks.

# SUMMARY

The literature about the beneficial functions of dance participation is found in many social science fields, from anthropology to education to dance therapy. Throughout this literature, there appears to be considerable concensus as to how dance benefits those involved. In primitive societies, dance has been interpreted as serving many ritual and religious functions. Dance participation has been advocated by dance educators and therapists because it is believed to enhance body and self concept through the development of physical competence, to provide an opportunity for the development of social competence and cooperative interpersonal contact, and to allow for the enhancement of aesthetic appreciation and creative abilities.

These benefits can be understood theoretically as the learning of attentional and attributional self control. The type of learning context which most effectively teaches children about their general self-regulative skills is one which dynamically combines the primary motive of affiliation with the secondary motive of mastery. We suggest that dance is an excellent activity for teaching children how to learn about learning.

# BIBLIOGRAPHY

Ashton, R. Aspects of timing in child development. Child Development, 1976, 47, 622-626.

Bainbridge, G., Duddington, A. E., Collingdon, M. & Gardner, C. E. Dance-mime: A contribution to treatment in psychiatry. Journal of Mental Science, 1953, 49, 308-314.

Bandura, A. Self-referent thought: a developmental analysis of self-efficacy. In J. H. Flavell & L. Ross (Eds.), Social Cognitive Development. New York: Cambridge University Press, 1981.

Bateson, G. Steps to an ecology of mind. New York: Ballentine Books, 1972.

Bateson, G. Mind and nature: A necessary unity. New York: Bantam Books, 1979.

Bender, L. & Boas, F. Creative dance in therapy. American Journal of Orthopsychiatry, 1941, 11, 235-244.

Bohrnstedt, G. H. & Felson, R. B. Explaining the relations among children's actual and perceived performances and self-esteem: A comparison of several casual models. Journal of Personality and Social Psychology, 1983, 45, 43-56.

Bower, G. H. Mood and memory. American Psychologist, 1981, 36, 129-148.

Brown, A. L. Learning and development: The problems of compatibility, access and induction. Human Development, 1982, 25, 89-115.

Brown, D. N. The dance of Taos Pueblo. CORD Dance Research Annual, 1976, VII, 199-272.

Chace, M. Dance as an adjunctive therapy with hospitalized mental patients. Bulletin of the Menninger Clinic, 1953, 17, 219-225.

Csikszentmihali, M. Attention and the holistic
approach to behavior. In J. S. Pope & J. L.
Singer (Eds.), The stream of consciousness.
New York: Plenum, 1978.

Duggan, A. S., Schottman, J. & Rutledge, A. The
folk dance library. Vol. 1: The teaching of
folk dance. New York: Barnes, 1948.

Emmerson, G. S. A social history of Scottish
dance. Montreal: McGill-Queen's University
Press, 1972.

Evan, B. Therapeutic aspects of creative dance.
Dance Observer, 1959, Nov., 1.

Feder, E. & Feder, B. The expressive arts therapies. Englewood Cliffs: Prentice-Hall, 1981.

Fine, R., Daly, D. & Fine, L. Psychodance: An
experiment in psychotherapy and training.
Group Psychotherapy, 1962, 15, 203-223.

Flavell, J. H. Cognitive monitoring. In W. P.
Dickson (Ed.), Children's oral communication
skills. New York: Academic Press, 1982.

Frazer, J. G. The golden bough. London:
Macmillan, 1911.

Gardner, H. The arts and human development. New
York: Wiley, 1973.

Griffin, N. S. & Keogh, J. F. A model for movement confidence. In J. Kelso & J. Clark
(Eds.), The development of movement control
and coordination. New York: Wiley, 1982.

Hambly, W. P. Tribal dancing and social development. New York: Macmillan, 1927.

Hamilton, J. A. Attention, personality, and the
self-regulation of mood: Absorbing interest
and boredom. Progress in Experimental
Personality Research, 1981, 10, 281-315.

H'Doubler, M. N. Dance: A creative art experience. New York: Crofts, 1940

Jensen, M. B. & Jensen, C. R. Folk dancing. Provo, Utah: Brigham Young University Press, 1973.

Kaslow, F. W. Dance and movement therapies: A study in theory and applicability. Unpublished doctoral dissertation, Bryn Mawr College, 1969.

Kaye, K. The mental and social life of babies. Chicago: University of Chicago Press, 1982.

Kennedy, J. M. & Silver J. The surrogate function of lines in visual perception: Evidence from antipodal rock and cave artwork sources. Perception, 1974, 3, 313-322.

Kraus, R. History of the dance in art and education. Englewood Cliffs: Prentice-Hall, 1969.

Kurath, G. P. Panorama of dance ethnology. Current Anthropology, 1960, 1(May), 233-254.

Lange, R. Dance folklore and the urbanized world. In Dance Studies Vol. 2, Les Bois, St, Peter, Jersey C. I.: Centre for Dance Studies, 1977, 1-13.

Levine, J. M., Snyder, H. N. & Mendez-Caratini, G. Task performance and interpersonal attraction in children. Child Development, 1982, 53, 359-371.

Lindkvist, M. R. Movement and drama with autistic children. In G. Shattner & R. Courtney (Eds.), Drama in therapy. Vol. 1, 1981, 95-109.

Lomax, A. Folk song style and culture. Washington, D. C.: American Association for the Advancement of Science, No. 88, 1968.

Melamed, L. All join hands: Connecting people through folk dance. Montreal: Melamed, 1977.

Nicoll, A. Masks, mimes and miracles: Studies in the popular theatre. New York: Cooper Square, 1963.

Osgood, C. E., Suci, G., Tannenbaum, P. The Measurement of Meaning. Urbana-Champagne: University of Illinois Press, 1957.

Royce, A. P. The anthropology of dance. Bloomington: Indiana University Press, 1977.

Ruble, D. N. The development of social-comparison processes and their role in achievement-related self-socialization. In E. T. Higgins, D. N. Ruble & W. W. Hartup (Eds.), Social cognition and social development. New York: Cambridge University Press, 1983.

Shaffer, L. H. Rhythm and timing in skill. Psychological Review, 1982, 89, 109-123.

Silver, J. A. Therapeutic aspects of folk dance: Self concept, body concept, ethnic distancing, and social distancing. Unpublished doctoral dissertaion, University of Toronto, 1981.

Thomas, A. & Chess, S. The dynamics of psychological development. New York: Bruner/Mazel, 1980.

Trevarthen, C. The primary motives for cooperative understanding. In G. Butterworth & P. Light (Eds.), Social Cognition: Studies of the development of understanding. Chicago: University of Chicago Press, 1982.

Uzgiris, I. Two functions of imitation during infancy. International Journal of Behavioral Development, 1981, 4, 1-12.

Wallock, S. Dance/movement therapy: A survey of philosophy and practice. Unpublished doctoral dissertaion, U. S. International University, 1977.

Weikart, P. S. Teaching movement and dance: A sequential approach to rhythmic movement. Ypsilanti, Michigan: High/Scope, 1982.

Response:   DRAMA:   DANCE OF LIFE
by
Joyce A. Wilkinson


Drama, in holding "as twere, the mirror up to nature," is a reflection of the "dance of life." It is in this context that the psychological benefits of dance and movement delineated by Silver and Baird converge with claims made by drama specialists for more than five decades.

In isolating the elements common to both drama and dance, the Venn diagram (Illustration I) shows that the anthropologically derived functions of dance are equally integral to drama. No dramatist would dispute this observation. Similarly, the benefits attributed to dance education as demonstrated in Illustration II are also viewed by drama researchers and practitioners as outcomes of the drama process. The numerous therapeutic results, outlined in Illustration III, as cited by dance therapists have also been documented by drama therapists, researchers and leaders. This overlap seems to denote dance as a component of drama. [Illustrations begin on page 144]

In citing psychological concepts from child development and learning theory to explain why and/or how such learning occurs through dance, Silver and Baird give us pause for thought. Their hypothesis that dance offers "a learning context of unusual promise for teaching general self-regulative skills" (p. 11) has merit and lends itself well to the rigours of scientific testing. I suggest this as the logical next step; the outcome of such scrutiny may be a significant contribution to the mutual benefit of both dance and drama. Meanwhile, what can we determine about 'drama and learning' from the authors' proposed connections between the benefits and/or functions of dance and learning theory?

Like dance, drama in which the teacher's philosophy dictates that no external evaluation occurs (Way, 1967) is a virtual laboratory of contextual learning. Within such spontaneous drama, participants are constantly assessing their status, role, impact and effect on others in the process. In the more pre-meditated theatrical process, players constantly evaluate others' responses as well as their own. Such metacognitive awareness is integral to both mastery and satisfaction. Both attentional and evaluative self-monitoring are components of this awareness gained through drama.

If motivation, a necessary adjunct to learning, depends as Kaye (1972) indicates on two different performance models, i.e. one that is just beyond the learner's competence and one that is familiar and composed of already-learned, enjoyable actions, then in drama, learning often does not occur because the teacher is not aware of or sensitive to the frontiers of the learners' competency.

But besides motivation, effective learning that promotes change involves learning about attentional and/or attributional processes. Attentional self-regulation, i.e. controlling attention or concentration, is key to mastery in any form of drama (Spolin, 1963; Stanislavski, 1949; Way, 1967; Wilkinson, 1982). The authors claim that access to concentration is via mood:

> The person who is successful at self-monitoring is the person who is able to use the mood (s)he is feeling as feedback about the effectiveness with which his/her attentional processes are being used. (p. 13).

Personal research on self-monitoring (Wilkinson, 1982) leads me to question this statement. Perhaps it is the value word 'successful' that jars. More likely it is the contradiction with Mark Snyder's (1982) empirical differentiation of high and low self-monitors as two contrasting types of people, both successful from their perspective of monitoring. My own research also contradicts this theory. In a Chi-square analysis of 92 secondary students, high and low drama achievers (categorized as such on the basis of concentration scores) were equally distributed throughout all four cells (24 HD/H-SM; 24 HD/L-SM; 23 LD/H-SM; 21 LD/L-SM; $X^2$ = .05; n.s.). These results portend that 'successful' self-monitoring in drama is not irrefutably an outcome of using mood as feedback on how effectively one is concentrating.

Learning more about situations and remembering them in greater detail when they are congruent with mood (p. 14) is worthy of our exploration. Children usually enjoy drama and know they are learning but if congruency of mood and incident increase learning, drama might be a superior method for learning content from other subject areas. Optimal Learning presently utilizes drama for this reason (Grey, 1982). But moods abound in drama. Does this congruency apply to all moods, only to joyful ones or only to incidents explored in a joyful context?

Consistent evaluation, an essential ingredient of a self-concept based on accurate self-appraisal skills (Bandura, 1981), helps children to learn the attributes that result in their 'performance outcomes,' i.e. to develop attributional self-regulation.

Since learning the impact of ability and non-ability factors on performance helps children improve self-concept, discovering one's own potential resources irrespective of others (Way, 1967) in drama is the essential first step in children's doing tasks requiring minimal external aid. The climate of NO RIGHT OR WRONG, ONLY YOUR OWN UNIQUE WAY prevents any "discrepancy between actual and perceived performance achievement" (p. 16) and the absence of 'fear of failure' in a 'no failure possible' atmosphere allows children the freedom to accept (know, learn about) themselves.

Other means of evaluation include social comparison processes that help children to acquire self-awareness. These abound in drama as in dance with personality dynamics very often dictating the achievement norms. Learners can also appropriate self-esteem through successful drama experiences based on suitable sub-goals and achievement norms. Interpersonal attraction can escalate when peers share successfully a cooperative drama task (Levine et al., 1982). Social support providing continuity and security fostering change (Thomas & Chess, 1980), characteristics of the learning environment, are also integral to the development approach to drama.

Learning to concentrate precedes learning to evaluate. Indeed, in drama, evaluation is seen as interfering with concentration (Way, 1967). Ruble's (1983) conclusion "that children do not spontaneously use information obtained from social comparisons to evaluate their own perform- ances before seven or eight years of age" (p. 19) offers validation for Slade's (1954) and Way's (1967) claim that young children should not be exposed to audiences. Guffin & Keogh (1982) justify this non-evaluative, lack of audience stage by defining 'movement sense' as "the pleas- urability of the sensory experience accompanying any movement activity" and the primary motivation in young children's trying new movements. As natural play evolves into dramatic play, metacog- nitive learning about behaviour norms through observations of others' performances occurs. Like Bateson's dolphin learning about learning, young children need the freedom to do drama for the sheer joy of it (the learning gained, a matter of individual choice), rather than for the entertainment or objective-achievements of adults.

In the brevity of space/time allowed this response, only major arguments have been addressed. Had we "but world enough and time", the following questions raised by this paper might well engage our attention:

Is there a parallel between the folk dance lesson structure, both in content and sequence, with that of the drama lesson?

What is the role of praise in deutero- learning? Is this evaluative?

Does self-monitoring, in fact, lead to trans- fer of learning?

Are there only two learning consequences to any drama activity?

Are drama skills only acquired through imita- tion? What is the role of discovery, intuit- ing, imaging and hemisphericity in drama?

142

In what ways are rhythmic activities a metacognitive context for learning to control one's arousal levels in drama? Is this why Slade often begins drama with response to time-beat and Way with strongly rhythmic music?

As it is, Silver and Baird have shown us how the learning theory supportive of dance techniques portends that metacognitive knowledge, attentional and attributional self-regulation are also outcomes of learning through drama.

*ILLUSTRATION I:* **THEORETICAL FUNCTIONS AS SEEN BY ANTHROPOLOGISTS**

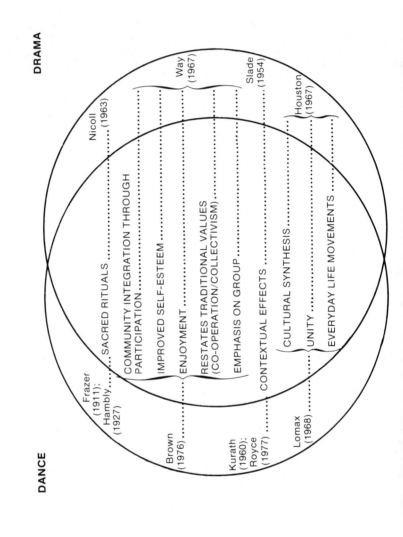

# ILLUSTRATION II: BENEFITS AS SEEN BY EDUCATORS

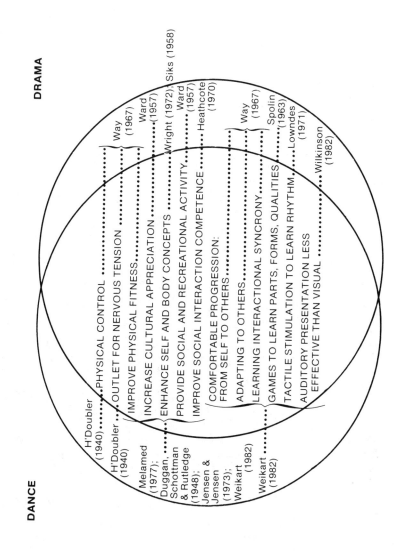

*ILLUSTRATION III*: **THERAPEUTIC OUTCOMES AS SEEN BY THERAPISTS**

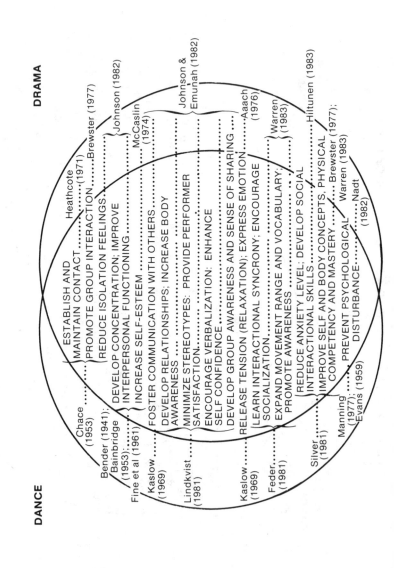

# BIBLIOGRAPHY

The following references are those cited by
Silver and Baird in their Bibliography for
"Psychological Benefits of Dance and Movement":
Bainbridge et al.; Bandura; Bender et al.; Brown;
Chace; Duggan, Schottman & Rutledge; Evans; Feder
et al.; Fine et al.; Frazer; Guffin & Keogh;
Hambly; H'Doubler; Jensen & Jensen; Kaslow, Kaye;
Kurath; Levine et al.; Lindkvist; Lomax; Manning
et al.; Melamed; Ruble; Silver; Thomas & Chess;
Weikart.

Aach, Susan. Drama: A means of self-expression
    for the visually impaired child. New Outlook
    for the Blind, 1976, 70 (7), 282-285.

Brewster, Jeff. Drama with physically limited
    children. In Geraldine Siks, Drama with
    Children. New York: Harper and Row, 1977.

Grey, John. Optimal learning. A presentation to
    the Faculty of Education Seminar Series,
    Lethbridge, Alberta: University of
    Lethbridge, 1982.

Heathcote, Dorothy, Putting in the Bone. A
    video-taped presentation to the Canadian
    Child and Youth Drama Association Conference,
    Fredericon, New Brunswick: University of New
    Brunswick, 1976.

Heathcote, Dorothy. Three Looms Waiting. New
    York: Time-Life Films 1971.

Houston, James. The White Archer: An Eskimo
    Legend. Toronto: Longman, 1967.

Johnson, David. Drama therapy. A presentation
    to the National Association for Drama Therapy
    Conference. New Haven, Connecticut: Yale
    University, 1982.

Johnson, David and Renee Emunah. Drama therapy
    with ex-psychiatric patients. A joint
    presentation to the National Association for
    Drama Therapy Conference. New Haven,
    Connecticut: Yale University, 1982.

Lowndes, Betty. _Movement and Creative Dance for Children_. Boston: Plays, Inc., 1971.

McCaslin, Nellie. _Creative Dramatics in the Classroom_. Second Edition. New York: David McKay Co., 1975.

National Association of Drama Therapists. Philosophy presented at conference. New Haven: Yale University, 1982.

Nicoll, Allardyce. _Masks, Mimes and Miracles: Studies in the Popular Theatre_. New York: Cooper Square, 1963.

Siks, Geraldine. _Creative Dramatics, An Art for Children_. New York: Harper and Row, 1958.

Slade, Peter. _Child Drama_. London: University of London Press, 1954.

Snyder, Mark. The self in action. An invited presentation to the Western Psychological Association. Sacremento, California, April 1982.

Spolin, Viola. _Improvisation for the Theatre_. Evanston, Illinois: Northwestern University Press, 1963.

Stanislavski, Constantin. _Building a Character_. New York: Theatre Arts Books, 1949.

Ward, Winifred, _Playmaking with Children from Kindergarten through Junior High School_. Second Edition. Englewood Cliffs, New Jersey: Prentice-Hall, Inc., 1957.

Warren, Bernie. Drama therapy in special education. A workshop presentation. Lethbridge, Alberta: University of Lethbridge, 1982.

Way, Brian. _Development through Drama_. Longmans, 1967.

Wilkinson, Joyce A. The evaluation of involvement in developmental drama and its relationship to self-monitoring and hemisphericity. Doctoral dissertation. Minneapolis: University of Minnesota, 1982.

Wright, Lin. The effects of creative drama on person perception. Doctoral dissertation. Minneapolis: University of Minnesota, 1972.

THE ARTS IN GUIDANCE THERAPY
FOR THE GIFTED
by
Sandra M. Shiner

I wonder sometimes
Who I really am
through the masks I have when I go out
to parties and to social affairs
and even when I go to school.
Do people know that though
I may be smiling brightly
and looking in their eyes unconcerned
with anything above trivial importance
that I am really struggling
and trying to live up to everyones'
expectations from the outside
and my expectations from the inside...

I want desperately not to be
cast in the mold
of a teenage girl
or a younger sister
or so-and-so's daughter
and I am worrying about and thinking
about and trying to understand
what is going on around me.

But people just pass me by
seeing only the outer shell
of my being
and not thinking or caring
about what inner thoughts motivate or
manipulate me.
                                Judy, age 12.


        What are the guidance needs of the creatively
gifted, and how can the arts play a specific role
in facilitating those needs?  These two questions
shall be the main focus of the following discussion,

## Guiding the Gifted Through the Arts.

        What is meant by guidance needs?  Khatena
(1982) makes a useful distinction between
psychotherapy and guidance.  Psychotherapy, it
can be generalized, deals with the abnormal
problems of adults.  Guidance deals with the

developmental problems of normal children as they strive towards self-actualization and higher states of mental health. Therapy situations are generally crisis oriented and remedial. John Gowan (1979) elaborates the misconceptions that many guidance practitioners have about their field. In the main, he charges that most guidance counselors either restrict themselves to very limited information-sharing about vocational or career options; or view themselves as clinical psychotherapists, having to deal with crisis stress problems. Gowan describes a developmental role for guidance officials in the schools, especially related to the needs of gifted students. He suggests that guidance for the gifted should encourage these students to develop the broadest and healthiest profiles, both cognitively and affectively. He claims that in order to provide such service, guidance counselors must delve into areas of vocational, educational and motivational needs to provide the right kinds of information that will facilitate students to higher levels of creative self-actualization and mental health.

These objectives seem theoretically recognized by the Ontario Ministry of Education. The Handbook, Intermediate Guidance (1978) describes the purposes of guidance as "a process of helping students gain a better understanding of themselves in order for them to take advantage of their opportunities and meet their social responsibilities." The guidance process emphasizes educational and career planning, personal development, and gives students assistance in managing the many environmental forces and influences they encounter. This Handbook further suggests that Guidance (at the Intermediate Level at least) should be integrated with the total school program, and should permeate daily classroom activities in every subject. It should be the responsibility of the whole school and not exclusively that of guidance personnel. Guidance services should be co-ordinated as a team effort on the part of the school, the home and the community.

The responsibilities for generating such a program, in this Handbook, is divided between the classroom teacher and the Counselor. It is suggested that classroom teachers should have a firm understanding of self and others in order to present a desirable role model; should have an understanding of the physical, intellectual, social and emotional development of the students at their particular stage of development; should provide opportunities for students to develop leadership qualities, decision-making skills, and self-direction; should integrate career awareness with regular classroom activities; and finally should work co-operatively with students to resolve individual and group problems arising in the classroom. The responsibilites of Guidance Counselors, then, are seen as mainly consultative, supervisory, information dispensing, record keeping, teacher-training and evaluative.

The Handbook describes a number of program suggestions to implement the described goals of Guidance. Various exercises, largely of a cognitive nature (e.g. questionnaires, checklists) are described, to delve into areas of self-awareness; values; social relationships; decision making; educational and career planning; and leisure planning. These activities are described for the general school population. Two assumptions are implicit: that classroom teachers have the skills and the desire to delve into these areas with their students; and that all students would react in a similar fashion to the experiences which a teacher might engage them in.

What resources exist in our schools for adequate guidance training? Guidance programs are scarce in our school systems, according to a host of researchers who have lamented this gap since the 1950's (Hildreth, 1952; Martinson, 1961; Gowan and Demos, 1964; Zafrann and Colangelo, 1977). The present writer (Shiner, 1982) reviewed proposed plans for gifted education by 14 Ontario School Boards. None had designed guidance programs for their gifted students. A Skills Inventory of Guidance Needs has been presented by the writer to more than 100 Masters' Level teachers within the context of a course on the Educational Needs of the Gifted. Over 90 per cent of the respondents (a variety of teachers with from two to twenty years of teaching experience) expressed the need for specific training in the areas of personal awareness; group dynamics; communication skills; and specifically in understanding the distinctively different needs which gifted students might have beyond those of the average school population.

The need for specific guidance training to help all students understand and use their best potentials is therefore clearly evident in the literature. Two problems now remain to be examined: the specific guidance needs of the gifted; and the role the Arts can take in facilitating those needs.

Why do we talk about guidance needs for the gifted? Aren't the gifted those students in our general school population who already have more going for them than the average populace? Those familiar with Terman's studies on the gifted (1925; 1947; 1959) might be led to believe that gifted students are those who already have greater academic and personal strengths, and who do indeed achieve above the general populace. But recent studies have shed light on a group of individuals who may not even have been identified as gifted in the Terman studies. This is the population often called "high creatives" or creative intellectuals. These students have been typified by various researchers (Drews, 1965; Khatena, 1978; Shiner, 1981; Simonton, 1978). Torrance (1977) draws up the following list of characteristics which his many studies of the creative personality have generated. Along with advanced intellectual functioning, these individuals often display a large number of the following tendencies:

1. ability to express feelings and emotions.

2. ability to improvise with commonplace materials and objects.

3. articulateness in role playing, story telling, and sociodrama.

4. enjoyment of and ability in visual arts (drawing, painting, sculpture).

5. enjoyment of and ability in creative movement, dance and drama.

6. use of expressive speech.

154

7. fluency and flexibility in figural media.

8. enjoyment of and skills in group activities, problem solving, etc.

9. rich body language.

10. humour

11. problem centredness and persistence in problem-solving.

12. emotional responsiveness.

Drews (1964) warns of the unpredictable nature of the motivation of these "types" of gifted students. Unlike their counterpart, the Studious Achiever, who is conforming, studious, likes high marks and traditional teaching, Creative Intellectuals are often resistant to the other peoples' ideas and teaching formats. They are generally unmotivated by the goals of high marks unless they are "turned on" to teacher and subject matter. They are more interested in pleasing themselves than others; are often outspoken about their dissatisfaction with a system and will volunteer "constructive criticism" without being asked. The difficulties that such students might have in traditional school systems are obvious.

However, not all high creatives have the strength to act out their needs. Khatena (1978) describes another possible experience which repressed creative children can manifest:

> Repression of his creative needs may lead the highly creative child to become outwardly conforming, obedient and dependent, with damaging consequences to his concept of self. It may also led to serious learning disabilities and behavioural problems. In preferring to learn by authority, he sacrifices his natural tendency to learn creatively by questionning, guessing, exploring and experimentation. Much of the aggressive behaviours in the classroom that the highly creative gifted child exhibits can be traced to the creative thinking strategies he uses to overcome his tensions.
>
> (p. 78)

Khatena, Gowan and Torrance all express the concern that repressed high creatives may develop emotional problems, neurosis and even psychosis. The struggles of the creative individual to maintain a symbiotic balance with a society whose worldview is very different from his own, is graphically described in works such as Colin Wilson's The Outsider (1972) or Rollo May's study of The Meaning of Anxiety. (1977) Briefly, Rollo May points out that creating always involves destroying the status quo, destroying old patterns within oneself, and creating new and original forms of living. Therefore, every experience of creativity has its potentiality of aggression or denial toward other persons in one's environment, or towards established patterns within oneself. The creative experience, therefore, is always accompanied by anxiety and guilt. The more creative the person, the more anxiety and guilt are potentially present.

The problems of the creatively gifted are becoming of increasing interest to researchers. Ritchie, Bernard and Shertzer (1982) suggest that "guidance needs for the gifted" is too broad a designation. Gifted individuals are as unlike each other, as they are different, en masse, from the generalized population. This study suggests that a focus be developed towards students who could be described as those with special gifts of "interpersonal sensitivity". Using a group of 10 to 12 year old gifted and average students, Ritchie et al were able to distinguish qualitatively different reactions by the "interpersonally sensitive" students to a variety of taped sociodramas. In the main, students with superior interpersonal sensitivity, gained significantly higher ratings in the following areas:

the ability to perceive the emotions of others
                    nonverbal cues
                    veiled intentions of others
                    defensiveness
                    insensitivity
                    effective communication skills.

To summarize, it has been discussed that most teachers are poorly trained to meet the guidance needs of the general student population. The guidance needs of gifted students are even less clearly defined and understood. It has further been suggested that gifted students are as different from each other as they are from the general populace. The group of gifted students who may experience the most acute need of, and benefit from Guidance Therapy through the Arts are the types of gifted students which are variously described as Creative Intellectuals or Interpersonally Sensitive.

Frasier (1979) has stated that the gifted encounter four main counselling needs:

(1) coming to terms with their identity as a gifted person.

(2) difficulty in making academic and vocational decisions.

(3) problems of making social adjustments.

(4) problems in facing and resolving inter-personal and social conflicts.

One might observe that these conflicts are faced by all developing personalities. In what specific ways are the concerns of the gifted different from those of the general population? It is not within the parameters of this paper to dwell extensively on the differences. But a brief example from the mouths of gifted students them-selves might illustrate the specific nature of the conflicts that gifted students face. The following quotes are taken from a collection of thoughts (Krueger, 1978) that gifted students have generated about various aspects of "being gifted."

On identity:

"Now, let's be blunt: We are not normal and we know it; it can be fun sometimes, but not funny always. We tend to be much more sensi-tive than other people. Multiple meanings, innuendoes, and self-consciousness plague us. Intensive self-analysis, self-criticism, and the inability to recognize that we have limits, make us despondent. In fact, most

157

times our self-searching leaves us more
discombobbled than we were at the outset."
(p. 9)

On academic and vocational decisions:

> I'd heard it said, "the sky's the limit".
> But how was I to know that, for I did not
> have anything to compare it with. The sky
> was limitless. As far as I could surmise,
> the ninety was close to the sky...of my
> English class. I'd come so close with so
> little effort. I knew my English and history
> classes were not challenging. I knew all my
> teachers were not challenging me. I knew
> their skies were not my skies.
> (p. 12)

> If you are like us, you know that when you
> exhibit extraordinary abilities, other people
> tend to exaggerate them. In their minds, you
> become a "genius" and/or an eccentric. While
> your work may be exceptional, you may not be
> able to achieve at the level on which others
> may expect you constantly to operate. With
> the passing of time, you may find your per-
> formance is farther and farther from what is
> expected of you. Pursuing one course of
> action, you may attempt to do things beyond
> your reach. At some point, you will probably
> tell yourself that you have no talent, which
> is, of course, untrue. Your mind will
> vacillate between believing that you are a
> genius and believing you are a failure.
> Neither being true, you may become extremely
> depressed or confused and your opinion of
> yourself will begin to break down.
> (p. 31)

On social problems:

> It's a rotten feeling to have people just
> turn against you when they find out you're
> gifted...one problem is that kids think of me
> differently. I absolutely don't want to be
> considered better than them, and I don't want
> teachers to think I am better either. This

makes me feel alone and different. I want to
feel "with it".

(p. 22)

On interpersonal conflict:

Eventually, I began to withdrawn more and
more each day. I wouldn't talk. I ate very
little. I stayed in my room too much. I did
have friends, but I couldn't match their
standards all the time. Though I tried
desperately to make the same jokes, talk the
same slang, enjoy the same pastimes...I'd hit
bumps and just have to admit to myself just
how phony it was. It was a bore. I got
bored with my very closest friends and left
no one to confide in.

(p. 27)

These excerpts from the lives of the gifted
themselves are a small sample of the problems
which gifted children encounter in their development. More extensive descriptions and research
into these areas can be found in the work of
Bridges, 1973; Colangelo and Zafrann, 1979;
Newland, 1976; Shiner, 1978.

Must the creatively gifted suffer lives of
despair and alienation in order to make their
creative contribution? Herman Hesse, it is said
had a loneliness and an "inward dying" not due to
any defects of nature, but rather a profusion of
gifts and powers which had not achieved harmony.
Kubie (1958) in his study of creative individuals
notes that many of his subjects mistakenly
believed that suffering was necessary to stimulate their creative output. As our understanding
of the possibilitiies of positive self-actualization develops (through theories of Maslow,
Rogers, Arieti, etc.) we must now educate highly
creative individuals to prize their creative
differences; to understand more about the
structure and development of creative thought
processes; and to develop strong self-worth about
themselves and others. We must bring them out of
their isolated shells of differentness and help
them see their place in a world that can be taught
to value creative expressions of the artist.

The arts has an intrinsic role to play in this important task. The remainder of this discussion shall suggest ways in which involvement with the arts can specifically provide instructional models to assist with the afore-mentioned counseling needs of the gifted -- personal identity; academic and vocational decisions; social adjustments; and interpersonal conflicts.

The role that the arts can play in developing self-awareness and self-esteem has been described by Courtney (1979) in a document about the impor-tance of the arts in education, as follows:

> To create art is to state our personal identity-the students' painting or dance says something about himself. It reflects his confidence, and thereby helps to build his self-esteem...The arts increase his self-awareness...at the same time they develop his awareness of others. In the group arts in particular (drama and dance) his personal relationships are strengthened and these, in turn, reinforce his sense of self...From his creation of the arts, the student extends his awareness into his immediate group, the local environment, his community and his culture as a whole. This leads him to understand others ---their similarities and differences with himself.
>
> (p. 17)

The need for the gifted to discover themselves through the arts has been documented in the studies of eminence carried out by the Goertzels (1978). They made the following observations about the 700 eminent personalities whose back-grounds they examined:

> Children who become eminent love learning but dislike school and school teachers who try to confine them to a curriculum not designed for individual needs...they like to go to special schools that train actors, dancers, musicians and artists...they need and manage to find periods of isolation when they have freedom to think, to read, to write, to experiment,

to paint, to play an instrument.
freedom can be obtained only by ᴸ
illness.

(pp.

How often do gifted children have to "ᴸ
to gain these required periods of creᴀ
energizing?   Shiner (1979) found that
experiences for the gifted in the arts werᴠ
and happenstance.  A few exemplary programᴮ
be found in the literature however.  List (1ᴸ
describes a unique summer writing program ᴛ
gifted and talented youth at the University oᴼ
Connecticut.  This workshop provided gifted young
writers with the tools for more effective writing.
Writing was seen as an attempt to approximate how
we know things and to revive them in writing.
Thirteen year old Sue Campbell began a poem
called <u>Portrait</u> this way:

> Eyes that pierce through the heaviest mask
> Make you feel your thoughts aren't secret
> anymore
> But they never allow you to see
> behind them.

(p. 28)

Journal writing is another tool which can
provide release and insight into personal awareness and talents of the gifted.  Techniques
described by Progoff (1975) and Rainer (1976) can
be introduced to gifted students to assist them
in using journal writing as a therapeutic tool.

The main benefits of the use of writing for
young gifted individuals is to provide tools and
experiences for self-development.  That is, it is
the <u>process</u> which is important.  Occasionally,
however, the <u>products</u> of the young stand as
universal works of art alongside the product of
their more mature counterparts.  <u>The Diary of
Anne Frank</u> is an outstanding example of the
writings of a gifted and sensitive 14 year old
girl who documented the horrors of the Holocaust
tragedy:

> Why do I dream of the most terrible things?
> My fear makes me want to scream out loud
> sometimes.
> If you think of your fellow creatures, then

you only want to cry, you could really cry the whole day long.

Career guidance for the gifted can be assisted ⅃y the many role models which exist in literature and film. A course of study could be developed around inspiring creative figures in these media. One young girl describes her successful "escape into literature":

> I realized early that my parents were not interested in discussing (death, religion, the Universe) with me... and that my peers were incapable of doing so. I withdrew into literature, and had read all of Dostoevsky by the age of fourteen. I then became absorbed in the French existentialists... Although I had friends, I was lonely and depressed through my teen years. I was emotionally incapable of coping with the issues which intrigued me intellectually.

> (Hollingworth, 1942, p. 68)

Films such as <u>All That Jazz</u>; <u>Man For All Seasons</u>; <u>Being There</u>; <u>Galileo</u> and <u>Fame</u> could be utilized to depict the struggles of the creative personality with himself and society. Richert's review (1981) of the film <u>Simon</u> is an example of understanding the plight of the gifted through film.

Problems of academic and vocational decision-making could be examined through role-playing, fantasy and guided imagery. Courtney (1979) points out that specific involvement with the arts allows individuals to experience themselves in wider frames of reference. Involving gifted students in sociodramas around current world issues (e.g. aging, immigration) can help them develop their awareness of, and reactions to a variety of critical social issues.

Social adjustment can be explored through the use of bibliotherapy. Bibliotherapy is the use of books to help a person to solve a personal problem; develop skills needed for living; and/or bolster self-image. Olsen (1875) points out that the bibliotherapeutic process consists of IDENTI-FICATION (with a major character of the book);

CATHARSIS (release of emotional tension); INSIGHT (achieving new perspectives on a problem). A number of books are available listing titles suitable for gifted children (e.g. Baskin and Harris, 1980; Dreyer, 1979). With appropriate guidance, gifted children can be helped to find literary peers who share their lifestyles.

The use of film is also appropriate to assist in social adjustment. Films such as The Outsiders which focuses on the "rebel" gifted.; Flashdance which depicts the struggles of an aspiring young dancer; or Breaking Away the story of bright young boys from the "wrong side of the tracks" who compete with the local college population, are all vehicles which can spur discussion about the social and emotional adjustments of accomplishments.

Finally, interpersonal and humanistic concerns of the gifted can be aided through drama and dramatic techniques. The play Amadeus focuses on societal reactions to the gifted, by examining the tensions and jealousies which the young Mozart generated amongst his artistic peers. A Man For All Seasons portrays the struggles of a man of principle against social convenience; Galileo also depicts the conflicts which a man of inventiveness and vision experienced by bucking the conventions and attitudes of his day.

Sociodrama can be used by gifted students to explore conflicts about current political, social and ethical concerns. For example, one group of bright high school students recently experienced social, psychological and economical aspects of aging in contemporary society through a sociodrama which they wrote and acted in after collecting data through many interviews with senior citizens in a variety of settings. The play was performed for both student audiences (in Junior High and High Schools) as well as Seniors in retirement and nursing homes. The experience enlightened the students about the dilemmas inherent in the perils of "growing old." It also gave many of the performers the satisfaction of making a real educational contribution to alleviate a social problem which they had previously expressed concerns about.

In conclusion, it has been shown that the arts, specifically Creative Writing, use of Journals, drama, film, bibliotherapy, and sociodrama have a therapeutic and instructive role to play in Guidance for the creatively gifted. Involvement with these experiences can provide insight and companionship for this isolated group. Many of their inherent tendencies previously described (articulateness, role playing, expressive speech, sense of humour, emotional responsiveness) can be ventilated and strengthened through these arts activities. As the gifted see themselves mirrored in their own activities with the arts, they may gain strength to go on using their talents in, as yet, undiscovered areas.

What remains to complete this scenario is an awareness for the potentiality of the use of the arts in the training of Guidance counselors. Arts educators have a critical role to play in this endeavour. They already have a deep awareness of the potentiality for development which enactment with and through the Arts can engender.

In what ways can arts educators and guidance personnel collaborate to develop techniques and implementation strategies to marry the technology of the two fields into a course of Guidance Therapy for the Gifted? The need is clear. Providing the answer can be a dramatic and creative challenge.

The following questions illustrate the areas which should be thoroughly explored:

(1) What education is necessary to ensure that both guidance personnel and arts educators have a sound and intensive understanding of the guidance needs of the creatively gifted?

(2) Clear curriculum goals are essential for an effective plan of action. How can arts educators and guidance personnel work together from the earliest planning stages to ensure that the goals of guidance and the goals of effective arts experience are well-coordinated?

(3) What new techniques, experiences, attitudes must arts educators and guidance personnel develop in order to share and utilize the perspectives of their individual and combined fields?

(4) What provisions for in-service can be developed? Who will finance such undertakings? Where will time, material and resources come from to support such undertakings?

(5) What incentives (emotional, intellectual, financial) can be developed to ensure the interest and commitment of guidance and arts educators to a program of Guidance Therapy for the gifted through the Arts?

(6) What will be the role of the classroom teacher in these endeavors? How will school administrators view such programs? What will be administrative difficulties in evolving a program of guidance involving arts educators?

(7) How will the outcomes of such a program be evaluated? What will be objectives? Will formative or summative evaluation procedures be designed?

(8) How can gifted students themselves be involved with the design and evaluation of such programs?

(9) How will the educational milieu (parents, rest of student body, the media) view such a program? How can the milieu be informed and involved with such a program?

(10) In what ways can the objectives of a guidance program for the gifted using the arts be communicated to the rest of the school society? What are the implications for expanding or adapting this program to meet the needs of other specific groups in the school system?

(11) What support can be given to other groups outside the "formal educational community" which might have input or training facilities for expanding this program of guidance through the arts? (e.g. museums, art galleries, little theatres, TV stations, artists, actors, other creative mentors in the community, arts councils, business and the arts, etc.)

(12) How can objectives be developed to incorporate both cognitive aspects of the program (e.g. What will a course of study using Fame as a central stimulus contain?) and also affective concerns (e.g. Are guidance personnel emotionally prepared to utilize such different media to elaborate their original professional mandates?)

This discussion has focussed on presenting the needs for developing a course of Guidance Therapy for the creatively gifted through the Arts. Such a course would incorporate the technology, insights and sensitivities of two traditionally separate fields. It is an exciting professional challenge to attempt to breach the gap. The successful development and implementation of such programs could greatly enhance the sound emotional and vocational development of a promising, but largely neglected portion of our student population.

# REFERENCES

Baskin, B. and Harris, K. Books for the gifted child. New York: Bowker, 1980.

Bridges, S. Problems of the gifted child, IQ 150. New York: Crane, Russak & Co. 1973.

Colangelo, N. & Zaffran, R. T. (Eds) New voices in counseling the gifted. Dubuque, Iowa: Kendall Hunt, 1979.

Courtney, R. The face of the future. Report to Canadian Conference of the Arts. Ottawa, 1979.

Dreyer, S. The bookfinder; a guide to children's literature about the needs and problems of youth aged 2-15. Circle Pines, Minn. American Guidance Services. (2 vols) 1979.

Drews, E. M. The four faces of able adolescents. Saturday Review. Jan. 19, 1963, pp 68-71.

Drews, E. M. The creative intellectual style in gifted adolescents; being and becoming; a cosmic approach to counseling and curriculum. Research Report. Michigan State Univ. E. Lansing, Mich: 1965. ED 003182.

Frasier, M. M. Counseling the culturally diverse gifted. In N. Colangelo and R. T. Zaffrann (Eds) New voices in couseling the gifted. Dubuque, IA: Kendall/Hunt, 1978.

Goertzel, MG. Goertzel, V. & Goertzel, T. G. 300 eminent personalities. San Francisco: Jossey-Bass, 1978.

Gowan, J. C. & Demos, G. D. The education and guidance of the ablest. Springfield, Ill: Charles C. Thomas, 1964.

————, and J. Khatena & E. P. Torrance. (Eds) Educating the Ablest. Itasca, Ill: F. E. Peacock, 1979.

Hildreth, G. H. Educating Gifted Children. New York: McGraw-Hill, 1965.

Hollingworth, L. S. Children above 180 IQ. New
    York: World Book Co., 1942.

Khatena, J. The creatively gifted child. New
    York: Vantage Press, 1978.

Khatena, J. Educational psychology of the gifted.
    New York: John Wiley and sons, 1982.

Krueger, M. On being gifted. New York: Walker &
    Co., 1978.

Kubie, L. S. Neurotic distortion of the creative
    process. New York, Noonday, 1958.

List, L. J. Writing: the journey and the dance.
    G/C/T. Jan/Feb 1983, pp 27-31.

Martinson, R. A. Educational programs for gifted
    pupils. Sacramento, California: State
    Department of Education, 1961.

May, R. The meaning of anxiety. New York: W. W.
    Norton, 1977.

Newland, T. E. The gifted in socio-educational
    perspective. Englewood Cliffs, N. J.
    Prentice-Hall, 1976.

Olsen, H. Bibliotherapy to help children solve
    problems. Elementary School Journal, April,
    1975. pp 423-429.

Ontario Ministry of Education. Intermediate
    guidance curriculum guidelines. Toronto,
    1978.

Progoff, I. At a journal workshop: the basic
    text and guide to using the Intensive
    Journal. New York: Dialogue House, 1975.

Rainer, T. The new diary. New York: J. P.
    Tarcher, 1978.

Richert, E. S. Media mirrors of the gifted. in
    Gifted Child Quarterly, 1981, 25, 1, 3-4.

Ritchie, A. C. Bernard, J. M & Shertzer, B. E.  A
    comparison of academically talented children

and academically average children on interpersonal sensitivity. <u>Gifted Child Quarterly</u>.
1982, <u>26</u>, 3, 105-109.

Shiner, S. M. <u>Curriculum implications of the</u>
<u>profiles of gifted high school students</u>.
Ph.D. dissertation, U. of Toronto, 1978.

Shiner, S. M. The gifted and talented and the
arts. In R. Courtney (Ed.) <u>The Face of the</u>
<u>Future</u>. Canadian Conference of the Arts,
Ottawa, Canada, 1979.

Shiner, S. M. Creative intellectuals: anxious
misfits in our schools. Paper presented to
Fourth International Conference on the
Gifted. August, 1981, Montreal, Canada.

Shiner, S. M. Provisions for the gifted in
Ontario Faculties of Education and some
Ontario School Boards: Paper presented to
24th annual conference of Ontario Educational
Research Council. Toronto: December, 1982.

Simonton, D. K. The eminent genius in history:
the critical role of creative development.
<u>Gifted Child Quarterly</u>, 1978, <u>22</u>, 2, 187-195.

Terman, L. M. <u>Mental and physical traits of a</u>
<u>thousand gifted children</u>. <u>Genetic studies of</u>
<u>genius</u>. Stanford, Calif: Stanford Univ.
Press, 1925.

Terman, L. M. & Oden, M. H. <u>The gifted child</u>
<u>grows up: twenty-five years follow-up of a</u>
<u>superior group</u>. <u>Genetic studies of genius</u>
(Vol. 4) Stanford, Calif: Stanford
University Press, 1947.

Terman, L. M. & Oden, M. H. <u>The gifted group at</u>
<u>mid-life</u>. <u>Genetic studies of genius</u> (Vol.
<u>5</u>) Stanford, Calif: Stanford University
Press, 1947.

Torrance, P. <u>Discovery and nurturance of gifted-</u>
<u>ness in the culturally different</u>. Reston
Va: Council for Exceptional Children, 1977.

Wilson, C.  The outsider.  London:  Gollancz, 1972.

Zaffran, R. T. & Colangelo, N.  Counseling with gifted and talented students.  Gifted Child Quarterly, 1981, 20, 3, 305-320.

Response To:  DR. SANDRA SHINER"S PAPER
by
Holly N. Giffin

In her paper Dr. Shiner introduces us to the field of guidance therapy and specifically to a particular group of young people, the "creative intellectual or the interpersonally sensitive" for whom she has special concern.  She expresses her own sense that experience in and with the arts should be incorporated into a guidance therapy program for this gifted group.  She suggests some specific ways in which journal writing, drama, socio drama, and film, have been or could be used to help the creatively gifted transcend their sense of alienation while stimulating their natural powers.  Finally, she provides us with a detailed outline of issues we must address in order to implement such a collaboration between therapists and arts educators.

As dramatic educators we can recognize many parallels between the goals of drama and the goals of guidance therapy.  Dr. Shiner affirms that the goal of guidance therapy is to facilitate the development of children as "they strive towards self-actualization and higher states of mental health."  Likewise, Brian Way asserts that we as drama teachers are interested in developing people rather than drama.  As facilitators of human growth we have focussed our investigations on the process involved in creating drama (Way, 1967).  Leaders in our field such as Richard Courtney (1968) and Virginia Koste (1978) have described this process of dramatic imagination as the source of all creative expression and learning.  In contributing our perspective we may be able to elaborate and strengthen Dr. Shiner's argument for the use of arts experiences in guidance therapy for the gifted.

Dr. Shiner suggests that plays and films about creative persons who had similar problems may offer role models to gifted students.  Sociodrama is suggested as a vehicle by which the gifted can explore other people's lives.  Further, since the creative intellectuals seem to have a flair for expressiveness in movement, speech, and story telling, drama should enable them to ventilate and strengthen these traits. It seems however, that as drama specialists we can offer some other reasons for why dramatic education may have something special to offer the gifted.

The profile of the creatively gifted child that Dr. Shiner presents us suggests a person whose preferred and perhaps incorrigible mode of learning is akin to that which is encouraged in drama. The creative child rebels against learning by rote. Drama is learning through experiencing imaginately. The creative child may automatically feel with others. Drama leads participants to hone this empathic ability into a powerful tool for learning. The creative child sees many possibilities. Drama relies on the power of the imagination to transform, to generate a multiplicity of answers. The creative child enjoys becoming absorbed in solving problems. Drama is explored through various "problems" of exercises. Each child solves them in his or her own way. The creative child may respond especially emotionally to the environment. Drama teaches students to value and respect the intuition. Beyond developing the natural capacity of the gifted for expressing, drama may provide an affirmation of and challenge to their natural mode of experiencing.

Perhaps indeed "repressed creatives" who hitherto have not allowed themselves expression may be discovered in the course of doing drama. Richard Courtney (1978) has articulated the belief of many drama experts that dramatic education, learning by doing, by acting, by experiencing is the natural mode of learning for all children and the source of all creative thinking. If this is so there may be a large number of repressed high creatives. One definition of the creatively gifted child might be: a child whose natural affinity for the dramatic mode of investigation is so strong that traditional education, in its relentless push for right answers and approved products, has not been able to squelch it.

Another concern which Dr. Shiner expressed was that the gifted frequently feel isolated by their giftedness. Drama can provide a safe setting in which each individual's experience is accepted. There are no right answers, thus everyone's response is accepted as true for him or herself no matter how innovative they may be. Drama sessions tap basic abilities of all human beings to sense, to imagine, to move, etc. and essentially provide the structures through which each individual can explore these powers at his or her own level. Thus the gifted child is able to feel an integral part of the group yet is challenged to use his or her abilities fully. The kind of mutual appreciation of each other's creativity that tends to be generated during drama sessions can provide the gifted child with a sense of community and belonging. In drama individual differences are accepted and participants are free to meet each other at the level of their shared humanness.

Dr. Shiner concludes by enumerating a number of questions which must be considered in the creation of a guidance therapy-arts program for gifted students. These concern, among other things, defining the curriculum, establishing a system for evaluation, motivating guidance personnel and teaching staff to participate in implementing such a program. These are practical realities that indeed we must take into account.

However, in addressing these issues it is essential for dramatic education specialists to be alert to implicit differences in values between drama and traditional education. Drama is concerned with subjective process which is possible only in an atmosphere safe from premature evaluation. Often the traditional educational establishment is concerned with concrete, objectively measurable and evaluable products. Drama is child-centered and wholistic. Traditional education tends to be subject-centered and organizes learning into separate areas. Drama relies on and develops the intuition. Traditional education tends to value intellectual or cognitive knowledge.

Virginia Koste cautions that an observer can only see and hear the valuable flow of dramatic experience "if he is willing to believe it (suspend judgment) and if he can accept that it is impossible to understand it all. This life-study (like all study) is in fact an act of faith, postulated on the basic assumption that meaning is there waiting to be discovered" (Koste, 1978, p. 116). A program which must subordinate the values of drama to those of traditional education loses much, possibly most, of its potential effectiveness.

A major task in the collaboration between dramatic educators and guidance therapists will be to develop appropriate curriculum goals and evaluation methods. The categories of the curriculum must be responsive and subordinate to the organic development of the child. Methods of evaluation must be sensitive to the creative process if they are to avoid destroying it. However, in training school personnel to implement this program we must recognize that we may be asking them to espouse perhaps a radically different set of values and assumptions.

In conclusion, Dr. Shiner has introduced our discipline to a potential ally, the field of guidance therapy. She has alerted us to the special needs of the creatively gifted. Finally she has proposed a collaboration between guidance therapists and educators in the arts which challenges us to probe more deeply and articulate more fully the nature of dramatic education.

# Bibliography

Courtney, Richard. Play, Drama, and Thought:
    The Intellectual to Dramatic Education.
    (London: Cassell, 1968).

Koste, Virginia Glasgow. Dramatic lay in
    Childhood: Rehearsal for life. (New
    Orleans: Anchorage, 1978).

Way, Brian. Development Through Drama.
    (London: Longman Group, 1967).

# DRAMA AS A CONTEXT FOR TRANSFORMATION
by
Bradley Bernstein, Ph.D.

## Introduction

Journal Notes. A drama workshop in a special
education class for emotionally disturbed
children. We are playing the Spolin exercise,
"Mirror."[1] First there is a random selection of partners: we count off -- teacher
included -- and everyone gets in pairs around
the room. In each pair one person is the
initiator and the other the mirror. We
switch back and forth until everyone is
initiating and mirroring simultaneously. In
the Spolin lexicon this is called "follow-
the-follower." The group enjoys the game:
focus is strong and body movements are full
and fluid. When the exercise is over we move
into another game. We count off again; new
groups form.

A week later I ask the teacher if anything happened as a result of the last
session. "You know," she says, "when we
played Mirror I got as a partner a boy who
previously I had had no contact with. He
doesn't raise his hand, ask me questions,
whatever. In the Mirror exercise we both did
it together, and once or twice we smiled at
each other. In the last week since then he
has come up to me twice to talk about what he
is working on, and once was just hanging
around my desk. I think it had something to
do with the Mirror. Even though we didn't
talk I think we established some kind of
link."[2]

*

Community should be thought of as a phenomenon of the spirit which comes and
goes and must be deliberately sought
after.

Viola Spolin, Theater Game File[3]

176

Through drama a group can transform into a community.

A group is a collection of people characterized by isolation, that is, people are isolated from each other, and each from his/her own creativity. In a group each individual is ultimately pursuing what is best for him/herself. A group can be manifest in any of the following contexts: a marriage; a family; a business corporation; a school classroom; a dramatic production; or a nation-state.

The same structures can transform into communities when we who participate in them act for the benefit of each other. In those moments we become networks of persons-in-relation, characterized by spontaneous and deliberate action for connection and contribution. Each individual is valued for the contribution s/he makes to the whole, and everyone has a positive sense of belonging and building.

We have reached the point in contemporary civilization when we must choose to express ourselves as members of a world community, or to remain in separated groups. In the latter we live in fear and aggression and face perilous results in the not-too-distant future. Continued separation results in degeneration and collapse. If we work towards achieving community, however, we have the possibility of entering the present and creating the future simultaneously as the expression of contribution, combination, and unity. Connection creates life and growth.

To correct confusion at the start: the community, or world-as-a-whole, implies individuality, but expresses it as the inseparable pairing of opposites. This is symbolized by the yin-yang, the linga and yoni, the crux ansata, the cross, and the double triangle. As a phenomenon of the spirit on the human plane, community comes about through the movement of opposites in harmony: this is the transformation to community. Transformation must be regarded as movement -- literally "moving across form" -- particular kinds of human action in a context which values community and allows it to occur. Through our actions together we move toward -- or away from -- community.

A context for community can appear in many forms, as already stated, and drama is one of them. In the I Ching, the Chinese Book of Changes, written almost five thousand years ago, we find reference to the transformative power of drama in its early expressions:

> Religious forces are needed to overcome the egotism that divides men. The common celebration of the great sacrificial feasts and sacred rites, which gave expression simultaneously to the interrelation and social articulation of family and state, was the means employed by the great rulers to unite men. The sacred music and the splendor of the ceremonies aroused a strong tide of emotion that was shared by all hearts in unison and that awakened a consciousness of the common origin of all creatures. In this way disunity was overcome and rigidity dissolved.[4]

Drama is the fabric of interpersonal existence, the interplay of each of us with one another and all of us with the world and cosmos. It takes place within our individual selves as well. "Drama is a universal activity."[5] It comes in daily life, and can also be created theatrically, in a workshop exercise or a production.

For the last six years I have been exploring the uses of drama-as-theater with "emotionally disturbed" individuals -- people who have been labeled depressed, schizophrenic, psychotic, manic, learning disabled, hyperactive, and withdrawn. This exploration has been conducted through drama projects in special education classes and in residential psychiatric facilities in Canada, Australia, and the United States. The projects have included creating original theater pieces, filmmaking, exploring Shakespeare's plays, and on-going theater workshops for students and teachers, and patients and staff.

The principal inspiration for this exploration is Viola Spolin's work, as published in

Improvisation for The Theater, and the Theater Game File. Spolin's landmark contribution has been immeasurably influential in theater training for the last twenty years, and is increasingly used with groups outside of usual theater activity: in prisons; old-age homes; programs for underpriviledged youngsters; teacher training classes; and in hospitals. The Spolin work values, and is a structure for, action and agency, as well as involvement and mutuality. It is a context for the transformation to community.

The students and patients with whom I've worked have had little or no positive contact with their own creativity or with one another and the surrounding world. They tend to view themselves as being defeated, unable to create and achieve. Their energy output is low and lifeless, or high and unfocused. Their similarity is their isolation -- from their own powers and potential, and from one another and the possibility of being effective contributors to a developing community. These people, segregated from society as well, represent the alienation from self and others that is characteristic of our age.

The study of community is engaging a number of contemporary psychologists, interested in psychology as "intersubjective understandings."[6] We seek to discover how shared meaning is brough about, and how contexts are created in which a person can experience his/her individuality and be part-of-the-whole as well.

This is a paper about drama as a context for transformation in psychiatric settings. Since drama activities are so closely related to all forms of human activity, they can be very useful in psychotherapeutic situations. Writing about her first experiences using drama with hospitalized psychiatric patients, Gertrud Schattner states:

> I recognized the almost magical outlet that drama gave those patients and realized once again the curative powers of the creative arts in the treatment of the emotionally disturbed...I learned what happiness some of the patients felt when they believed that

179

they had something to contribute and that they were part of a team.[7]

When drama functions this way everyone -- students, patients, inmates, teachers, staff, parents, relatives, and the public -- has a sense of community. What are the characteristics of drama as a context for transformation? I will address this question through considering some theoretical issues, practical requirements, and through field-study observations. I hope the reader will actively consider his/her own response to what appears in the following pages.

The quest for community involves all of us and is limitless. The view given here, through the clarifying lens of Spolin's work, is an offering to our understanding of how community comes about, and the importance of drama in that process.

<u>Point-of-View: Learning through Action and Involvement</u>

The most important prerequisite for trans-formation is a context which values agency and community and creates conditions to bring them about. This is a point of philosophy which gets directly translated into practice: Do we adhere to a "classical view" of persons, or do we promote its alternative?

The classical view of man, then, is at once a view of him as an isolated, thinking subject set over against an objective world, facing an essentially theoretical task, and a view of him as a mechanism, operating according to laws. Epistemologically, we feel that the only form of real knowledge we can have about the world is that which we have in thought, reflection, or contemplation, i.e., objective knowledge. And, ontologically, everything that exists in the world as we know it exists as an entity constituted from a determinate set of independent elements in lawful motion.[8]

Most of contemporary schooling is organized according to this view. We describe the world, and in so doing acquire a knowledge of "the facts." This is a rather passive, verbal-type of learning. It advances the notion that the world is separated into discrete parts. It also leads to another kind of separation -- of people. We learn to compete and out-do one another. We gauge and reward learning by virtue of amount: "right" answers; test scores; courses completed; degrees earned. This leads to detached and isolated individuals each determined to do the best for him/herself rather than for society. We educate for individual survival.

The alternative is to develop the person's sense of being an active agent in the establishment of community:

As an alternative to this classical view of man as primarily an isolated an egocentric contemplative, separated from the world of practical affairs, we may view him as primarily a doer, immersed in the world as agent...in a state of exchange with other agents both like and unlike himself, forming communities such that together they can do more than they could ever do along...Such an image of man involves not only a shift in standpoint from one in thought to another in action, it is also intrinsically a social view of man. Rather than an egocentric self, it is a view of man as a person among other persons.[9]

Such a shift in standpoint has far-reaching implications: Learning is not a function of contemplation, but comes from action. Through a person's action in the world s/he develops knowledge of the world: "We know existence by participating in existence...there can be no knowledge without an activity which supports it."[10]

A context for transformation is geared to an individual learning through his/her actions with others. For example, a patient whom I shall call Paula (a twenty-two year-old artist with a history of severe psychotic episodes) becomes ill and stays in her room each week on the day of the drama workshop. After the first three weeks she comes to the theater room, but sits on the sidelines. However, she is engaged and animated, as is obvious by her facial expressions, body movements, and spontaneous cries of delight as she encourages the other players. By the sixth session she participates in some of the exercises. Two weeks later she is participating fully. When we begin planning for a production, Paula spontaneously contributes excellent suggestions for scenery. Everyone is very enthusiastic about her original ideas. In the production, some two months later, Paula plays an important character, and most of her work is determined in her spontaneous interaction with the audience.

Paula became progressively active and involved -- by her own choice and at her own pace. This development -- from being ill and isolated to being spontaneous and fully engaged -- occurred as Paula had the choice (and opportunity to choose) to exercise herself and learn through action that she is capable of spontaneity, that her spontaneity can be creative, and that her creativity can be a contribution to the whole of which she is part. A context for transformation offers these opportunities. Each participant can realize him/herself as an agent, and as a member of a developing community. "Everyone can act," states Spolin, "the combination of individuals mutually focusing and mutually involved creates a true relationship."[11]

## Action Through Focus

The context for transformation requires that each person becomes an active participant in solving a group problem: "Any game worth playing is highly social and has a problem that needs solving within it -- an objective point in which each individual must become involved." The objective point is the focus -- the player is not thinking about him/herself, but full-body attention is directed to the problem to be solved: e.g., "focus on keeping the ball in space and out of the head"; "focus on silently mirroring partner's words"; "focus on communicating and on showing -- not telling."[12]

Focus directs attention and action to something between players rather than within individuals. In the Spolin work, as in the projects inspired by it, the problem to be solved is in the exercise or production. Rather than isolate the individual's "problem" the players solve a problem together. This has a certain curative effect. "In the course of playing a game or exercise a door is opened and the player's 'problem' dissolves as a new action (insight) emerges."[13]

A problem is an opportunity for further exploration. The previously mentioned production in which Paula participated was called "The Jungle Play" and involved all patients and staff in one of the units in a small psychiatric treatment center for young adults. Roles for the production presented a problem.

Journal notes. Asking the players what roles they want to play meets with dead stares. A different approach must be taken. We do a "free writing" exercise: "Would you like to be a plant, an animal, or a person in the jungle? What's your first choice? For five minutes write down whatever you imagine." Some examples:

"I am a medicine man. Big black cauldron with wooden stirring stick, talisman attached to the end. Exotic smelling smoke -- burning eucalyptus. I'm stripped to the waist, bermuda shorts, bare feet. Back and chest tatooed, various junglesque accoutrements like beaded bracelets, necklaces, earrings, nose rings. Hair pulled up and tied around a bone."

"I am a tiger mad at man. Man who could make me snap with his gun and snake who could threaten me. I am lean and slick. I don't often go after prey. When I do I am careful about what I pick, judging something that has grown sadistic which must run in mad flight. Then I become all claws and teeth and stained with blood. I have made my hideous kill."

"I am a tall willowing avocado tree, with big oval leaves that are shiny and of the color green. I have a delicate bark that scars easily. I bear the fruit avocado. I have many at one time. When ripe, this food is rich and delicious to the taste. Its skin is smooth and oily. the pit inside roots within the fruit and is the beginning of a tree like me."

These become the springboards for exercises, explorations, characterizations, costume designs, and scenarios. The free writing exercise also reveals that one player would rather do lighting than act on stage; another prefers to be the stage manager. Everyone has a role; and everyone is also on one of the production teams for costumes, scenery, and sound. The work of each team gets defined and grows as the project develops, bringing everyone into an increasing number of inter-personal contacts. There is confrontation, discussion, and resolution as we work together over agreed tasks, all solving problems as we go along.

Focus sparks creative spontaneity and mutual involvement. In a workshop for difficult nine year-olds we are playing "Building a Story." When it is his turn to contribute to the developing story, Darryl, a hyperactive and rebellious child, starts making abrasive noises. His contribution cannot be integrated and the game is disrupted. We begin again. This time when it is his turn Darryl starts a different story. The other children are frustrated: "Come on, Darryl," "Cut it out!" "He always does that," are some of their comments. On the third go-around Darryl's contribution is lively and integrated. It is also very funny, and the group enjoys a good laugh.

Players, particularly those patterned psycho-logically and culturally to view themselves as being isolated, often try to pull the focus to themselves, as Darryl did. Such actions call attention to the player's isolation. The value of drama activities conducted through focus and mutual problem-solving is that action and attention are drawn to a <u>common</u> ground. Each person supports and becomes part-of-the-whole. As we read in the <u>I Ching</u>, "disunity was overcome and rigidity dissolved [through] cooperation in great general undertakings that set a high goal for the will of the people; in the common concentration on this goal, all barriers dissolve, just as, when a boat is crossing a great stream, all hands must unite in a joint task."[14]

184

Part-of-the-Whole:   The Sense of Community

To function as a context for transformation,
a drama activity or production must allow for and
nourish the sense of being part-of-the-whole.
This sense -- ultimately what we experience as
community -- is an outcome built through action
and relation on three interdependent levels:
with others; with the environment; and within
one's self. Although an analysis of each level is
well beyond the scope of this paper, we will
highlight three common elements essential to
becoming part-of-the-whole.

Communication.   "The techniques of theater
are  the  techniques  of  communicating."[15]
Through Spolin's exercises such as "Mirror,"
"Give and Take," "Involvement in Twos," and
others, communication is promoted on verbal and
non-verbal levels. In playing we develop sensitivity to the communications of others and also
become attuned to how we send out signals and
messages:   Each of us is a receiving/sending
set.   In-coming and out-going channels of
communication are opened.

Observation.   Exercise:   "Play Ball."   No
props; instead, a ball is created out of
"space substance."  Terry, 10 , hyperactive,
starts throwing the ball very quickly and
without direction, soon losing the ball and
his partner, Les. Les gets angry, and he and
Terry begin to bicker. I start the game
again, this time coaching the class to play
in slow motion. Terry regains contact with
the ball and throws it directly to Les. The
two play catch across the space. When
regular speed resumes both are clear where
the ball is, when it drops, and where it
rolls to if one of them misses it. Their
irritation with one another turns into
delight in playing.

We clarify and heighten communication through
developing our senses. "Peripheral Vision,"
"Sending Hearing Out," "Listening to the Environment," are all designed to bring about clarity
and depth to what we receive from each other and
our surroundings. Through opening our senses we
come in touch with ourselves as well. This can

be pleasurable or disturbing, as shown in the following examples, taken from an on-going workshop series with seven year-olds in a special education class:

Observation: "Feeling Self with Self." When the children are coached to feel their feet in their shoes and to feel the hair on their heads everyone is focused and there is complete silence. Then there is some surprised and delighted laughter as some children experience the sensory feelings as if for the first time.

Observation: "Listening to the Environment." In response to the coaching, "Send your hearing outside the room," Craig disrupts the game by calling out, "I hear your momma on the toilet."

In both cases the players' actions give us clues for further work in communication. For Craig, who was unable to listen without being disruptive, the exercise was restructured so that players closed their eyes and each child -- Craig included -- had a turn at making a sound in the room (closing the door; the on/off of a light switch; rustling papers, etc.). On the next occasion, the children were coached to listen to sounds in the hallway outside, and so on, until the range broadened. In this way Craig was brought into increasingly direct contact with what was going on in the outer environment. He became less preoccupied and more calm -- able to focus and interested in playing. Loss of contact can be experienced as frightening. As one's senses are activated -- rehabilitated? -- channels of communication are opened; clarity of focus and increased participation result. Body therapies, massage, dance, and music can all be helpful in opening the body to receive and send communications.

Roles. Drama activities allow us to shed our usual roles and role behaviors and enter into present-time playing and experiencing. This is as true for patients and students as it is for staff and teachers.[16]

Field Notes. In a reformatory for adolescent boys, Clyde, aged 13, is playing "Involvement in Twos" with Gerry (a unit guard). They are folding a bed sheet made from space substance. The audience greatly enjoys watching them. Is it to see a guard doing a mundane task? Or to watch Clyde, whose room is always a mess, become involved in straightening up? Gone are the usual commands and resistances. Both players work together -- making jokes, enjoying themselves.

As Paula, the patient mentioned earlier, dropped her role behavior of being "ill" she was able to participate freely. Likewise when players give up role behaviors of being withdrawn, domineering, aloof, and authoritative. However, it is not unusual to find that a person is resistant to shedding his/her usual role behavior during an exercise. This appears to be particularly true for group leaders. In observations of teachers and children in special education classes playing the Spolin exercises (where all were under the direction of an outside specialist), teacher action fell into four categories, only one of which was "focused playing." The others were "withdrawal," "policing," and "teaching." Teachers lost focus during the exercises by becoming involved in other tasks, daydreaming, scolding children, disciplining during the exercise, or instructing children how to play. One of the teachers, Mrs. Percy, was virtually unable to give up her usual role and had continuing difficulty in becoming a fellow player:

Observation: "Relay Where." Focus is on the game: the players are adding to pieces of a stage set, working with space substance. When James makes an addition to the set Mrs. Percy calls out from the sidelines, "Nice work James!" The focus shifts to Mrs. Percy.

During the playing there is some talking amongst the players, but it is about the game and does not disturb its flow. Nevertheless, talking of any sort displeases Mrs. Percy, who gets up and starts handing out little plastic counters. These are part of her usual behavior modification program and represent points. The game is disrupted.

Mrs. Percy walks across the room and hands the leader a counter as well, saying, "You get one too."

Her manner is firm and patronizing. The intrusion is sudden and forceful.

Conditions for experiencing: In the preceding example the teacher was unable to give up control. Instead she made her presence felt through compliments, disagreeable looks, rewards, and the threat of punishment. Such behavior directs focus to the leader's actions and reactions rather than to the on-going process. This also separates players and fosters competition.

In a context for transformation we must be wary of competition and its sources since "it makes group harmony impossible; for it destroys the basic nature of playing by occluding self-identity and separating player from player."[17] Authoritarianism, prejudice, assumptions, judgments, criticisms, and personal interpretations are also anathema to developing the sense of community. When we act in these ways we intrude on playing and mutual focus. Our intrusions can be very subtle -- they are well ingrained in our systems of teaching and learning and in the treatment we provide in institutions. We must continually bring our awareness to dissolving barriers, not creating them.

If we want to stimulate spontaneity and creativity we should attend to the problem to be solved and to the process of which we are part -- rather than to the self-importance we may give our attitudes and personal judgments. This is not meant to suggest that evaluation should be avoided, for it can be one of the most useful tools available to the whole group, if handled properly. "True evaluation that is based on whether the problem (focus) was solved does away with criticism and judgment values...a player on stage either communicates or does not. The audience sees the book in his hand or does not see it. This is all we ask. The very simplicity of this is what confounds most [people]."[18] Evaluation must open a door for continued action and relation.

The conditions of a drama activity -- the structure, atmosphere, tone, and style of presentation -- are primarily the leader's responsibility. These aspects deserve careful thought, planning and continued attention on his/her part. The leader can create a supportive, nourishing environment -- one that is a context for transformation to community -- or s/he can create a context for actions which are self-aggrandizing, judgmental, and divisive, thus perpetuating the isolation that is characteristic of our culture. There is no question that the conditions set by the leader have a pervasive influence on the participants -- on what they do during the activity, and on what they learn from the activity and carry into their lives. "What I have discovered," stated another teacher after playing Spolin exercises with her class,

> ...is that an adult can be responsible for causing behavior in a child. I am beginning to be much more aware of how a definite pattern gets set up between the children and me, and how it ends up with me controlling everything.

*

In becoming part-of-the-whole, we -- leaders and players -- dissolve personal resistance and interpersonal barriers in the moments when we are focused and mutually involved. In this way, we facilitate the transformation to community rather than withhold against it. We withhold ourselves from transformation in a variety of ways, all of which are manifestations of fear: fixed attitudes; rigid belief systems; narrow perceptions; and muscular holds. All of these limit our possibilities for action and relation. With any of these limitations a person literally "holds back." The person is concerned for his/her own survival and creates conditions to ensure it. At the core of psychotherapy -- and any context for transformation -- is the dissolution of resistance, and the coming into contact with one's self, with others, and with the world-as-a-whole.

Through action in such a context the person learns to value his/her spontaneity and creativity. Furthermore, the person learns that through one's creativity s/he is responsible to the whole. There are many possibilities for individual expression and interpersonal relations in a drama activity or project. All channels need to be kept open for mutual fulfillment and mutual growth.

## Improvisation:  Including the Audience

Through the Spolin work players create improvised, spontaneous theater. Nothing is prearranged, "no outside device is to be used... All stage action must come out of what is actually happening on stage."[19] When "The Jungle Play" ran for six public performances, parents, friends, townspeople and fellow patients and staff members came to be part of the event. Instead of sitting and observing, the audience moved around the jungle, involved in the action as it unfolded. From a newspaper review:

> Unlike a conventional stage play, the audience gets actively involved with the creatures it meets in the jungle. It becomes a release of each person's imaginative expression as the jungle creatures coax and cajole the participants...The actor's characterizations are, in fact so inspiring of humor or thought, one has to pull oneself away to interact with other jungle creatures.

After each performance a reception is held for the players to meet the audience. Conversation is animated, experiences are shared. The bouyant feeling is one likely to be found in a professional theater which has just opened an unqualified hit rather than a usually sober (if not morose) psychiatric institution.

Improvisation springs from trust -- in one's own spontaneity, and in the support of one's fellow players. Focus, involvement, open communication, shedding roles, and setting the proper conditions for play and experiencing all are vital to improvisation. The audience too becomes part-of-the-whole. No one knows what is going to happen; all are participating in present-time creation. A context for transformation is ever-widening to include more participants in the growing sense of community.

## The Indeterminate World

In the first section of the paper we called for a shift in viewpoint -- from seeing the person as an "isolated thinking subject," to viewing him/her as a "socially responsible agent."[20] In this view, action is primary. We shape the world through our actions together:

> In acting we do something: using something as a tool or instrument we make something else, some materials, take on a form different from the form it would have if we had not acted. Thus, in acting, we determine at least some small aspect of the world. For this to be possible the world must be capable of being given a structure it does not already possess. That is...the world must be in some sense essentially indeterminate. If real human action is to be possible, the world cannot have an eternally fixed character, it must be a world that can be developed in a direction "pointing" from a certain past, through the moment of action in the present, to a more or less uncertain future -- with it being really possible at the present time for the world to be developed in any one of a number of different possible ways in the future by the actions of agents.[21]

The sense of the world as indeterminate is consistent with improvisation and is vital to any context for transformation. We are responsible for our actions and their consequences. We can transform from isolation to community. The choice is our action, "the future is the field of possibility."[22]

## Summary

When we conduct drama activities the question of purpose should be paramount: What are we seeking to create? If we conceive of drama as a context for the transformation of a group into a community, then we create opportunities for individuals to come into full and coordinated contact with each other, with the surroundings, and with themselves.

191

In the quest for community we must be willing
to recognize that much of what we promote and
transmit through our culture leads to separation
and isolation. We need also recognize that our
attempts at self-protection and survival are
ultimately useless, and in fact, do not promote
growth. Each of us, like everything else on this
planet, has a life. The greater transformation
-- birth/death/birth with living flowing throughout -- is occuring all the time and we are part
of it. When we fully realize this we no longer
protect ourselves, but instead promote conditions
for life and growth for ourselves and others. We
live for the other. Transformation to community
occurs through love, through acts of communion.
The religious connotation here is purposeful:

> An artist is one who creates new visions of
> beauty hitherto unguessed. Surely a reli-
> gious man must be one who creates in the
> religious field -- who understands and
> reveals what has been hitherto hidden and
> secret, and who creates new possibilities of
> communion, who integrates human society in
> new forms of shared experience, who experi-
> ments in the world of human community and
> discovers the conditions and methods of new
> and deeper intimacies between man and man,
> and between man and the world.[23]

We always return to the people whom we serve:
Are we nourishing them properly, individually and
together? Do we give the group every opportunity
to transform into a community? The emotional
disturbance of psychiatric patients is a function
of their isolation. They do not value themselves
and they feel unloved by others. They are discon-
nected from their own potential, and from the
world about them. Often these are people of
startling creativity which has never been properly
recognized and developed. Thus, their creative
energies turn inward and become dark, full of
rage, fear, and pain.

Contexts for transformation such as the
Spolin work and drama projects inspired by it can
release this well-spring of creativity so that
the person is able to give his/her expression
positive shape in the world, connecting with
others and the environment. Everyone wants to

belong.  Everyone already does belong.  The
deepest learning is to experience interrelation.  The greatest teaching affords the
opportunities for this to occur.

> Existence is infinite, not to be defined;
> And, though it seems but a bit of wood in
>       your hand; to carve as you please,
> It is not to be lightly played with and
>       laid down.
> When rules adhered to the way of life,
> They were upheld by natural loyalty:
> Heaven and earth were joined and made
>       fertile.
> Life was a freshness of rain,
> Subject to none,
> Free to all.
> But men of culture came, with their grades
>       and distinctions;
> And as soon as such differences had been
>       devised
> No one knew where to end them,
> Though the one who does know the end of all
>       such differences
> Is the sound man:
> Existence
> Might be likened to the course
> Of many rivers reaching the one sea.[24]

## FOOTNOTES

1.    Viola Spolin, Improvisation for the Theater, (Evanston, Ill.:  Northwestern University Press, 1963); idem, Theater Game File (St. Louis:  CEMREL, 1975).  The reader is advised to consult the Spolin works for complete descriptions of the exercises referred to in this paper.

2.    "Journal notes," "Observations," and "Field Notes," are taken from the author's personal and unpublished accounts of his work in special education classes and psychiatric treatment centers.  See also, Bradley Bernstein, "Action, Relation, and Transformation:  A Study of Viola Spolin's Theater Games" (Ph.d. diss., University of Toronto, 1979).

3.    Spolin, Improvisation for the Theater, 37.

4.    Richard Wilhelm, trans. The I Ching (Princeton:  Princeton University Press, 1977), 227-228.

5.    Richard Courtney, "The Universal Theater: Background to Drama Therapy," in Drama in Therapy, vol. 2, ed. Gertrud Schattner and Richard Courtney (New York:  Drama Book Specialists, 1981), 2.

6.    John Shotter, Images of Man in Psychological Research (London:  Methuen & Co., Ltd., 1975), 33.

7.    Gertrud Schattner, "Introduction," in Drama in Therapy, vol. 2, xiii.

8.    Shotter, Images of Man in Psychological Research, 30.

9.    Ibid., 31.

10.    John Macmurray, Persons-in-Relation (London:  Faber & Faber, 1961), 17.

11.    Spolin, Improvisation for the Theater, 3-4.

12. Spolin, Theater Game File. Sources for all foci and exercise titles are Spolin, Improvisation for the Theater; idem, Theater Game File.

13. Viola Spolin with Mary Ann Brandt, "Theater Games," in Drama in Therapy, vol. 2, 214. Note that Spolin does not consider her work a system of therapy, like Psychodrama, created by J. L. Moreno, where the individual's problem of personal growth or adjustment is the subject or "work" for the group.

14. I Ching, 228.

15. Spolin, Improvisation for the Theater, 14.

16. See also David Read Johnson, "Drama Therapy and the Schizophrenic Condition," in Drama and Therapy, vol. 2, 47-64. Johnson's treatment of role relationships in drama activities is useful in understanding the multiplicity of relationships between players.

17. Spolin, Improvisation for the Theater, 10-11.

18. Ibid., 28.

19. Ibid., 39.

20. Shotter, Images of Man in Psychological Research, 30-31.

21. Ibid., 108.

22. John Macmurray, The Self as Agent (London: Faber & Faber, 1957), 133.

23. John Macmurray, Reason and Emotion (London: Faber & Faber, pp. 1935), 253-254.

24. Laotzu, The Way of Life, trans. Witter Bynner (New York: Capricorn Books, 1944), 45-46.

BIBLIOGRAPHY

Bernstein, Bradley. "Action, Relation, and
     Transformation: A study of Viola Spolin's
     Theater Games." Ph.D. diss., University of
     Toronto, 1979.

Boyd, Neva L. Play and Game Theory in Group
     Work. Edited by Paul Simon. Chicago:
     University of Illinois, 1971.

Courtney, Richard. Play, Drama & Thought.
     London: Cassell, 1974.

Giorgi, Amadeo. Psychology as a Human Science:
     A Phenomenologically Based Approach. New
     York: Harper and Row, 1970.

I Ching. Translated by Richard Wilhelm and Cary
     F. Baynes. Princeton: Princeton University
     Press, 1977.

Laotzu. The Way of Life. Edited by Witter
     Bynner. New York: Capricorn Books, 1944.

Leont'ev, A.N. Activity, Consciousness, Persona-
     lity. Englewood Cliffs, New Jersey:
     Prentice-Hall, Inc., 1978.

Macmurray, John. Persons in Relation. London:
     Faber & Faber, 1961.

Macmurray, John. Reason and Emotion. London:
     Faber & Faber, 1935.

Macmurray, John. The Self As an Agent. London:
     Faber & Faber, 1957.

Schattner, Gertrud, and Richard Courtney, eds.
     Drama in Therapy. 2 vols. New York: Drama
     Book Specialists: 1981.

Shotter, John. Images of Man In Psychological
     Research. London: Methuen & Co., Ltd., 1975.

Spolin, Viola. Improvisation for the Theater.
     Evanston, Ill.: Northwestern University
     Press, 1963.

Spolin, Viola.  Theater Game File.  St. Louis:
        CEMREL, 1975.

Wexler, Philip.  Critical Social Psychology.  London:
        Routledge & Kegan Paul, 1983.

Response. L'EXPRESSION DRAMATIQUE
PRIVILEGED AREA OF CHANGE AND FAVORED
INSTRUMENT IN THE TRANSFORMATION OF THE MILIEU
by
Gisele Barret

A Response translated from the French paper.

It gives me great pleasure and honor to have the opportunity to respond to Dr. Bradley Bernstein's paper. The topic treated by Dr. Bernstein is, in my opinion neither problematic nor disputable, but seems rather to be a clearly defined, humanistic and coherent topic both within modern psycho-educational alternatives as well as within the 'classic' examples inspired by the practice of Viola Spolin.

If, in effect, at first glance, the proposed title "Drama as a context for transformation" suggests a vast terrain to be explored, and demarcated if not outright defined, then Dr. Bernstein's paper offers precision and delineates the limitations of a more reassuringly circumscribed field of application.

It is not a question of seeing the process of transformation in its broad sense in which l'expression dramatique would be its context (we shall return to this choice of terminology, the meaning of which is not clearly evident to me; privileged context: possible context? - here again we shall have to posit a few hypotheses).

It is more a matter of a specific change by which "through drama, a group can transform into a community" ... As for the theoretical basis, the commentaries, be they philosophical or psycho-sociological, I cannot but state my total support for a subtle and pertinent analysis of a classical learning problem: that of socialization seen from a humanistic view point (we shall come back to the underlying ideology).

This field of exploration, and - to use the terminology of my distinguished colleague - this context, is already a vast terrain in which l'expression dramatique is seen as a preferential instrument - as simple, quick, attractive and efficient. I will try to give evidence of this as well as a few examples.

But in fact, the subject is seen in a new light when we discover that it utilizes "drama as a context for transformation in psychiatric settings", confirmed in the examples offered dealing with "disturbed" individuals, disturbed to differing degrees and dependent upon special education, psychological, or psychiatric treatment.

If, despite the general theoretical analysis, valid in all cases, I focus on the therapeutic aspect of the process of transformation, it is not a means to relativize its manifestation, but to justify it as one of the major problems facing educators, remedial educators and therapists and which they try to resolve by turning specialty to l'expression dramatique.

A question that quickly arises is whether the specialist in expression dramatique is competent to deal with the kind of intervention that the milieu and the objectives require. Is s/he educated for this purpose or will further specific education be necessary and if so, how much will be needed and how will it be provided? I ask this question as a person responsible for educating these specialists of expression dramatique and as an expert on education programs for teachers - teachers who seemingly deal with this specific problem in a scrupulous and unsure manner (I regret I haven't time to truly elaborate on this subject which exceeds the scope of my intervention).

Just as the specialists of expression dramatique called upon to practice in a milieu outside their realm of competence, I could have declined to give an opinion after having read Dr. Bernstein's paper since I was only prepared to answer to a subject to which I have given a different meaning and extension.

Unfortunately, the refusals are usually due to personal tastes as opposed to a conviction or a recognition of lack of competence and experience.

As for myself I have accepted to respond in order to justify this state of affairs, or at least, to bear witness insofar as a useful or productive questionning or criticism can be put forth.

I esteem that the beneficial effects obtained under these difficult conditions can be as productive as the effects obtained under less strenuous conditions.

Is an educational institution a less difficult milieu than a psychiatric institution? I don't think this is immediately evident. If yes - less difficult for whom? Probably for the specialists of expression dramatique. It remains to be seen.

If we take the advice of the common educator who is, in fact, a specialist in expression dramatique we will have to recognize that the problems encountered in socializing a "normal" individual are less serious than the acute problems of global socialization.

On the other hand I feel that the therapists who are interested in expression dramatique would find it to their advantage to work with well-educated specialists instead of psycho-educators however well-meaning they be. In order to promote efficiency, it would be interesting that the therapist be aware of what the specialist has to offer in this case the notion of Dr. Bernstein's "context".

It would also be advantageous to precisely define the notion of 'context' since expression dramatique is defined as: "Drama as a context". I find this concept especially appropriate.

L'expression dramatique is a framework (contextus), a weaving (texere) of circumstances in which the transformation of the individual and the group fits in and thereby evolves.[1] This environment, this privileged place of discoveries, of influences, of all kinds of stimulations, plays a primary role, not only in perception, expression, interrelation and communication, but above all - in learning.

In this case, we will then make reference to
a facilitating educational context, or preferably,
a psycho-educational context (transformation of
the individual) or better yet, a psycho-socio-
educational context (transformation of the group
through the transformation of the individuals or
the transformation of the individuals through the
transformation of the group). One does not occur
without the other and it isn't crucial to know
which manifests itself first or which is of
primary importance given the fact that expression
dramatique allows this double transformation
without hierarchy and with no other ideology save
humanism. I would add that if one clearly under-
stands the notion of "group"[2] that the objective of educating a group of individuals would
seem entirely adequate. On the other hand, the
concept of 'community' is interesting if only to
indicate the present erosion of the notion of
'group', but it is still too entrenched in a
mysticism not wholly pertinent in an educational
milieu. Why not re-evaluate the meaning of
'society' instead of risking the entanglements of
the word 'congregation' and then finding ourselves dealing with too-specific objectives.
While on this topic I would add that, while
appreciating the poetry of mystical quotations, I
would hope for quotations, just as forceful and
explosive, to arise from the pure or applied
sciences. For example, to illustrate an important part of Dr. Bernstein's paper: "The inseparable pairing of opposites ... The movement of
opposites in training" which provides innumerable
themes to expression dramatique[3] I would have
expected parallel to the mystical images, examples
of philosophy,[4] of psychology,[5] of physics[6]
and mathematics (concepts of antagonism, of contradiction, of paradox all within their simultaneous positive and negative aspects).

It is time to attempt answering Dr. Bradley's
question: "What are the characteristics of drama
as a context for transformation?... The theoretical issues, the practical requirements, the
field, study observations." I will not re-state
the examples of my colleague, but will mention
our many points of agreement dealing primarily
with the concept of man, of the world, of society
which underlies my activities as a practitioner,
as a didactician and as a researcher. The

fundamental philosophy of expression dramatique follows the same path and gives a profound justification to our work.[7]

I will adopt the concepts of activity and involvement of the educational basis and methodological structure as my own (even though they are not at the same level). In order to concretize these objectives, expression dramatique makes use of play therapy in which freedom, benevolence and pleasure (within a framework of rules) permits a simple union of expression and communication.

A reminder that for most of us, in the francophone as well as the anglophone milieu (as in many other milieux) the word drama is understood in its etymological sense which, in Greek, signifies activity; a second reminder that our interventions are in the form of workshop exercises (as opposed to course, seminars and labs.)

Unlike Dr. Bernstein and other practitioners of creativity, I have a tendency to speak of "living situations" instead of problems to be resolved which too often bring back bad memories of school work.

Outlining basic principles is often insufficient since one has to find methods of applying these principles. A solution to this practical problem, and one I have proposed to the specialists of expression dramatique, would be a technical referent called "double structure"[8] a way of avoiding the pointillism of rote exercises which offer no visible progression. The initiation, the significance, the consciousness-raising, the desire to enter into relationships and the fact of doing so are processes which develop slowly throughout the duration and proposing ways to facilitate this development in terms of meaningful stages is important.

Unfortunately I haven't the time to develop this much-needed methodology judging by the general anarchy predominant amongst practitioners; however I would like to specify that my approach tries to bypass the pitfalls of traditional education. The verbal exchanges at the end of each workshop do not take on the form of confrontations, discussions or resolutions, but are more in the nature of personal expression offered to the group as a gift and which will blend in with others' personal expressions in a non-competitive, non-hierarchial and non-judgmental manner. Each individual learns to speak, to listen, to appreciate his/her differences all the while appreciating the uniqueness of others; each discovers his/her own space while respecting the space of others; each learns the dialectics of speaking and listening, of teaching and learning, of giving and taking. It is from the implicit nature of confrontation that one's sense of being, of belonging is developed and so one can thereby attempt to arrive at a solution to the paradox: myself and others/myself with others.

Another important point to be made is the fact that verbal exchanges do not precede the activity in order to avoid the phenomena of anticipation, rationalization and intellectualization. Collective activity is taken on with the implicit agreement that each individual will be attentive to or conscious of others and that the results will be an unpredictable union of individualities including whatever opposition, contradiction and conflicts that may arise. The nature of man's coexistence with others is, in fact, the questionning of the dialectics between the individual and the collective, of its rapport of convergence and divergence where the individual is able to respect him/herself all the while respecting others.

If the 'free expression' approach is then essential for the development of the processes of expression and communication, the indirect or oblique approach is a significant auxiliary. It would be better to begin with the mediation of objects, through an intervention of identities, recurring to the theme before daring to exploit the situation hic et nunc which is, after all, the final objective. After having played with a simple chair, after swaying in the breeze like a bush by the pond, only then may it be possible to examine oneself and to realize this as a 'real' authentic experience, who can discuss the perceptions, the feelings and the ideas of the group as a whole.

For, if there is transformation, it is total
and affects the individual in his/her complexities even though it is easier to identify the
zones more obviously affected by the change.
This learning to become a whole, a total being,
is critical in a time when traditional education
has a tendency to separate the individual into
pieces. Here the group leader's role becomes
clearly evident - he is the leader, the one who
holds the key in the search for unity, this unity
we need to find, to rebuild. S/he is the guide
through contradictions, leading or following but
always present, a discreet catalyst and active
witness to the change.

I have been practicing expression dramatique
for more than fifteen years and each day I am
awed by its inherent mysteries - be they phenomena or miracles - it becomes too difficult to
define. In spite of today's popular tendency to
veer in the opposite direction I continue on -
for everyday I have new proof of the changes and
new evidence that expression dramatique is a
privileged area of change as it is a favored
instrument in the transformation of the milieu.
Just as the flux and the reflux, the cyclic
breathing patterns, just as the passing of day
into night and the rhythmic changing of the
seasons, all change within the individual contributes to the transformation of the collective
just as all transformation of the group provokes
a change in the individual and expression dramatique is a weaving of these exchanges, a meeting
place of ideas - the context for natural transformation. How extraordinary!

(1) I use the definitions from the 'Robert' and from 'Vocabulaire de l'Education' de Gaston Mialaret.

(2) Group: number (assembly-context) of persons having something in common (independently of the presence in a shared area). Personally I utilize the concept of 'collective' (pararallel to individual) which for me seems more open and neutral (that is which diverse connotations according to usage).

(3) For nearly ten years I have used the following proposals for workshops which I define as "le couple neutre" up/down; inside/outside; heavy/light; opened/closed; centripetal/centrifugal; full/empty; positive/negative or giving/receiving; going up/coming down; pull/push - notions which can be deneutralized by key images re: key/keyhole; flux/reflux; or which can complement each other by the concept in in-betweeness (doorway, stairway, road, bridge, door, etc.)

(4) M. Beigbeder: Contradiction et nouvel entendement (Bordas).

(5) Psychologie Humaniste No. 23 - Fev. 83. Bulletin de l'Association Francaise de Psychologie Humaniste. Entire issue dealing with the antagonist logic of Stephane Luspasco.

(6) J. Piaget: Recherches sur la Contradiction

B. Nicolescu: Science et Contradiction (C.N.R.S.)

S. Luspasco: Logique et Contradiction (P.V.F.)

S. Luspasco: Le principe d'antagonisme (Hermann)

(7) G. Barret: L'expression dramatique: Pour une theorie de la pratique, Montreal, Universite de Montreal, 1976.

(8) G. Barret: <u>Pedagogie de l'expression drama-
tique</u>. Montreal, Universite de Montreal,
1973. Revision in Press, 1982.

# FROM RITUAL TO REASONING:
## A PROLEGOMENA TOWARDS ESTABLISHING LINKS
## BETWEEN RITOLOGY AND SCHOOLING
### by
### Peter McLaren

Those societies which cannot combine reverence to
their symbols with freedom of revision, most
ultimately decay either from anarchy, or from the
slow atrophy of a life stifled by useless shadows.


-- Alfred North Whitehead


A woman patient who has been a patient in a mental
hospital for over twenty years, approaches me at
the same time each day, curtsies and hands me a
piece of cardboard on which is stuck a small
effigy. I take it, appraise it, smile, say 'thank
you', bow, hand it back. She takes it back,
smiles, curtsies, walks away. Almost every day
for about eighteen months the same scene is
repeated.
 The effigy is surrounded by captions with
arrows directing the reader to different sections:
 'These limbs are made with wax from my
 ear and hair from my armpit,'
 'The genital area is made with my
 menstrual blood and my pubic hair.'
 'The face is made with my tears, my
 saliva, my catarrh, and hair from my
 head.'
 'The body is made with my shit, my
 sweat, and my blood.'
 I play my part in this ritual to humour her,
somewhat patronizing and embarrassed. I might
have taken the palms of her hands and licked her
sweat, I might have drunk her blood, swallowed
her tears. But I was a psychiatrist.


--- R. D. Laing

...But even though the Oilers intend to change a number of things, they won't alter their pregame ritual.

Like most athletes, the Oilers are superstitious, and because they have done well with a ritual, they will use it again tonight.

When it's time to line up for the national anthems, most teams simply rush towards their goalie and urge him to come through for them...

...Players approach the goalie in an accepted order. Dave Semeneko, meanwhile, stands to the goalie's right. Mark Messier stands in the corner.

Most players tap the goalie's pads with their sticks. Gretzky taps the goalie's head with his right hand. Then the starting players, including the goalie, stand on the blueline for the anthem. The exception to this is when Lee Fogolin is in the starting lineup. In that case, Gretzky stands behind him.

Using this ritual, the Oilers went through the season without losing three games in a row. Obviously, the ritual has let them down...

--Al Strachan, <u>The Globe and Mail</u>

I received a letter containing an account of a recent suicide:

"My friend...jumped off the Golden Gate Bridge two months ago. She had been terribly depressed for years. There was no help for her. None that she could find that was sufficient. She was trying to get from one phase of her life to another, and couldn't make it. She had been terribly wounded as a child...Her wound could not be healed. She destroyed herself."

The letter had already asked, "How does a human pass through youth to maturity without breaking down?" And it had answered, "help from tradition, through ceremonies and rituals, rites of passages at the most difficult stages."

-- Wendell Berry, <u>The Unsettling of America</u>

Hence, though man's environment greatly varies in the corners of the planet, there is a marvelous monotony about his ritual forms. Local styles of the century, nation, race, or social class obviously differ; yet what James Joyce calls the "grave and constant in human sufferings," remains truly constant and grave.

-- Joseph Campbell
The Flight of the
Wild Gander

The teacher is an exorcist confronting a panoply of dybbuks.

--- Ira Shor

The general orientation of this paper rests on an analogy between ritual or rite and school instruction. Laing (1982) underscores the fact that theories built on analogies are a tricky scholarly business when he reminds us that "The net is not the sea, the map is not the territory, the menu is not the meal..."[1] And while I am sympathetic to Laing's admonishments that, as scientists, we "fumble for metaphors and paradigms which are less analogous to the process of reality than the barking dog resembles the dog star, or the howling wolf resembles the moon,"[2] I am nevertheless reminded of a quote from the notebook of Samuel Butler: "Though analogy is often misleading, it is the least misleading thing we have."[3]

This paper's fundamental assumption is that the modern expansion of mass communications and industrialization has made for a wide and rapid diffusion of novel ritual systems which have been disseminated into the whole of contemporary culture. Following on the heels of this assumption are three further assumptions: (1) that in modern industrial societies, schools are symbolically saturated and serve as major repositories of rituals and ritual systems; (2) that rituals play a crucial and ineradicable role in the whole of a person's existence: inner/outer, private/ public, mystical/ political; and that (3) these variegated dimensions of ritual are deeply implicated in the events and transactions of institutional life and the warp and woof of school culture. Furthermore, it is assumed that the student, as animal symbolans, articulates his being-in-the-world through participation in school- based ritual, with religious and public symbols providing the mise en scene. Rituals are posited as pregnant with significance for the school researcher and regarded as ideological guardians of symbol systems which have been nurtured by the wider society and augmented by the dominant culture. Moreover, they can, _mutatis mutandis_, be examined as a way of gaining a fruitful perspective on how social actors construct and codify their life-worlds. It is my conviction, therefore, that an understanding of ritual can be of signal importance in an understanding of both student and teacher behaviour.

My own work in ritual studies has evolved out of the belief that a greater critical understanding of ritual will enable educators to pattern and repattern cultural symbols so that they may begin to mollify the negative symptoms of modern techno- cracy, and communicate to students in today's conflict ridden and often timorous educational climate. I believe that in the context of educational research, ritual studies may not unfittingly serve as a unique conceptual prism - or set of lenses - through which enculturation may be sensed and grasped, and which will enable hitherto unprecedented insights to be made into the process of schooling.

The main theme defining the scope of this paper concerns the relationship of ritual to the pedagogic encounter. Years ago - when I first came into contact with the works of the polymath Victor Turner (whom I regard as one of the most distinguished exponents of ritual exegesis) - I became intrigued by the idea of bringing about a rapproachment between educational research and some of the insights gleaned, both theoretical and methodological, from the nascent discipline of ritual studies. But it wasn't until I became familiar with the writings of Ronald L. Grimes (especially his book _Beginnings in Ritual Studies_), Roy Rappaport's cybernetics of the holy, and to a lesser extent, Richard Schechner's iconoclastic musings on the roots of performance, that I became convinced that such a theoretical collusion between educational research and ritual studies (or "ritology" as Grimes calls it) was ripe.[4] The work of these academicians, and others, has convinced me that ritual -- when properly understood -- can serve as an exceedingly profitable aid in the analysis and evaluation of student and teacher interaction.

From whatever disciplinary perspective (e.g., anthropology, liturgical exegesis, sociology, semiology), and with whatever theoretical equipment (e.g., structuralism, comparative symbology, phenomenology, hermeneutics), ritology is making serious inroads into the traditional preserves of cultural studies. Many contemporary "ritologists" could be described as symbolic consocites of Victor Turner (since they work largely under the spell of the Turnerian vulgate whose doctrines are composed of a 'processual' explanation of ritual). These scholars persist in probing the cultural core of ritual, stripping ritual of its derisory religious connotations, making the topic conceptually exciting to scholars from a wide variety of academic backgrounds, and creating an unprecedented interest in ritual in general. Highly important and significant studies are now being penned by scholars other than Turner and their work has developed to the extent that it may be considered more than just footnotes or adjuncts to Turner's seminal work. I refer to studies by such ardent ritual exegetes as Ronald L. Grimes, Sally Falk Moore, Robert Bocock, Barbara Myerhoff, and Richard Schechner.

The overarching task that lies ahead can be summarized in a single question: How effectively can ritual studies assist the educational researcher or classroom instructor in understanding school culture? To answer that question adequately, one must endeavour to delicately steer a course between the Scylla of a substantial lack of empirical research connecting secular ritual with schooling, and the Charbydis of transferring data already accrued in anthropological fieldwork undertaken in tribal societies to conform to educational settings. My own empirical research among grades seven and eight Azorean students in a Catholic school fieldsite, will provide me with initial direction.

I shall attempt to forge my connections between ritual and schooling in three stages: first, by dispelling some of the misconceptions surrounding the term ritual; and secondly, by providing a brief overview of my own research. In conclusion, I will sketch out some future directions for educational research from a ritological perspective.

## Misconceptions Surrounding the Term Ritual

The word ritual is tantalizingly ambiguous. Long-hallowed by repeated liturgical and anthropological use, the term 'ritual' continues to prove troublesome to scholarly commentators. And while conflicting schools of thought remain at daggers drawn, the term ritual has not ceased to provoke the most alarming connotations among laymen. This longstanding definitional problem is no doubt caused by a strong oscillation between various poles of anthropological and lay explanations of ritual - poles which have often been merged, interrelated, intermixed, or cross-referenced. Veiled by ambiguity, the one word "ritual" has frequently been substituted by what a number of commentators have distinguished as routine, habit, schedule, or superstitious behaviour. Because of the wide-ranging use of the term ritual, it is not surprising that we find a variety of definitions, or as often as not, no explanation at all of what ritual means. As a "catch-all" phrase for anything repetitive or habitual, the term ritual has been diluted and trivialized to such an extent that it has become common cultural property and continues to present serious problems for the scientific examination of social relations. And psychoanalytic tradition has proferred a rather distasteful view of ritual, conflating the term with symptoms of private pathology, idiosyncracy, and neurosis (a view which first emerged from Viennese consulting rooms at the turn of the century). These conceptions have done little to enhance the reputation of ritual as a process of noteworthy social significance. Some of the misunderstandings surrounding ritual stem, at least in part, from varying undifferentiated explanations of the nature and significance of ritual which have caused the concept to be solely connected to vital religions, or restrictedly defined, as in the stillborn image of somebody perfunctorily going about simple routine such as washing one's hands. Scholars and laymen alike have over-emphasized its picayune and superficial nature (e.g., as synonymous with artifice or empty gesture). Within the literature on ritual there exists a theoretical skepticism, regarding the appropriateness of applying conceptual advances gathered from anthropologists studying rituals in preindustrial societies to societies existing in complex industrial settings. In addition, ritual's trail of supernatural associations, a condition resulting from the preponderance of anthropological investigations of religious ceremony, has surrounded the term in a miasma of mystification - as if ritual belonged in a feretory along with holy relics or vials of a martyr's blood. In view of these misperceptions of ritual, it should come as no surprise that a sociological hypothesis that conceives of ritual honorifically, as more than a cultural artifact or a peepshow in an anthropological circus, tends to ruffle the academic feathers of those regnant lords of quantitative research who couch social process in algorithmic terminology, who flinch at the sound of the word "symbolic," and who regard the term "performance" at the bête noire of contemporary social science.

The analysis of ritual in the social sciences labours under various theoretical handicaps. "Ritual," laments Mary Douglas (1973), "has become a bad word signifying empty conformity. We are witnessing a revolt against formalism, even against form."[5] The grievous imbalance which exists in favor of pre-ordinate studies in the social sciences, has not only provoked researchers from deferring to the conceptual richness of ritual, but has impaired respect for associated disciplines as well. Thus, mythology, dramaturgy, thaumaturgical arts, and folklore - which are not easily studied in quantitative terms - have, up to and including the present day, frequently been abjured as topics of serious inquiry, branded as unnecessary scholarly accretions, shunned as otiose relics or peripheral additions to serious "hard" research, and consigned to the realm of social insignia - gargoyles perched upon the structural foundations of the social order. As Guy Davenport (1982) so sardonically puts it: "The arts can look after themselves; they are used to neglect and obfuscation."[6]

Many of the conventionalized and sloganized renderings of ritual not only do violence to the work of contemporary ritologists, but continue to prejudice the use of ritual as an important variable in scientific research.

216

Lurking around the edges of the anti-ritual arguments posed by the scholarly gloseur is a penumbra of doubt in the efficacy - or even the existence of ritual in a post traditional, postmodern world. In some scientific circles rituals are overwhelmingly regarded as existing in only putatively diminished, debilitated, or denatured forms, denuded of their pre-symbolic plentitude; they are regarded as innocuous, part of a bygone era - leftovers perhaps from some former vaunted age of ritual replete with golden idols, smoking cauldrons, and the proverbial sacrificial virgins. Rituals have supposedly retreated in our society to the periphery of culture to serve as ancillory appendages to the forces that created them - a position any ritologist worth his salt would find defammatory. Because of the standard assignment of ritual to the occult, the mysterious, and the ineffable, some critics still associate it with images of hooded Rosicrucian adepts, e.s.p. equipped spoon benders, joss sticks and other cultic paraphernalia - recrudescent symptoms of a spiritually impotent age where man is chained to a soul-less postmodern body, is steeped in restlessness and anomie, and is in need of some fancy symbolic props to assuage his emotional emptiness. But rituals do not serve solely as some type of sacerdotal stilts or metaphysical protheses that celebrants can spiritually strap on in their frantic scramble towards the divine. Anthropologically sterile conceptions such as these continue to fetter the study of ritual in conceptual shackles. Indeed, the concept of ritual has been mired in so many unwarranted assumptions that it creates more confusion than illumination. Hence, we must come to the crucial decision of determining just what ritual is really all about.

## What A Ritual Is

According to Grimes (1982), a ritual is a form of symbolic action composed primarily of gestures (the enactment of evocative rhythms which constitute dynamic symbolic acts) and postures (a symbolic stilling of action). Gesture is formative; it is related to everyday action and may oscillate between randomness and formality. Not all ritual meaning is symbolic.

Within a ritual, the relation between a signal and its referent many also be indexical or self-referential (Rappaport, 1980). Symbols, in order to be considered ritualistic, must evoke gestures (Grimes, 1982). Ritual gestures are always concerned with the genesis of action; they "constitute a class of mediating actions which transform the style and values of everyday action, thereby becoming the very ground of action itself."[7] Rituals may be considered as gestural embodiments of the inner cognitive or affective states of the performers. Grimes claims that gestures are metaphors of the body: they display the identifications which constitute the performer. In addition, they generate corresponding thought and feeling patterns as well as reinforce particular values. Rituals may equally be considered as the gestural embodiments of the dominant metaphors of the wider social structure.

A routine is more than a ritual surrogate; a habit, more than a psyhoanalytic stepchild. But while routine or habitual actions fall under the morphological umbrella of ritual, they must necessarily be considered as paler, less authentic, more 'wraithlike' forms of ritualization. "Habituation," says Grimes, "is the bane of ritualization...imposed on the form of ought-filled, unmindful, heteronomy, and then the secret of this imposition is glossed over."[8]

## What A Ritual Is Not

I conceive of a ritual as a series of encoded movements that oscillate between rigid structure (high redundancy) and excessive randomness (high entropy). In the former instance, the ritual actions may amplify the uniformity and symmetry of social process. In the latter instance, the actions may draw our attention to the tenuousness and arbitrariness of social life (as in the carnival or rites of inversion). Non-ritual action is a form of "gestural noise" in which entropy is so high that all possible meanings for the gesture are equally probable. Gestural noise results from random movements lacking in predictability, syntax, codes, or patterns of meanings.

## Towards A Working Definition

The quest for a definition of ritual becomes a rather daunting task, especially since the literature on ritual reveals a concatenation of sometimes paradoxical and contradictory definitions bristling with such juxtaposed polarities as sacred and secular, structure and antistructure, rituals of intensification and rites of rebellion. The process of ritual remains refractory to any overall proclamation; the result is that there is no one conceptual organon that has achieved agreement of all and sundry. The attempt to set in order the armoury of contestible categories and hypotheses surrounding ritual and forge them into a single _ex cathedra_ definition has yet to be achieved; however, Grimes' division of ritual into six modes or sensibilities (ritualizing, celebration, ceremony, liturgy, decorum, and magic), and his distinction between hard and soft definitions of ritual, have at least cozened the campaign for definitional closure into a theoretical truce.[9]

In order to simplify matters, I shall posit a minimal operational definition.[10] This definition should not, however, be viewed as a brute and intractable formulation of ritual - some blueprint by which to distinguish it antiseptically from all other aspects of social life. I share with Delattre (1979) his perspective that "definitions serve best as relatively compact points of departure for systematic inquiry rather than as conclusions, and that they will therefore call in time for redefinition."[11]

> Rituals are strategic clusters of symbols which are linked together as models or root paradigms, propelled into action through formative bodily gesture and language, in order to enable individuals or groups to frame, negotiate, and articulate meanings in social settings in an atmosphere of sanctity.

Some critics have objected that by conceiving of ritual as a type of symbolic activity, the term may serve as a type of blank cheque on which almost any explanation of social and cultural processes may be written. But rituals do not simply inscribe or display symbolic meanings or

219

states of affairs but <u>instrumentally bring states of affairs into being</u>. To argue that a ritual simply reflects or mirrors meaning in an <u>ex post facto</u> manner is to trip philosophically over the same stumbling block that has impeded many students of ritual. To hold such a view is to separate the medium of ritual from its message. Rituals do not reflect – they <u>articulate</u> (Delattre, 1978). By ignoring this aspect of ritual, we are mortgaging our understanding of contemporary cultural forms.

What, then, does the conceptual map of ritual look like? The base-line provisional conception of ritual in my own work incorporates twenty-two characteristics of ritual (nine properties and thirteen functional attributes) which have been ferreted out of the ritual literature – some of which conflate several discipline-specific uses of the term. The summary that follows, which I have advanced as a series of postulates, serves as a common backcloth of theoretical assumptions about ritual.

---

### (1)  Properties of Ritual

1)  Rituals have a distinct <u>form</u> in which its medium (morphological characteristics) is part of its message (Myerhoff, 1977; Van Gennep, 1960; Myerhoff and Metzger, 1980; Rappaport, 1979).

2)  Rituals are primarily clusters of <u>symbols</u> and can best be understood using symbolic analysis (Turner, 1969).

3)  Rituals are inherently <u>dramatic</u> (Courtney, 1980; Perinbanayagam, 1974; Turner, 1979; Peacock, 1968; Harrison, 1915; Young, 1965).

4)  Rituals are important aspects of psycho-social integration leading to personality development. (Erikson, 1966; Worgul, 1980; Kavanagh, 1973; Schechner, 1982).

5)  Language codified into texts may possess an inherent ritual <u>authority</u> over readers (Olson, 1980).

6) Many rituals may be termed secular and exhibit the formal qualities of repetition, "special behaviour" or stylization, order, and evocative presentational style or staging (Moore and Myerhoff, 1977; Turner, 1982).

7) Rituals embody a repertoire of choices or "tokens" which centre around specific rules or "types" (Lewis, 1980).

8) Ritual codes (restricted and elaborate) are related to family structures and grow out of social class divisions. (Douglas, 1973; Bernstein et al., 1966).

9) Rituals invariably partake of six modes (ritualization, decorum, ceremony, liturgy, magic, celebration). While these modes overlap, one mode generally dominates (Grimes, 1982).

(2)  Functions of Ritual

1) Rituals serve as a framing device. Framing establishes a centre/periphery or figure/ground relation which is metacommunicative; the characteristic of frame enables the ritual participants to interpret what occurs within it (cf. Myerhoff, 1977; Turner, 1979; Myerhoff, 1977; Handleman, 1977; Turner, 1982).

2) Rituals encourage holistic involvement in the form of flow which implies a "willing suspension of disbelief" (Turner, 1979; 1982).

3) Rituals communicate by classifying information in different contexts (DaMatta, 1979).

4) Rituals have the ability to transform participants into different social statuses as well as different states of consciousness. This is usually achieved in ritual's liminal state (Moore and Myerhoff, 1977; Turner, 1979; Partidge, 1972; Myerhoff, 1975; Holmes, 1975; Myerhoff, 1978; Bilmes and Howard, 1980).

5) Rituals negotiate and articulate meaning through distinctive rhythms (Delattre, 1978; 1979).

221

6) Rituals provoke an aura of sanctity through their morphological characteristics and by addressing themselves to supernatural entities - entities which are not necessarily spirits but which are more or less synonymous with aspects of "transcendence," "ultimate importance," or "unquestionability" (Nagendra, 1975; Moore and Myerhoff, 1977; Pannikar, 1970; Turner, 1982; Goffman, 1981; Smith, 1974; Rappaport, 1971, 1976, 1979, 1980).

7) Undergoing a ritual experience endows the participant with a unique type of "ritual knowledge" (Wallace, 1966; Jennings, 1982).

8) Ritual language possesses a performative force which is capable of bringing about conventional effects (Worgul Jr., 1980; Rappaport, 1978, 1979; Ray, 1973; Bloch, 1974; Gill, 1977; Tambiah, 1969; Finnigan, 1969).

9) Rituals are capable of reifying the socio-cultural world in which they are embedded (Dolgin et al., 1977; Munn, 1973).

10) Rituals may invert the norms and values of the dominant social order (Babcock, 1978; Yinger, 1977; Moore and Myerhoff, 1977; Gluckman, 1963; Ortiz, 1972).

11) Rituals enable participants to reflect on their own processes of interpretation as well as their location in the dominant culture (Geertz, 1973; Turner, 1974; Rappaport, 1980).

12) Rituals have a political aspect to them and may embody and transmit certain ideologies or world views (Lukes, 1974; Piven, 1976; Olson, 1976; Edelman, 1974, 1977; Cox, 1969).

13) Rituals have the capability of fusing polar domains of experience, such as the physical and the moral (Turner, 1982; Worgul Jr., 1980).

* * *

The extent to which any of the above features are present in any ritual will depend to a great extent on the context in which the ritual is enacted. Moreover, to state that all these

222

characteristics of ritual are manifest (to a greater or lesser extent) in every ritual is to imply that the conclusions of ritual are built into its very concepts. These descriptive characteristics and their functional attributes are neither foreordained nor omnipresent in the enactment of every rite. Such characteristics should not be looked upon as dyed-in-the-wool definitions but as potentialities of the ritual process (keeping in mind the difference between what a ritual does and what it is capable of exercising in performance). These characteristics can also prove useful points for the discussion of school events. The importance of the latter looms large if we are to focus on the heuristic usefulness of ritual in our discussion.

## Ritual and Schooling

The long history of anthropological and theological association with ritual contrasts with the relatively short history of interest to educators. You will not find the term ritual among the in-house slogans in the school staffroom. Despite the growing interest among educational researchers in ethnographic portrayals of classroom life, the classroom ethnographer has so far failed to realize the potential to incorporate ritual as a conceptual instrument in classroom analysis. The symbolic self-awareness that Victor Turner has brought to the study of cultural process has been slow to filter through to the investigators of classroom practises. This state of affairs has no doubt been influenced by the fact that so many conventional assumptions about rituals are made almost unassailable by the hyper-discursiveness or positivistic bent of modern educational research.

While there exists a long list of researchers who have attempted to use the term ritual in discussing school life (e.g., studies by Leemon, 1972; Courtney, 1980, 1982; Phenix, 1964; Blackham, 1966; Shipman, 1968; Clancy, 1977; Illich, 1977; Eddy, 1969; Olson, 1979; Lancy, 1975; Hill Burnett, 1969; Willower, 1969; Clifton, 1979; Moore, 1976; Weiss, 1976; Lutz and Ramsey, 1973; Kapferer, 1981; O'Farrell, 1981; McLaren, 1982; Foster, 1974; and Grumet, 1978), few commentators have tried to forge connections

223

between classroom instruction and secular ritology. One exemplary exception is Lawrence
Patrick O'Farrell's comprehensive examination of
the use of ritual in conjunction with creative
drama in school settings - including "hands on"
classroom activities and curriculum development.[12]

## A Typology of Ritual Forms

My work with grade eight Azorean students in
a Metropolitan Toronto Catholic School revealed
the existence of a complex ritual system in
operation. A number of ritual types emerged from
my investigation which I have termed micro rituals
(individual lessons), macro rituals (individual
lessons examined collectively over a school day),
and grand rituals (major school-wide ceremonials).
All three types may be said to comprise the
school's rites of instruction. The analysis of
the rites of instruction hinged conceptually on
the identification of a number of states of
interaction among students which I have termed
the streetcorner state, the student state, the
sanctity state and the home state. The streetcorner state and the student state were by far
the most predominant.

Before school, after school, and in between
micro rituals, students enter into particular
roles and statuses and engage in certain distinctive behaviours which I have termed the "streetcorner state." By use of the word "state," I do
not mean to suggest some type of trance or state
of consciousness in the clinical or psychological
sense of the term. By the term "state," I am
referring more specifically to a particular style
of interacting with the environment and with
others which could perhaps be appropriately
labelled behavioural clusters or complexes.
Heralded by the physical setting in which the
students find themselves, the streetcorner state,
as the name suggests, is evocative of behaviour
students exhibit on the street (e.g., hanging
around the local neighbourhood, outside the plaza,
etc.). The student state, in contrast, charac-
terizes most of the student behaviour inside the
school building (listening to a lesson, writing
an exam, etc.). When in the streetcorner state,
students characteristically unleash and give vent

to their pent-up frustrations. The streetcorner state is therefore cathartic - ritual forms are often underdistanced (cf. Scheff, 1977). Relationships between individuals frequently approach unmediated intimacy; activity often bears a close approximation to primary experience: Bodies can often be seen to twist, turn, and shake in an oasis of free abandon. There is a great deal of physical contact. Boundaries between spaces, roles, and objects are transparent, plastic, adaptive, pliable, and malleable. Students are unpredictable, boisterous, obstreperous, and loud. There are more frequent and exaggerated instances of kinesethic activity, including pronounced postural configurations. In addition, there are greater instances of irregular speech and body rhythms (e.g., spontaneous and ejaculatory expressions of feelings and emotions). Time becomes polychromatic as individuals "create" their own schedules. Symbolization is mainly iconic or emotional (cf. Courtney, 1982). The mood is "subjunctive" (in the sense described by Turner, 1982). There is apt to be more "flow" (after Csikszentmihalyi) in the matching of skills and abilities since students do things at their own pace. Students spend time experimenting with different roles - playing "as if" they were others. Yet students are most decidedly themselves in this state. Consumerism constitutes the prevailing ethos. Spontaneous communitas is frequently present and this state could be said to possess a liminal or liminoid dimension. Locomotion is characterized by movement as opposed to gesture (see Brenneman et al, 1982). The kernel metaphor of this state is ludic or of the nature of play.

Following entrance into the building, students realign and readjust their behaviour, shifting from the natural flow of the streetcorner state to the more formal and rigid precinct of the "student state." It is here that the students give themselves over to the powerful controls and enforcement procedures available to teachers - controls which allow teachers to dominate students without recourse to brute force. Students move "offstage" from where they are more naturally themselves to the proscenium of the classroom where they must write their student roles and scenarios in conformity to the teacher's master script; they move from the "raw" state of streetcorner life to the more "cooked" or socialized state of school existence.

The student state refers to an adoption of the manners, dispositions, attitudes, and work habits expected of "being a student." The kernel metaphor of the student state is work. The teacher's control mechanisms constitute the boundaries between the streetcorner state and student state. These boundaries are seldom permeable - and only during prescribed times (such as between classes or outside the school building). Most often, the students are compelled to enter into the student state through a highly ritualized and institutionalized punishment and reward system which serves to guy the hoopla, gibing, kibbitzing, ribaldry, scurrilous bantering and general effervescence of the streetcorner state. Youngsters in the student state are generally quiet, well-mannered, predictable, and obedient. Gestures (scientientific, academic, and industrial) replace movements (see Brenneman et al, 1982). The mood of this state is "indicative" - meaning it prevails in the world of actual fact (in the manner employed by Turner, 1982). Symbolization is primarily through use of signs and symbols (in Courtney's terminology). There is little physical movement unless on the cue of the teacher. There is a distinct separation between mind and body and a stress on the work ethic. Ritual forms are, for the most part, invariant and conventionalized. Communitas is rare. Elements that partake of liminal or liminoid ritual genres are usually those associated with pain or discomfort.

The students spent approximately 76 minutes of the school day in the streetcorner state, and 298 minutes in the student state.

The macro ritual was discovered to constitute a bastard version of Van Gennep's classic rites of passage -- a mutant similitude or refined variant of the classic ritual process. The performative sequencing of separation (preliminal), threshold rites (liminal), and rites of re-aggregation (postliminal) were effectively altered both structurally and qualitatively. As in Van Gennep's tripartite schema, transformation from one state to another entailed a "separation" and a change of status and behaviour on the part of the students. But the change from streetcorner state to student state is a change from a more natural state with characteristics of spontaneous communitas to an institutionalized state constituted by uncomfortable, painful, and oppressive liminal characteristics often associated with initiatory rites. I have referred to the student stage as a "culture of pain" - a type of symbolic cicatrization of the mind. Lancy has warned that "whenever we find school practices that resemble the rites of initiation, these should act as red flags stopping us and forcing us to reconsider the rationale that created them."[13]

Three variant teacher types were identified within the micro ritual: teacher as liminal servant; teacher as entertainer; and teacher as prison guard. When students responded with a sense of immediacy or purpose, either verbally or gesturally, to the teacher's performance -- when, for instance, they become the "primary actors" -- then they engaged in an authentic ritual of instruction: the surroundings were sanctified, the students became co-celebrants of knowledge with the teacher (who had adopted the role of liminal servant), and the class was transformed into a congregation. As in religious ritual, where the meta-congregation is God, the meta-congregation of a successful instructional ritual is the Logos (in Christian theology the Logos is equivalent to the second person of the Trinity and its functions are associated with the creative activity of Christ). In this sanctified curriculum "moment" during which students bore witness to the universal wisdom embodied in the rites of instruction, the teacher was transformed into a rabbi or priest of knowledge (the sole mediator between the Logos and the student).

When students were actively engaged by the instructor, but - due to various obstacles inherent in the ritual structure and performance - remain isolated viewers of the action, then the students were being entertained. The classroom was transformed into a theatre and the students became an audience. In this instance, the teacher lost his priestly function and became a paid entertainer, or sometimes a propagandist for the dominant culture.

When, however, the students were not provoked to respond to the teacher's instruction - either verbally, gesturally, or silently in their heads (e.g., when they ceased to think at all about what went on) - then the students no longer figuratively sat in a church or a theatre but in Max Weber's iron cage. The teacher was reduced to a prison guard and knowledge was passed on perfunctorily - as though it were a tray of food passed under a cell door. In such a situation -- one that is all too common in our classrooms -- the few feet surrounding the student might as well have been a place of solitary confinement -- a numbing state of spiritual and emotional emptiness.

With his usual clarity, Rappaport (1976) distinguishes between ritual and theatre:

> Rituals may also be distinguished from drama by the relationship of those present to what is being performed. While an audience is in attendance at a drama, a congregation is present at a ritual. An audience merely watches but a congregation participates, usually in some degree actively...And while those who enact a drama are "only acting" in a play, those who celebrate rituals are "not playing" or "play-acting", they are taking action, and it is often very serious action.[14]

Making a similar point, Turner (1982) writes:

> Ritual, unlike theatre, does not distinguish between audience and performers. Instead, there is a congregation whose leaders may be priests, party officials, or other religious or secular ritual specialists, but all share formally and substantially the same set of beliefs and accept the same system of practices, the same sets of rituals or liturgical actions.[15]

Again Turner articulates the difference between ritual and theatre, this time drawing on a quote from Schechner:

Theatre comes into existence when a separation occurs between an audience and performers. The paradigmatic theatrical situation is a group of performers soliciting an audience who may or may not respond by attending. The audience is free to attend or stay away -- and if they stay away it is the theatre that suffers, not its would-be audience. In ritual, stay-away means rejecting the congregation -- or being rejected by it, as in excommunication, ostracism, or exile.[16]

When a teacher becomes a liminal servant, an added vitality is brought to the rites of instruction. A teacher becomes a liminal servant when he or she is able to transform the context of a lesson from the indicative (a stress on mere facts) to the subjunctive (a stress on the dramatic "as if" quality of learning), from resistance to undifferentiated "humankindedness," from within the confines of social structure to the seedbeds of creativity located within the antistructure (a receptive mode of consciousness in which we exist in a state of undifferentiated human totality). The liminal servant is a spiritual director as much as he is a school pedagogue. He does not shun the ambiguity and opacity of existence. He is also androgynous, which means he draws upon both feminine and masculine modes of consciousness. Much depends on his personal charisma and his powers of observation and diagnosis. He becomes aware of the strengths and weaknesses of his students by observing and diagnosing their ritual needs. The liminal servant presents an array of symbols which have a high density of meaning for the student; he creates a "felt context" by promoting conditions which will allow the student to internalize both exegetical (normative) and orectic (physical) meanings. By thus creating a particular posture towards symbols, he is able to ensure that symbols are adequately encountered by students through both cognition and affect.

The liminal servant is aware of his shamanic roots; he is mystagogue more than an ideologue. He does not eschew theory (which would be a form of pedagogical pietism); nor does he avoid intuition that comes with practice (where avoidance would amount to a moribund intellectualism or "siege mentality"). The metier of the liminal servant is the clearing away of all obstacles to the embodiment of knowledge. The liminal servant is wary of too much ratiocination and leans towards helping students enact metaphors and embody ritual rhythms that will have meaning and purpose for them -- not just as an abstraction, but as a "lived" form of consciousness. Modes of symbolic action are employed that do not betray a cleavage between the passive "reception of facts" and the active participatory ethos of "learning by doing." The liminal servant encourages students to enact metaphors and embody rhythms that bypass the traditional mind/body dualism so prevalent in mainstream educational epistemology and practice. The liminal servant does not put a high priority on structure and order (although his classes may be highly structured and ordered) and he is able to 'conjure' conditions amenable to the eventuation of communitas and flow. He knows that he must not merely present knowledge to students; he must transform the consciousness of students by allowing them to "live" knowledge viscerally. I should point out, however, that by using the term liminal servant to describe the successful teacher, I am not trying to wrap the classroom instructor in a shroud of mysticism, nor are my observations coloured by an affinity towards Vitalism, Transcendentalism, or neo-Gothic revival. I am definitely not suggesting that teachers abrogate their duties of teaching basic academic skills such as reading and writing. I am suggesting, though, that teachers be willing to take more risks. They must cross the antistructural divide. However, it would be too simplistic to view the liminal servant as the "good guy" and the other models as the "bad guys" within the ritual scenario. Sometimes these roles shade into one another. In addition, the liminal servant is an explosive and potentially dangerous role to play; it could easily "blow up" in the teacher's face, leaving both teachers and students emotionally scarred. The liminal servant is a role to which teachers should aspire only so long as the values being embodied are productive and beneficial for the growth of the students and the community at large.

230

Rituals were found to serve two basic functions: engendering creativity and serving as agents of social control. Teachers, as ritual officiants, possessed a powerful two-edged sword. Ritual stood in relation to the students as half benefactor, half monster: It could both sanctify and criminalize, befog and illuminate, immure and liberate, engage and estrange, empower and take away. Instructional rituals thus functioned in the manner of Shiva, the God of Shivaite Hindus - they both polluted and purified, destroyed and created.

Students were also seen to partake of a distinct form of <u>ritual knowledge</u>. Ritual knowledge is more than a solipsistic tingle one sometimes gets while genuflecting before a church altar or being titillated by a private revelation. Neither is it necessarily linked with enlightenment gained through ecstacy, Maslovian peak-experiences, epiphanies, or petaphysics. One does not have to ascend Mount Caramel or descend into Dante's pit to acquire it.

For Anthony Wallace (1966), ritual knowledge is basically a form of <u>cognitive re-synthesis.</u>[17] For Theodore Jennings (1982), "Ritual knowledge is gained through a bodily action which alters the world or the place of the ritual participant in the world"[18] - a concept similar to Polanyi's "tacit knowledge." Jennings describes ritual knowledge as possessing three significant characteristics: It is 1) primarily corporeal rather than cerebral, 2) primarily active rather than contemplative, and 3) primarily transformative rather than speculative. It is a knowledge that is distinct from reflective knowledge, contemplation and mytho-poesis. It is also different from scientific reflective-critical knowledge. <u>It is a knowledge gained from an alteration and transformation of that which is known.</u>[19]

Jennings notes that when engaged in a ritual action, one does not first think through the action and then perform it. Rather, the body discovers the fitting gesture. When taking part in the Eucharist, for example, my hand "discovers" the fitting gesture of grasping the chalice. On

the disco floor, my feet "find" the fitting step.
For Jennings,

> Ritual knowledge is gained not by detached
> observation or contemplation but through
> action. It is in and through the action
> (gesture, step, etc.) that ritual knowledge
> is gained, not in advance of it, nor after
> it...To say that there is such a thing as
> ritual knowledge is to say that it is
> knowledge which is identical with doing or
> acting, with a bodily doing or acting.

> Ritual knowledge is gained through the
> alteration of that which is to be known. I
> do not discover what to do with the chalice
> by observing it but by "handling" it. (Just
> as I discover how to use an axe to chop fire-
> wood - unless to speak metaphorically, the
> axe "teaches me" through my hands, arms, and
> shoulders how it is to be used).[20]

Jenning's discussion of ritual knowledge
serves as a conceptual mooring for what Richard
Courtney (1982) terms "dramatic knowledge." As
in the acquisition of ritual knowledge, dramatic
knowledge possesses an incarnate character and is
gained through practical involvement. It works
noetically, provides a pattern of doing, and has
the power to create and transform the world.[21]
Ritual, as Zuesse (1975) notes, "gestures forth
the world..."[22] It is both consciousness and
body, both pre-reflective and reflective."[23]
Ritual inheres in what Dixon (1974) has called
"the erotics of knowing."[24] Another way of
putting this is to say that the distinction
between participant (as a somatic being) and act
(as symbolic activity) is nominal: the participant is both the means and ends of the ritual.
Thus, to speak of "creating" rituals is somewhat
redundant. A better way of putting it perhaps is
that rituals "create us" by providing the metaphors and rhythms through which we attend to the
world. Rituals are contantly in motion; they are
better understood as "verbings" rather than
objective or frozen accounts that one might
discover in an anthropologist's logbook. The
power of ritual always remains concealed in its
very form; ritual can erase its traces from that
which it effects. Rituals are perhaps best seen

as temporal events: they are successive symbolic transformations over time. Described as such, they bear a striking similarity to what Courtney (1982) has termed "the curriculum moment." Such rites or moments cannot be adequately conceptualized as either subjective or objective (emic or etic) but as a "temporal unit uniting the two."[25] Like light, ritual is pure action: it can transport meaning and leave no residue. A ritual uses objects to project messages, but is not attached to any object: it remains a smile without a face, a kiss without lips.

To use the vocabulary of ritual in the context of acquiring knowledge is to speak of students as human agents, who, separately or collectively, are either manipulating and/or being manipulated by an aggregate of symbols or who are enacting metaphors through a series of bodily gestures. We must remember that while symbols point beyond themselves, metaphors are embodied viscerally: they embody what they mean (Grimes, 1984). In speaking thus, one can rightly assume that ritual knowledge promotes the development of a distinctive bodily and cognitive style and way of attending to the world.

In the case of the Azorean students, the mind sets they acquired by participation in the dogmatic mediations of the instructional rites were those in which reality was perceived as segmented, rationally organized, insulated and atomized. This was partially due to the fact that teachers rarely embodied the role of the liminal servant. More often than not, teachers served as either entertainers or prison guards. Consequently, knowledge that was to be held as valuable - even hallowed was, in essence, a public fiction created and refined - and ultimately mystified - by the ritualized forms of its presentation. The ritual appurtenances of instruction imbued this knowledge with a sense of sanctity. Therefore, the instructional rituals were only tangentially part of the instrumental act of teaching; rather, they were more important in creating a cultural world, a dominant and restrictive moral order. Under the ritual exigencies of instruction, the mental templates of the students were galvanized by conventional, technocratic thinking.

The frail character and operative sterility of the "hyper-cognitive" classroom rituals paled in comparison to the "bodily" characteristics of the working-class cultural forms of the street-corner state. Students became fed up with pustular and jaundiced modes of interacting with experience - with learning things hypothetically and interacting in a milieu of ersatz feelings. They wanted to embody knowledge viscerally and experience a style of knowing that was devoid of excessive abstraction and doctrinal baggage. From the perspective of the students, the rituals of instruction constituted degradation ceremonies. However, knowledge gained through the street-corner state was qualitatively different from the knowledge acquired through the instructional rituals of the student state precisely because the students in the streetcorner state made more use of bodily exploration and organic symbols. True, ritual knowledge in the student state was more symbolically sophisticated; but because such knowledge was not "lived," it remained removed, distant, abstract. For the Azorean students, bodily participation was necessary for knowledge to be real. Epistemology was born of the flesh.

Properly speaking, ritual knowledge is not something to be "understood"; it is always, whether understood or not, something which we feel and to which we respond organically. The mechanical formality, regimentation, and invariance which was part of the instructional rites, to a large degree defoliated the cultural land-scape of the classroom of its organic symbols. Is it any wonder, therefore, that the major social drama in the classroom was the battle to prolong the streetcorner state during the time alloted for the student state? Student re-ritualization in the form of rites or resistance was a typical reaction to the anti-incarnational characteristics of school instruction.

Conclusion

Analysis of the instructional rites of the school underscored the importance of creating a "felt context" between the transmission of know-ledge and the embodiment of that knowledge. Congruent with the conception of ritual knowledge outlined above is the belief that knowledge is more than just words - more than just being told. Practical experience also plays an important part in learning. Teachers should consider the symbolic culture of the classroom, the morphology and medium of instruction, and the bodily engagement of students - in short, the performative domains - as prime candidates that contribute to their students' learning. This view supports Dewey's notion that knowledge is not acquired independently of the means of instruction. Learning includes a physiognomic/somatic meaningfulness - a "posturefulness" as well as "mindfulness."

Clearly, an important direction in which instructional rituals should proceed is in the creation of situations destined to spawn <u>liminal zones of learning</u> in the form of either <u>spontaneous or institutionalized communitas</u>. Myerhoff and Metzger announce that liminality is fundamental to the teaching act:

> Liminality is not only reflexive, it is also reflectiveness. Here, we think about things previously not pondered, not even raised to the level of questions. For this reason, <u>liminality is the great moment of teachability</u>...[italics mine][26]

Urban T. Holmes (1977) reminds us that liminality and communitas

> describe an existence <u>outside</u> structural definition. Liminality and communitas are both antistructural in nature...the individual or collectivity in that state are <u>open</u> to a reality that is <u>not controlled</u> by society and its hierarchy. <u>The imagination is freed!</u>[27]

Furthermore, Holmes writes that

> communitas is a 'generative centre,' the goal of pilgrimage, the experience of one another ouside of structural relations (including comaraderie) and the place of ritual leveling and humilation...To move into the antistructure is to experience one's humanness. It is to return to a source in order that one might come back more deeply aware of who he truly is.[28]

The key, it seems, is to find the correct balance "between communitas, the trip into the world of symbols, and the social structures, life amid the univocal signs."[29]

Knowledge gained through the liminal zone would replace the linear knowledge of mainstream schooling with metaphoric knowledge (the kind which Schechner describes as being released through engagement in the arts).[30]

Rituals are the symbolic artifacers of culture. Like mirrors fastened to the back wall of Plato's cave, they reflect back cultural meanings, revealing the source of their own creation, and permit participants to engage in a reflexive dialogue with the process of culture itself.

A further suggestion for the improvement of instruction would be replacing the image of the student as a passive recepticle of facts with the paradigm of the student as pilgrim and the teacher as liminal servant. Urban Holmes (1973) has described the characteristic of the pilgrim as one of "active waiting, hopeful expectation, power in innocence and weakness, and acceptance of strangeness of others as a possible source of transcendence."[31]

> The pilgrim is an incongrous, ambiguous person, for whom no category fits. To be a pilgrim means to move out of the institutional structures and their roles and statuses that define the person and to free the imagination for the discovery of what is new.[32]

Instruction that primarily consists of listening to facts delivered by teachers too often amounts to a psuedo ritual bereft of organic symbols and gestural metaphors. Knowledge of this sort remains unembodied and hence removed from the student's corpus of felt meanings. The student's path to knowledge should be an incarnate, bodily journey, rich in gesture as well as contemplation. The seed of each student's creative liberation - perhaps even his perfectibility - requires liminality for successful germination.

236

In an age of educational crisis, and in view of my far reaching claims for the significance of ritual as a factor in classroom interaction, it would be reassuring to look with bouyant optimism to ritology as the much-heralded theoretical device that explains the hitherto unexplainable, that reconciles the irreconcilable, that truly totalizes and comforts, and which has the propaedeutic potential to revolutionize the teaching profession. Could ritology be the answer to the search for ultimate closure, to the bringing together of disparate analytical elements into a single, unifying instrument of pedagogy and performance? Unfortunately, ritology does not, at present, offer the heady promise of providing educators an instantaneous, clear, and commanding vision for future classroom programming. While we should not discredit the potential of ritology to eventually alloy comparative symbology with learning theory into a renewed classroom lituriology, to chart out new areas of school reform, or to ramify into other academic domains, we must admit that, before ritological anlysis can proceed apace in our research departments, much more work needs to be done. Considering the dramatic qualities of ritual, it would appear constructive for both drama teachers and educator-anthropologists to begin to forge connections between ritual and drama which could be applied to the creation of improved curriculum programming - programming which will allow the educator to pose solutions to the practises of teachers who continue to coerce reality for students through calcified and conceptually shallow forms of ritualized instruction.

Solutions could incorporate techniques from drama theory via Stanislavski, Burkman, Brecht, and Grotowski, to promote a greater awareness and sympathetic understanding among teachers towards the view that students are active body-subjects who engage the world not just in their heads, but in their hands, their hearts, their guts, and in their loins. Researchers and programme designers could examine the works of these authors in conjunction with Turner's theory of the ritual symbol, Grimes' modes of ritual sensibility, Goffman's interaction ritual, and Bellah's symbolic realism to lay the groundwork for an emergent epistemology of ritual knowledge.

Since, as Holmes warns, "liminality feeds the vision of revolutionaries, reformers, and prophets,"[33] there always looms the danger of ritual analysis being lost in revolutionary praxis. Whether or not ritology is destined for diachronic deployment in the schools for purposes of social reconstruction is better left for future researchers to decide. Educational ritology has yet to find its Turner, its Rappaport, its Schechner, or its Grimes who could help to solidify the status of schooling as a ritual event.

Choices involving how teachers ritualize their lessons are fateful and important for the future of education, and an ignorance of the consequences of each choice continues to pockmark the performance of our schools. Without a greater understanding of the power of ritual, we will continue to demand that our students yield to our mechanical classroom arrangements, to our didactical and rigid instructional rituals, or insist that they genuflect before a phalanx of oppressive and petrified symbols. We must, at all costs, decry the fettering of the human spirit in our classrooms. It is in the exegesis of particular pedagogical rituals that we will be able to mine the rich veins of both sacred and secular symbols that disclose and shape the multiplicity of behaviours and transactions that are operative in our classrooms.

It remains the task of schools to become strongholds of purposeful symbols. The realm of school ritual must illuminate these symbols, fire them in a crucible of wisdom, and shape them on an anvil of love. Only then will we, as a community of teachers and students, move towards the brink of the abyss that Victor Turner calls the antistructure. Only then will we be able to propell ourselves to the other side where knowledge and faith meet once and forever.

FORMS OF STUDENT INTERACTION

| STREET STATE | STUDENT STATE |
|---|---|
| Tribal | Institutional |
| Emotional, Non-Rational | Cognitive, Rational |
| Random, Imprecise Gestures | Nonrandom, precise gestures |
| Ludic | Serious |
| Forms of Symbolization (Icons, Symbols) | Forms of Symbolization (Signs) |
| Play (Ritual Frame) | Work (Ritual Frame) |
| Spontaneous Action | Teleological |
| Tapping Own Inner Resources (Right Lobe Emphasis) | Imitation of Teachers (Left Lobe Emphasis) |
| Away from Formality | Formal, Technical |
| Sensuous | Mechanical |
| Multi-Signifiers (Hyper-Intensity) | Multi-Signified (Low Intensity) |
| Cathartic | Frustrating, Tension Inducing |
| Whimsy, Frivolity | Task Oriented |
| Status Determined by Peers | Status Determined by Institution |
| Liminal/Liminoid | Hierarchical |
| Communitas (Repartee) | Anomie, Anxiety |
| Subjunctive Mood | Indicitive Mood |
| Flow | Flow-Resistant |

| | |
|---|---|
| Ritual Forms (Elastic, Flexible, Haphazard, Improvisational) | Ritual Forms (Conventionalized, Stereotyped, Formal) |
| Motion | Gesture |
| P-Time | M-Time |
| Informal Space | Fixed Feature Space |
| Pediarchic | Pedagogic |

FOOTNOTES

1. R. D. Laing, The Voice of Experience: Experience, Science, Psychiatry (New York: Pelican
Books, 1983), p. 68.

2. Ibid., p. 66

3. H. F. Jones, ed., The Notebooks of Samuel
Butler (New York, 1921), p. 94. As cited in
Jonathan Z. Smith, Map Is Not Territory (Leiden:
Brill, 1978), p. 241.

4. The last ten years have been particularly
prolific in innovative studies of contemporary
secular events. Ronald Grimes tells us that the
term "ritual studies" was possibly first used at
the Ritual Studies Consultation during the
American Academy of Religion's annual meeting in
1977.

While one hesitates to burden the syntax of ritual
discourse with yet another neologism, Grimes' term
"riology" - meaning the study of ritual - is a
fecund one given the conceptual orientation of
this paper. Grimes, however, acknowledges that
the word is "a bit of rhetorical magic." For a
further discussion of ritology, see Ronald L.
Grimes, Beginnings In Ritual Studies. Washington,
D. C.: University Press of America, 1982.

5. Mary Douglas, Natural Symbols (New York:
Random House, 1973), p. 19.

6. Guy Davenport, The Geography of the Imagination (San Francisco: North Point Press, 1981),
p. 134.

7. Ronald L. Grimes Beginnings In Ritual Studies
(Washington, D. C.: University Press of America,
1982), p. 61.

8. Ibid., p. 38.

9. See Ibid., pp. 35-51.

10. See Peter McLaren, "Education As Ritual Performance." Unpublished Ph.D. dissertation,
University of Toronto, 1983. Some excellent definitions of ritual are as follows: "Ritual: Rule-

governed activity of a symbolic character which draws the attention of its participants to objects of thought and feeling which they hold to be of special significance" (Lukes, 1975:291); "Ritual is the symbolic use of bodily movement and gesture in a social situation to express and articulate meaning" (Bocock, 1974:37); ritual is "nondiscursive gestural language, institutionalized for regular occasions, to state sentiments and mystiques that a group values and needs" (Klapp, 1969:121); ritual is "the acting out of metaphoric predication upon inchoate pronouns which are in need of movement" (Fernandez, 1972:56); ritual is "the performance of more or less invariant sequences of formal acts and utterances not encoded by the performer" (Rappaport, 1980: 62-63); ritual is an "intermediary process between analogic and digital communication simulating the message materials in a repetitive and stylized manner that hangs between analogue and symbol: (Watzlawick, 1967:104); a ritual is "a relatively rigid pattern of acts specific to a situation which constructs a framework of meaning over and beyond the specific situation meanings" (Bernstein et al. 1966:429); rituals are "formal behaviour prescribed for occasions not given over to technological routine that have reference to mystical beings or powers" (Turner, 1967:19); rituals are "Those carefully rehearsed symbolic motions and gestures through which we regularly go, in which we articulate the felt shape and rhythm of our humanity and of reality as we experience it, and by means of which we negotiate the terms or conditions for our presence among and our participation in the plurality of realities through which our humanity makes its passage" (Delattre, 1978:282); a ritual is "a means of performing the way things ought to be in conscious tension to the way things are in such a way that this ritualized perfection is recollected in the ordinary, uncontrolled course of things" (Smith, 1982:63); and rituals are "dramatic actions performed in imitation of models" (Courtney, 1982:23).

11. Roland Delattre, "The Rituals of Humanity and the Rhythms of Reality," Prospects: An Annual Review of American Studies, 5 (1979), p. 36.

12. Lawrence Patrick O'Farrell, "Ritual in Creative Drama," Drama Contact (May, 1981), pp. 3-29. See also O'Farrell, "Ritual In Creative Drama," Master of Arts thesis, Arizona State University (August, 1980).

13. David Lancy, "The Social Organization of Learning: Initiation Rituals and Public Schools," Human Organization, 34, No. 4 (Winter, 1975), p. 379.

14. Roy Rappaport, "Liturgies and Lies," International Yearbook For The Sociology of Knowledge and Religion, 10 (1976), p. 86.

15. Victor Turner, From Ritual To Theatre: The Human Seriousness of Play (New York: Performing Arts Journal Publications, 1982), p. 112.

16. As cited in Turner, From Ritual To Theatre, p. 112.

17. Anthony Wallace, Religion: An Anthropological View (New York: Random House, 1966), p. 236.

18. Theodore Jennings, "On Ritual Knowledge," The Journal of Religion, 62, No. 2 (April, 1982), p. 115.

19. Ibid., p. 127.

20. Ibid., pp. 115-116.

21. Richard Courtney, "Performance: Meaning and Knowledge," forthcoming.

22. Evan M. Zuesse, "Meditation On Ritual," Journal of the American Academy of Religion, 44 No. 3 (1975), p. 518.

23. Ibid.

24. John W. Dixon, "The Erotics of Knowing," Anglican Theological Review, 56, No. 1 (January, 1974), pp. 3-16.

25. Richard Courtney, <u>Re-Play: Studies of Human Drama in Education</u>. Toronto: OISE Press (The Ontario Institute For Studies in Education), 1982, p. 171.

26. Myerhoff and Metzger, "The Journal As Activity and Genre: On Listening To The Silent Laughter of Mozart,"
<u>Semiotica</u>, 30, Nos. 1/2 (1980), p. 106.
<u>Liminality</u> is the second stage in Turner's tripartite ritual schematic consisting of separation, margin or limen, and reaggregation. In the liminal state the ritual participants (or liminars) are stripped of their status and are removed from societal scruples and constraints of authority; they exist in a state of "social limbo." <u>Communitas</u> (a name which Turner borrowed from Paul Goodman) is a quality of liminality which refers to a sense of comaradship and communion between liminars - a type of I-Thou ethos. Turner uses the term <u>liminoid</u> to refer to genres found in industrial leisure that have features resembling those of liminality.

27. Urban T. Holmes, "What Has Manchester To Do With Jerusalem:" <u>Anglican Theological Review</u>, 59, No. 1 (January, 1977), p. 95.

28. <u>Ibid</u>., p. 83.

29. <u>Ibid</u>., p. 95.

30. Richard Schechner, "Performers and Spectators Transported and Transformed." <u>The Keynon Review</u>, 3, No. 4 (Fall, 1981), p. 113.

31. Urban T. Holmes, "Revivals Are Un-American: A Recalling Of America To Its Pilgrimmage," <u>American Theological Review</u> (Supplementary Series), No. 1 (July, 1973), pp. 63-64.

32. <u>Ibid</u>.

33. Urban T. Holmes, "What Has Manchester To Do With Jerusalem?" <u>Anglican Theological Review</u>, 59, No. 1 (January, 1977), p. 95.

BIBLIOGRAPHY

Babcock, Barbara (ed.). The Reversible World:
Symbolic Inversion In Art and Society.
Ithaca: Cornell University Press, 1978.

Bernstein, B.; Elvin, H. L.; and Peters, R. S.
"Ritual in Education." Philosophical Trans-
actions of the Royal Society of London,
Series B. 251, No. 772 (December, 1966), pp.
429-436. Also reprinted in Schools and
Society, Open University with Routledge, 1972.

Bilmes, Jacob, and Howard, Alan. "Pain As A
Cultural Drama." Anthropology and Humanism
Quarterly, 15, Nos. 2 and 3 (June-September,
1980), pp. 10-13.

Blackham, H. J. "Ideological Aspects: A Reeval-
uation of Ritual." Philosophical Transactions
of the Royal Society of London, Series B, 25,
No. 772 (December, 1966), pp. 443-446.

Bloch, Maurice. "Symbols, Songs, Dance, and
Features of Articulation." European Journal
of Sociology, 15 (1974), pp. 55-81.

Bocock, Robert. Ritual In Industrial Society: A
Sociological Analysis of Ritualism In Modern
England. London: George Allen Unwin Ltd.,
1974.

Brenneman, Walter Jr.; Yarian, Stanley O.; and
Olson, Alan M. The Seeing Eye: Hermeneu-
tical Phenomenology In The Study Of Religion.
Pennsylvania: The Pennsylvania State
University Press, 1982.

Burnett, Jaquette Hill. "Ceremony, Rites and
Economy in the Student System of an American
High School." Human Organization, 28, No. 1
(Spring, 1969), pp. 1-10.

Campbell, Jeremy. Grammatical Man: Information,
Entropy, Language, and Life. New York: Simon
and Schuster, 1982.

Clancy, P. G. "The Place of Ritual in Schools:
Some Observations." Unicorn, 3, No. 1 (March,
1977), pp. 36-42.

245

Clifton, Rodney A. "Practice Teaching: Survival In a Marginal Situation." Canadian Journal of Education, 4, No. 3 (1979), pp. 60-74.

Cox, Harvey. The Feast of Fools: A Theological Essay On Festivity. Cambridge: Harvard University Press, 1969.

Courtney, Richard. Play, Drama and Thought: The Intellectual Background to Dramatic Education. London: Casell; New York: Drama Book Specialists, 3rd ed., 1974.

─────── · The Dramatic Curriculum. London, Ontario: University of Western Ontario, Faculty of Education; London, England: Hienemann; New York: Drama Book Specialists, 1981.

─────── · Re-Play: Studies of Human Drama in Education. Toronto: OISE Press, The Ontario Institute For Studies in Education, 1982.

DeMatta, Robert. "Ritual In Complex and Tribal Societies." Current Anthropology, 20, No. 3 (September 1979), pp. 589-590.

Delattre, Roland A. "The Rituals of Humanity and the Rhythms of Reality." Prospects: An Annual Review of American Studies, 5 (1979), pp. 35-49.

"Ritual Resourcefulness and Cultural Pluralism." Soundings, 61, No. 3, pp. 281-301.

Dixon, John W. "The Erotics of Knowing." Anglican Theological Review, 56, No. 1 (January, 1974), pp. 3-16.

Douglas, Mary. Natural Symbols. New York: Random House, 1973.

and Wildavsky, Aaron. Risk and Culture: An Essay on the Selection of Technical and Environmental Dangers. Berkeley: University of California Press, 1982.

Eddy, Elizabeth M. Becoming A Teacher: A Passage
To Professional Status. Columbia University:
Teachers College Press, 1973.

Erikson, Erik H. "Ontogeny of Ritualization in
Man." Philosophical Transactions of the Royal
Society of London, Series B, No. 772 (1966),
pp. 337-350.

Fernandez, James W. "The Mission of Metaphor In
Expressive Culture." Current Anthropology.
15, No. 2 (June, 1974), pp. 119-133.

Fernandez, James W. "Persuations and Perform-
ances: Of The Beast In Every Body...And The
Metaphors of Everyman." Daedalus, 101, No. 1
(Winter, 1972), pp. 39-60.

Foster, Herbert L. Ribbin', Jivin', and Playin'
The Dozens: The Unrecognized Dilemma of Inner
City Schools. Cambridge, Mass: Ballinger
Publishing Company, 1974.

Geertz, Clifford. Local Knowledge: Further
Essays in Interpretive Anthropology. New
York: Basic Books Inc., 1983.

Gerhke, Nathalie J. "Rituals of the Hidden
Curriculum." In Children In Time and Space.
Edited by K. Yamamoto. New York: Teachers
College Press, 1979, pp. 103-127.

Grimes, Ronald L. Beginnings In Ritual Studies.
Washington, D. C.: University Press of
America, 1982.

_____ . Symbol and Conquest: Public Ritual
and Drama in Santa Fe, New Mexico.
Ithaca: Cornell University Press,
1976.

_____ . "Ritual and Illness." Canadian Journal
of Community and Mental Health, 3. No.
1 (Spring,1984), pp. 55-64.

Grumet, Madeleine R. "Curriculum As Theatre:
Merely Players." Curriculum Inquiry, 8, No.
1 (Spring, 1978), pp. 37-64.

Handleman, Don. "Play As Ritual: Complementary Frames of Meta-Communication." It's A Funny Thing, Humour. Edited by A. J. Chapman and H. C. Foot. New York: Pergamon Press, 1977, pp. 185-192.

Holmes, Urban T. "Liminality and Liturgy." Worship, 47, No. 7 (August-September, 1973), pp. 386-397.

"Revivals are Un-American: A Recalling of America To Its Pilgrimmage." Anglican Theological Review (Supplementary Series), No. 1 (July, 1973), pp. 58-75.

Illich, Ivan. "Schooling: The Ritual Progress." The New York Review of Books, 3 (December, 1970), pp. 20-26.

Jennings, Theodore. "On Ritual Knowledge." The Journal of Religion, 62, No. 2 (April, 1982), pp. 111-127.

Kapferer, Judith L. "Socialization and the Symbolic Order of the School." Anthropology and Educational Quarterly, 12, No. 4 (Winter, 1981), pp. 258-274.

Klapp, Orrin. A Collective Search For Identity. New York: Holt, Rinehart and Wilson, 1969.

Laing, Ronald D. The Voice of Experience: Experience, Science, Psychiatry. New York: Pelican Books, 1983.

Lancy, David F. "The Social Organization of Learning: Initiation Rituals and Public Schools," Human Organization, 34, No. 4 (Winter, 1975), pp. 371-379.

Lukes, Steven. "Political Ritual and Social Integration." Sociology: The Journal of the British Sociological Association, 9, No. 2 (May, 1975) pp. 289-308.

Lutz, F. W. and Ramsey, Margaret A. "Nondirective Cues as Ritualistic Indicators in Educational Organizations." Education and Urban Society, 5, No. 3 (May, 1973), pp. 345-365.

McLaren, Peter. "'Bein' Tough': Rituals of
Resistance in the Culture of Working-Class
Schoolgirls." Canada Woman Studies, 4, No. 1
(Fall, 1982).

_____ • Cries From The Corridor: The New
Suburban Ghettos. Markham, Ontario:
PaperJacks, 1982.

Moore, Alexander G. "Realities of the Urban
Classroom." Schooling In The Cultural
Context: Anthropological Studies In Educa-
tion. Edited by J. I. Roberts and S. K.
Akinsanya. New York: David MacKay Company,
Inc., pp. 238-255.

Moore, Sally F., and Myerhoff, Barbara G., (eds.).
Symbols and Politics in Communal Ideology:
Cases and Questions Ithaca: Cornell
University Press, 1975.

_____ • and Myerhoff, Barbara G., Secular
Ritual. Amsterdam: Van Gorcum, 1977.

Myerhoff, Barbara G. Number Our Days. New York:
Simon and Shuster, 1978.

_____ • and Metzer, Deena. "The Journal as
Activity and Genre: On Listening To
The Silent Laughter of Mozart."
Semiotica, 30, Nos. 1/2 (1980), pp.
97-114.

Norton, David. "The Rites of Passage From Dependence To Automony." School Review (November,
1970), pp. 19-42.

O'Farrell, Lawrence Patrick. "Ritual In Creative
Drama." Drama Contact (May, 1981), pp. 16-18.

Olson, David. "On The Language and Authority of
Textbooks." Journal of Communication, 30,
No. 1 (Winter, 1980), pp. 186-196.

Phenix, Philip, Realms of Meaning: A Philosophy
of the Curriculum for General Education.
Toronto: McGraw-Hill, 1964.

Rappaport, Roy A.  "Concluding Remarks on Ritual and Reflexivity."  Semiotica, 30, Nos. 1/2 (1980), pp. 181-193.

"Liturgies and Lies."  International Yearbook for the Sociology of Knowledge and Religion, 10 (1976), pp. 75-104.

"Ritual, Sanctity and Cybernetics."  American Anthropologist, 73 (1971), pp. 59-76.

Schechner, Richard.  Essays in Performance Theory, 1970-1976. New York:  Drama Books, 1977.

_____ · "Restored Behaviour."  Studies in Visual Communication, 7, No. 3 (Summer, 1981), pp. 2-45.

_____ · "Performers and Spectators Transported and Transformed."  Kenyon Review, 3, No. 4 (Fall, 1981), pp. 83-113.

_____ · and Shuman, Mady )eds.).  Ritual, Play and Performance:  Readings in the Social Sciences/Theatre.  New York: Seabury Press, 1976.

Shipman, M. D. The Sociology of the School. London and Harlow:  Longman's Green and Co. Ltd., 1968.

Smart, Ninian.  Worldviews:  Crosscultural Explorations of Human Beliefs.  New York: Charles Scribner's Sons, 1983.

Smith, Jonathan Z.  Imagining Religion:  From Babylon to Jonestown.  Chicago:  University of Chicago Press, 1982.

Turner, Victor W.  The Ritual Process:  Structure and Antistructure.  Chicago:  Aldine, 1969.

Dramas, Field and Metaphors:  Symbolic Action in Human Society.  Ithaca:  Cornell University Press, 1974.

The Forest of Symbols:  Aspects of Ndembu Ritual.  Ithaca:  Cornell University Press, 1967.

"Process, System and Symbol: A New Anthropological Synthesis." <u>Daedalus</u>, 1 (Summer, 1977), pp. 61-79.

<u>From Ritual to Theatre: The Human Seriousness of Play</u>. New York: Performing Arts Journal Publications, 1982.

Watzlawick, Paul. <u>The Pragmatics of Human Communication</u>. Edited by Janet Beavin and John Jackson. New York: W. W. Norton, 1967.

Weiss, Milford S., and Weiss, Paul H. "A Public School Ritual Ceremony," <u>Journal of Research and Development in Education</u>, 9, No. 4 (1976), pp. 22-28.

Wilden, Anthony. "Semiotics as Praxis: Strategy and Tactics." <u>Semiotic Inquiry</u>, 1, No. 1 (1980), pp. 1-34.

Willower, Donald J. "The Teacher Subculture and Rites of Passage." <u>Urban Education</u>, 4, No. 2 (July, 1969), pp. 103-114.

Zuesse. "Meditation On Ritual." <u>Journal of the American Academy of Religion</u>, 44, No. 3 (1975), pp. 517-530.

Response. FROM RITUAL TO REASONING:
A PROLEGOMENA TOWARDS ESTABLISHING
LINKS BETWEEN RITOLOGY AND SCHOOLING
by
Lawrence O'Farrell

The implications of this paper are at once
commonplace and staggering. Who among us is not
aware that young people behave differently in
school than they do in peer groups on the
street? Everyone can verify this observation
from personal experience. However, the suggestion that this change in behaviour is induced by
ritual structures and motifs which reside at the
very core of school life, has far-reaching implications for all educators and for child-drama
specialists in particular. In my response I will
endeavour firstly, to evaluate the paper, providing what insight I can into the development of
its thesis, and, secondly, to highlight the significance of its conclusions for the field of
drama in education.

I must begin by stating that in my opinion,
the study is thorough, well-organized and co-
gently argued. Moreover, I am largely convinced
by the principal thesis which holds that schooling and ritual have much in common and that the
elements of ritual can have a major impact on the
effectiveness of institutionalized education -
for better or for worse. It goes almost without
saying, therefore, that the study addresses a
significant issue. Indeed, perhaps the research
question in itself is the most important contribution of the present work, quite apart from any
specific conclusions. The assumptions point to
education as a predominantly formal experience
which can unwittingly defeat its own purposes in
spite of its enormous potential for stimulation
and control.

The survey of relevant literature presented
by the paper is not only thorough but also laud-
ibly up-to-date. I must concur that any serious
discussion of ritual cannot long ignore the works
of Turner, Moore, Myerhoff, Schechner, Grimes and
the other scholars who have most accurately and
appropriately been cited. In particular, I
appreciate the care taken to dispel some

253

lingering misconceptions regarding the characteristics and function of ritual. Cultural Darwinists of the nineteenth century including such famous names as James Frazer and Lucien Levi-Bruhl have left to posterity a degenerating picture of "primitive" ritual as a kind of magical substitute for productive effort, performed by deluded, "pre-logical", natives who were incapable of distinguishing between fact and fancy. Such patently biased theories have long since been discredited but their influence lives on. Therefore, it is useful to have the lesson reiterated as a prelude to renewed efforts to define the field of ritual in more defensible terms.

In keeping with current trends and a determination to remain open to further insights, the paper has posited a "soft" definition of ritual, one which attempts to indicate the general region of ritual practice without restricting the field by an intractible set of boundaries. Interestingly, this soft definition of ritual would suit admirably as a definition of theatre, also. The paper recognizes this and attempts to differentiate the two activities by stressing the view that audiences actively participate in the ritual process whereas theatre audiences merely observe. I cannot support this distinction, although it is widely accepted, because it fails to recognize the range of audience participation possible in both ritual and theatre. Indeed it is easy to demonstrate the inverse of the definition. Participational theatre for children and creative drama are only two branches of the theatre in which boundaries between actors and audience are either blurred or completely eradicated. Conversely, I have personally attended many rituals both sacred and secular, at which the actors were strictly segregated from their audience both spacially and functionally. The question of how to define ritual has not entirely been settled by this paper. However, the groundwork has been well established upon which a relative definition may yet be constructed.

I can attest to the assertion that the literature is rife with competing definitions of ritual and the confusion has not been alleviated by similarly contradictory views about the theatre

254

and its relationship to ritual. It has recently become clear that the term "ritual" can no longer be restricted to religious events, because anthropologists and philosophers have been able to detect the structure and imagery of ritual in many secular occurrences. This development has seriously undermined the conventional notion of theatre as a kind of secular replacement for ritual. To add to the confusion, we have theorists like Richard Courtney who maintain that the roots of human behaviour are essentially dramatic, while others like Ronald Grimes speak of the same phenomena as nascent or formative rituals. Not only is there a considerable overlapping in definitions of ritual and theatre but much of the same territory is also claimed by progressive educators and social psychologists as representing concepts unique to their particular fields. I believe that it has now become necessary to approach all of these events, and the theories which endeavour to explain them, from a fresh perspective, one which honours major differences while, at the same time, acknowledging fundamental similarities.

This diagram (Figure One) represents a preliminary attempt to schematize some of the relevant areas of human behaviour in relation to one another and to their traditional fields of operation. When we speak of the theatre we are generally understood to include both Classical Drama exemplified by the highly formal Noh Theatre of Japan, and variations of theatrical realism including the work of Anton Chekhov interpreted according to Stanislovski's acting methods. Sacred liturgies typified by funerals and secular ceremonies including political investitures comprise the traditional range of Civil and Religious Rituals. Games like football are joined by forms of social role-playing such as "hosting" a party in the general field of social interaction. And finally, one might reasonably expect to find experiences in Dramatic Play such as "playing house" to be grouped with Creative Drama, exemplified by improvisations on a social theme, under the category of Human Development and Education. This analysis is not expected to win universal agreement but it does serve to demonstrate the type of divisions which we have come to expect in discussing these related areas of human endeavour.

Conventional thinking would have us see these categories as essentially distinct with some interesting but minor similarities. Social role-playing has been seen to resemble theatrical performance just as creative drama and games have been thought to share common elements. But the emphasis has always favoured the autonomy of each division. As a result of recent scholarship, however, it is possible to postulate a macro-division which might be called Symbolic Action. This division would be a sub-set of Symbolism in general and could be distinguished from other forms of symbolism by the fact that people make this kind of symbol manifest by performing elements of human behaviour kinetically and/or vocally.

The present format will not permit me to develop this theory further now, but I am confident that a comparison of the literature related to various Modes of Symbolic action including ritual, theatre, games, etc. will produce a generic description incorporating most of the properties and functions of rituals enumerated in the present paper. Symbolic Action in every category is essentially formal, symbolic, dramatic and authoritative. It may be either sacred or secular in context. It appears to derive from and serve social structures while at the same time it is set apart from those same structures, formally, by framing or bracketing devices. It has the potential for generating an experience of flow and for transforming the consciousness and status of participants. Concepts and values can be negotiated and articulated by every branch of Symbolic Action. Therefore, distinctions between categories will be relative rather than absolute. Every category is subject to regulation but games can be said to rely especially on the authority of rules and on the consistency of their application. Every category can be seen to express meaning in various ways but drama would appear to place particular stress on communication. When ritual is included in creative drama it will be distinguished from other kinds of dramatization by the attention paid to bracketing devices including orderliness and stylization. This means that while the terminology may eventually change as the modes of symbolic action sort themselves out again according to their relatively minor distinctions, the main thrust of this study will retain its significance for education.

It would be natural for us to despair at the heavily negative impact which can result from the unconscious or merely inept application of ritual structures and elements in school settings. However, there is much for teachers of drama and performers of plays for young audiences to rejoice about as well. This is because we, more than any other group of educators, are equipped to take advantage of the enormous creative potential of ritual. In fact, to a considerable extent we are already providing an excellent example of how others can capitalize on the advantages of symbolic action in the form of ritual or otherwise. In saying this I am speaking not only of the contribution of a few exceptional teachers and performers, I am referring to the work of any competent member of our profession.

This point can easily be illustrated by reviewing the format of a classical creative drama lesson in terms of ritual structure, as it is described by Victor Turner following Arnold Van Gennep. A conventional opening to a creative drama lesson is the warm-up activity. This exercise typically involves much physical activity, often introduced as a game. It usually stresses intuitive, spontaneous behaviour. It is generally seen as a direct way to prepare the students for more demanding drama work by, firstly, separating them from the linear subject matter and social behaviour of the classes they have just concluded and, secondly, by re-introducing the alternative style and methods of creative drama. A dramatic warm-up of this type is virtually identical with the initial phase of a ritual sequence. This is the "separation" in which ritual subjects are formally divested of their previous status and released from the usual constraints placed on thought and behaviour by a structured society.

The main body of a creative drama lesson closely parallels the "liminoid" phase in the

ritual process. Once freed of customary limitations, students are encouraged to explore and
assess the inner meanings of human interaction
and to express their oservations and emotions
through the creation and performance of original
art works in the dramatic mode. Within this
context, students develop a genuine esprit de
corps, or what Turner calls "communitas". They
also have the opportunity to experience "flow",
which is the ritual equivalent of aethetic
pleasure.

Finally, the classical creative drama lesson
ends with a reflective exercise or discussion
sometimes called a "warm-down" which directly
corresponds to the ritual phase of "reaggrega-
tion." At this point, ritual subjects formally
re-enter conventional society having been transformed either in spirit or in social status,
often in both.

Seen in this light, creative drama appears to
be a useful example of how the elements of ritual
can be deliberately applied within a school setting. More importantly, however, it serves as an
illustration of how the school curriculum as a
whole can be structured to accommodate the arche-
typal process of truly "formal" education in such
a way as to place at the teachers' disposal the
unlimited creative, intellectual and social
potentials of the human mind.

The implications of Peter McLaren's thesis
will need to be drawn out in much greater length
and, as acknowledged in his paper, even initial
assumptions will require further testing and
modification. However, our attention has,
intractibly, been focused on the importance of
symbolic form in the structure of institutionalized learning. Research, in this area must and
will proceed and as it does child drama specialists can expect to play a central role.

(Figure One)

Modes of Symbolic Action

(In Four Areas)

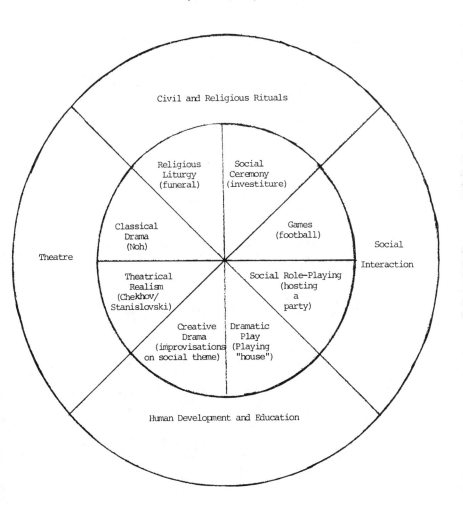

## Selective Bibliography

Courtney, Richard. _Play, Drama and Thought: The Intellectual Background to Dramatic Education_. London: Cassell, 1968.

Evans-Pritchard, E. E. _Theories of Primitive Religion_. London: Oxford University Press, 1965.

Frazer, James. _The Golden Bough_. New York: MacMillan Co., 1947.

Grimes, Ronald L. _Beginnings In Ritual Studies_. Washington, D.D.: University Press of America, 1982.

Levi-Bruhl, Lucien. _How Natives Think_. New York: Washington Square Press, 1966.

Moore, Sally F. and Myerhoff, Barbara G. _Secular Ritual_. Assen, The Netherlands: Van Gorcum and Comp. B.V., 1977.

O'Farrell, Lawrence. "Ritual in Creative Drama". _Drama Contact_ (May, 1981), pp. 16-18.

_____ . "Making It Special: Ritual as a Creative Resource for Drama". _Children's Theatre Review_ 33 (1):3.6

Rappaport, Roy A. "Ritual Sanctity and Cybernetics". _American Anthropologist_ 73 (1): 59-76.

Schechner, Richard. _Essays in Performance Theory, 1970-1976_. New York: Drama Books, 1977.

Turner, Victor W. _The Ritual Process: Structure and Anti-Structure_. Chicago: Aldin Publishing C., 1969.

Turner, Victor W. _From Ritual To Theatre: The Human Seriousness of Play_. New York: Performing Arts Journal Publications, 1982.

Van Gennep, Arnold. <u>The Rites of Passage</u>. Translated by Monika B. Vizedom and Gabrielle L. Caffee, London: Routledge and Keegan Paul, 1960.

KATHAK – THE CLASSICAL DANCE OF NORTH INDIA:
Its History, Technique, Training and
Educational Value
In Contemporary Society
by
Rina Singha

## Kathak:  Introduction and Brief History

The term KATHAK derives from the Sanskrit
work "Katha" or story. According to Hindu tradition, Dance began at creation with the Rhythm of
the Universe. As this story of creation was told
and retold in all its subtle shades and complexities, the Dance-word or "Katha" came into being
and along with it, the specialized art of making
the Katha come alive, not only through spoken
word but through the total dance experience,
using body movement, facial expression and
rhythmic interpretation.

This was the origin of Kathak, one of the six
major classical dance forms of India. Like the
other five, its fundamental structure in the laws
of theatre was codified and written down in the
3rd century B. C. in the Natyasastra.

Dance and drama were considered as a unified
art form in the very early times. At the long,
ceremonical, ritual sacrifices performed during
the Vedic period, two groups of priests elaborated hymns in the form of dialogues. Others
enacted the roles of the gods. Sometimes, this
combined art of dance and drama, was used purely
for entertainment as professional actors performed to break the monotony of the long rituals.

During the centuries that followed this
ancient dramaturgy of Kathak molded and revised
itself to suit the religious needs of the time.
The two major influences that gave Kathak its
present form were the Vaishnavite movement of
medieval Hinduism and Islam.

The Vaishnavite movement celebrated the God
Vishnu, particularly in his incarnations as King
Rama, hero of the epic, Ramayana and again as
Krishna, the cowherd Prince, the central figure
of the other epic, Mahabharata. During the

263

Bhakti Movement, when devotion to God was considered more important than elaborate ritual, Krishna became the presiding deity of the masses. His worship inspired great poetry, painting, music, imagery and art.

Islam was brought to India in the 8th Century by the Arabs and went on to become the state religion under the Moghul emperors. It professed one formless god, as opposed to the Hindu pantheon depicted in the human form by a host of gods and goddesses. It also preached the universal brotherhood of man instead of the caste system. The juxtaposition of two such opposing systems of thought had a profound effect on all the arts of North India including Kathak.

The Moghuls were great patrons of the arts and letters. The sophistication of their courts left its stamp on Kathak which is known today for its grace, beauty of line, rhythmic precision and subtlety of expression.

During the British rule, the Kathaks dispersed to find patrons among the feudal lords, and the art form degenerated to what the British termed "Nautch". This was a general period of decline for dance. Temple dancing was outlawed and dancers faced prison sentences for performing their art.

After Independence, in August 1947, the Government tried to preserve and popularize the arts and to provide patronage to the master artists. Government Institutes were founded to provide quality teaching and to rekindle the dying torches of the Indian music and dance heritage.

For Kathak, the government went a step further. With a deliberate policy to free it from its association to the Nautch, scholarships were given to educated young dancers who would hopefully elevate the Kathak image. Today, Kathak still enjoys government support, as do all the major dance forms. The Kathak Kendra in Dehli is staffed by India's top Kathak Gurus and choreographers who train dancers from across India and other parts of the world that have domiciled Indians, e.g., West Indies, Fiji, and East Africa.

Kathak:   An Ancient Art Relevant to Today's Needs

In this section of the paper, an analysis of the RANG MANJ, the opening ritual of Kathak, will illustrate how the goals, training techniques and performance of Kathak are relevant to society in the 20th century.

As stated earlier, Kathak like the other classical dances of India derived its authority from the Natyasastra, the codified laws of the theatre, written around the 3rd century B. C. Its goals, as stipulated, were to provide aesthetic delight of the highest form and also to inform and instruct the audience about the complexities and subtleties of life.

A key concept laid down by the Natyasastra was ABHINAYA (which means "to lead towards"). It referred to leading the audience towards the idea being expressed in the fullest possible way. Abhinaya had four elements: ANGIKA (physical), gestures, body movements, etc.; VACIK (verbal) words spoken or sung; AHARYA (decorative) costume and make-up; and SATVIKA (temperamental).

Also the art of dance-drama was seen as having 3 components: NRTTA, pure dance technique, NRTYA, pure dance combined with the dramatic element, and NATYA, or dramatic element alone.

The classical dances of India operated and developed within the above framework.

RANG MANJ:   The Cornerstone in Training, both for Technique and Attitude

The Rang Manj is the opening invocatory ritual of the Kathak repertoire of the Lucknow School. The word "Rang" means the stage or dancing area. The piece depicts the offering of flowers and prayers for the success of the performers. It starts at a very slow tempo and then is danced at double and four times the original tempo. The piece as danced today resembles closely the invocatory piece prescribed in the Natyasastra.

Until about 15 years ago, Kathak training of the Lucknow School always began with the Rang

265

Manj. The hand, foot and body movement for each beat were taught syllable by syllable and then in larger sections till finally the piece learnt in its entirety. Then came the painful grind. Each day for about 4-6 months, the same piece was danced over and over again for 2-4 hours at a time.

The slow tempo required a high degree of concentration and body control, while the double and quadruple tempo developed precision and speed. The Rang Manj thus laid the foundation for refined body awareness and a sound knowledge of the rhythm structure.

## Educational Value of the Rang Manj

The teaching of the Rang Manj is aimed not only at strengthening the dancers' technique but also at building an attitude of respect for knowledge and for excellence, and a regard for others.

Since these goals parallel our educational aims, it follows that a carry-over from the traditional Kathak training can have a beneficial effect in education.

For instance, it is generally accepted that a positive self image is the best starting point for learning. The Rang Manj develops grace and poise and builds self confidence. The proper execution of the Rang Manj demands great precision, concentration, and self control. As these qualities develop in the child, they bring about an awareness of the shortcomings of "instant" learning and the fact that it can only serve limited goals.

The movements of the Rang Manj suggest a humble salute to God and to the teacher, as the dancer recognizes a higher source of knowledge. This attitude of openness towards learning is absolutely essential if the child is to develop and grow in knowledge.

In education, we seek to motivate students to lifelong learning; Kathak training can promote this goal through its stress on self discipline, inner motivation and respect for knowledge.

Kathak also provides cultural insights and a link with past traditions. In today's world, many families find themselves domiciled away from their place of origin. This results in cultural alienation. Kathak dance and training enables Indian domiciles to better understand their cultural roots, values and traditions.

The Rang Manj ends in a salute to the audience. The principle of Abhinaya demands that a performance must touch the audience in a special way. Through the Rang Manj, the dancer asks for the audience's blessing and supportive thoughts so that together they can reach aesthetic fulfillment. This audience-performer relationship is a far cry from the each-one-for-himself attitude that engulfs today's society. The Rang Manj preaches an alternative message of cooperation and love.

Perhaps this is one of its greatest values.

# BIBLIOGRAPHY

Anand, M. R.: <u>Classical & Folk Dances of India</u>, Bombay, Marg Publications.

Aurbindo: <u>Rig Veda</u>, trans., London, Luzac, 1962.

Bharata: <u>Natya Shastra</u>, trans., M. Ghosh, Calcutta, Royal Asiatic Society of Bengal, 1950.

Bhatt, S.C.: <u>Drama In Ancient India</u>, New Dehli, Amrit Books, 1961.

Courtney, R.: <u>People In Performance: Perspectives on Drama & Culture</u>. Toronto: O.I.S.E., 1982.

Kabir, H.: <u>Indian Heritage</u>, London, Mendian Books, 1947.

Nandikesvara: <u>Abhinaya Darpananam</u>, trans., M. Ghosh, Calcultta, Metropolitain Printing House, 1934.

Row, Leela: <u>Nritta Manjari</u>, Calcutta, Indian Societ of Oriental Art.

Singha, Rina & Massey, R.: <u>Indian Dances, Their History & Growth</u>, London Faber & Faber, 1967.

# THE PRINCIPLES IN THE JAPANESE TEA CEREMONY
## WITH SPECIAL REFERENCE TO
## GIRLS' EDUCATION IN JAPAN
by
Hiroko Noro

## 1. Introduction

The Japanese tea ceremony (chanoyu) origi-nated in the religious tea serving to the gods at the Zen temple. The original purpose of tea ceremony was religious. After the tea ceremony became popular among laymen, its purpose was to entertain guests. The present tea ceremony has these opposing characteristics, i.e., religious and secular. Tetsuzo Tanikawa enumerates four factors forming the Japanese tea ceremony: (1) social; (2) ritualistic; (3) disciplinary; (4) artistic.[1] Chanoyu can be a social gathering, comparable with the western tea party on one hand, or it can be a religious ceremony to serve tea to the gods on the other. However, even though aimed at the communion between man and god, an element of social gathering is always involved with the religious ceremony. The social gathering aspect of tea ceremony needs a certain set of manners so as to accomplish the initial purpose. The Japanese chanoyu requires the par-ticipants to have an elaborate system of rules of conduct during the tea party: when to bow, how to fold the tea-serving napkin, how to walk around the tea-room, etc. A large amount of training is required to master how to properly participate in the chanoyu. In chanoyu, artistry is highly valued, but artificiality is not. The body movement of an expert appears to be natural. However, it is not an extension of everyday life. The naturalness of movement is the result of long-term training. Chanoyu in general exists in an equilibrium between these four factors.

This paper explores the interrelationship between the tea ceremony and girls' education in Japan. There are four main traits in tea ceremony: (1) self-discipline; (2) eating manners; (3) sex-role learning; (4) performance learning. These traits prevail in pedagogical principles in Japan. The tea ceremony has been used as an educational device for marriage preparation for girls.

269

The paper is organized in the following manner: first we examine why and how the tea ceremony has become a part of early female education (12 years -20 years), and second we analyze the four main traits in tea ceremony.

## 2. The Tea Ceremony and Girls' Education

In Japan for the last four hundred years there has been a certain point of view and life ritual associated with the tea ceremony. Kakuzo Okakura coined the word "Teaism" to describe the spirit of ceremonial tea-drinking.[2] "Teaism" may be regarded as direct teaching in taste and etiquette. This pursuit of good taste in life could not have come about without an organized education. It was the tea master who was largely responsible for this education. It is imparted and practised in the home under the ordinary conditions of life. The tea ceremony demonstrates that common domestic duties are not socially inferior or humiliating. The custom for girls to take domestic training for a few years before marriage to learn etiquette, which used to be common in Japan before World War II, is akin to the spirit of Teaism.

In early Meiji, Kakei Atomi, the founder of a girls school in Japan, introduced the tea ceremony into the curriculum.[3] She believed that the tea ceremony would be an ideal device for teaching etiquette. Promotion into the school curriculum and the domestic tendency of the tea ceremony itself led to it being regarded as the principal device for teaching manners. This includes table manners and serving manners, both indispensable to the Japanese girl.

## 3. The Four Traits in Teaism

### (1) Self-Discipline

The factor of self-discipline prevails throughout the tea ceremony, for example tea-serving, tea-drinking, walking, appreciation of the tea equipment. Teaism aims at creating a self-contained world wherein the human being can be freed from the impurities of ordinary life. Teaism like Zen Buddhism seeks for liberty of the human mind.   Self-discipline   is   stressed   to attain such a goal.

(2)   Eating Manners

If we define drinking as a variation of eating, the tea ceremony principally deals with eating manners.  These manners differ from ordinary table manners.  But the tea ceremony manners and everyday eating manners share the same root in being closely related to the image of the sacred.   In the sphere of mythology, eating is often regarded as the mediation between men and gods.[4]   In Japanese myth, there is a description of eating as an initiation into society.[5] Eating is a token of membership.  Eating has to do not only with the mediation between men and gods but also with that between men and their peers.

(3)   Sex-Role Learning

Since Kakei Atomi incorporated the tea ceremony into girls' education, it has played an important role in marriage preparation.  It is an ideal device for female education because of its domestic tendency.   Besides, tea ceremony provides opportunities for attaining an ability to perceive one's taste without verbal clues.   In the tea room, the hostess and the guests are not expected to converse.  The hostess is required to be perceptive of the guests' preferences.   Such sensitivity to another's taste, feeling and mood is regarded as one of the criteria of the ideal Japanese woman.

(4)   Performance Learning

The teaching method in the tea ceremony is demonstrative.   In the beginning, the disciples imitate what the tea master does.  Being observant is emphasized throughout.   In the tea room, the participants are the audience and at the same time the actors and playwrights. The ceremony values the process, not the result.  It is possible to say that the teaching method of the tea ceremony is dramatic, in that the disciples perform the ways of tea-serving and also experience the stage atmosphere in the tea room.  The disciples are encouraged to imitate a certain model.

This learning process takes a long time. Hence, the factor of self-discipline is vital. Once the disciples acquire the model technique, they are allowed to seek their own originality.

## 4. Conclusion

We conclude this paper with the following summary. In the first part, we posited two reasons why the tea ceremony became a part of girls' education. They are: (1) the domestic nature of the tea ceremony and (2) Kakei Atomi's introduction of the tea ceremony into the school curriculum. In the second part, the four main traits in the ceremony were analyzed. These factors are: (1) self-discipline; (2) eating manners; (3) sex-role learning; (4) performance learning.

These four main traits are also found in traditional Japanese parenting. The Japanese family puts emphasis on conformity. The child is expected to imitate the model behaviour performed by the adult. This process requires self-discipline. In sex-role learning, the conformity-oriented pattern enhances the difference between sexes. Eating manners, important for boys and girls, play an integral part in the parenting process, since eating is closely related to the communion between men and gods, and men and their peers. Thus, these traits found in the tea ceremony permeate in the life of Japanese since early childhood.

-NOTES-

1)  Tetsuzo Tanikawa, <u>Cha no Bigaku</u> (Aesthetics
    of Teaism), (Kyoto: Tankosha, 1977).

2)  Kakuzo, Okakura, <u>The Book of Tea</u>, (Tokoyo:
    Kenkyusha, 1939).

3)  Isao Kumakura, <u>Kindai Sadoshi no Kenkyu</u> (A
    Study of Modern History of Teaism), (Tokoyo:
    Nihon Hoso Shuppankai, 1980), pp. 298-304.

4)  Jan Kott, <u>The Eating of the Gods: An Inter-
    pretation of Greek Tragedy</u>, trans. by
    Boleslwa Taborski & Edward J. Czerwinski,
    (New York: Random House, 1970), p. 19.

5)  Masao Yaku, <u>The Kojiki in the Life of Japan</u>,
    trans. by G. W. Robinson, (Tokoyo: The Centre
    for East Asian Cultural Studies, 1969).

-BIBLIOGRAPHY-

Ellis, Michael J. Why People Play. Englewood
     Cliffs, N.J.: Prentice-Hall, Inc. 1973.

Hiratsuka, Masunori (ed.). Nihon no Katei to
     Kodomo (Japanese Family and Children).
     Tokyo: Kaneko shobo, 1973.

Iguchi, Tatsuo. Kurashi no Kisetsu (Seasons in
     Life). Tokyo: Jitsugyono-nihonsha, 1976.

Ikeda, Yasaburo. Sezoku no Geibun (Secular
     Literature). Tokyo: Seigabo, 1973.

Kott, Jan. The Eating of the Gods: An Interpre-
     tation of Greek Tragedy, trans. by Boleslaw
     Taborski & Edward J. Czerwinski. New York:
     Random House, 1970.

Kumakura, Isao. Kindai Sadoshi no Kenkyu (A Study
     of Modern History of Teaism). Tokyo: Nihon
     Hoso Shuppankai, 1980.

Levi-Strauss, Claude. The Raw and the Cooked.
     New York: Harper & Row, 1969.

Matsuda, Michio. Jiyu o Kodomo ni (Freedom to
     Children). Tokyo: Iwanami shoten, 1973.

Moriya, Tsuyoshi (ed.). Cha no Bunka: Sono Sogo
     teki Kenkyu (Tea Culture: A Comprehensive
     Study of Tea). Kyoto: Tankosha, 1981.

Okakura, Kakuzo. The Book of Tea. Tokyo:
     Kenkyusha, 1939.

Negishi, Kennosuke. Shitsuke to Asobi no Minzoku
     (The Folklore of Parenting and Play). Tokyo:
     Ohusha, 1980.

Noguchi, Takenori & Shigehiko Shiramizu. Nihonjin
     no Shitsuke (Japanese Parenting). Tokyo:
     T-ikoku chiho gyosei gakkai, 1973.

Tada, Michitaro. Asobi to Nihonjin (Play and the
     Japanese). Tokyo: Chikuma Shobo, 1978.

Tanikawa, Tetsuzo. Cha no Bigaku (Aesthetics of
     Teaism). Kyoto: Tankosha, 1977.

Umesao, Tadao (ed.).   Shokuji no Bunka (Culture of
    Eating).   Tokyo: Tokyo: Asahi shimbunsha,
    1980.

Whiting, Beatrice B. (ed.).   Six Cultures:
    Studies of Child Rearing.   New York &
    London:   John Wiley & Sons, Inc., 1963.

Yaku, Masao.   The Kojiki in the Life of Japan,
    trans. by G. W. Robinson. Tokyo; The Centre
    for East Asian Cultural Studies, 1969.

Yanagida, Kunio.   Teihon Yanagida Kunio shu
    (Collected Works of Kunio Yanagida).   Tokyo:
    Chikuma shobot, 1962.

Yoshimura, Teiji.   Cha no bi no hakken (Discovery
    of Beauty in the Tea Ceremony).   Kyoto;
    Tankosna, 1972.

# CEREMONY PAYING RESPECT TO TEACHERS
## (THE WAAI KHRUU CEREMONY)
### by Poranee Gururatana

Ceremony Paying Respect to teachers is a Thai Ceremony that is distinct from those known in Western Culture. The ceremony would be of special interest to those in the field of education. The ceremony can be observed as a dramatization which reinforces social roles of self as student and others as teacher.

The Waai Khruu ceremony or ceremony Paying Respect to Teachers is an ancient one. The ceremony was instituted as a way to present oneself as a pupil or protege, and also to remember those who were responsible for teaching. Teaching here includes cognitive knowledge, manipulative skills, and the affective area as well as dealing with social conduct and moral development. It was a way for an apprentice to express thanks for the knowledge and skills imparted by the master teacher.

Before the establishment of the formal school system in Thailand, boys were sent to study reading and writing with the monks in the Buddhist monasteries. If a child lived far from the monastery, he would even board there.

The children sent to study at the monastery were called luuk sit phra. The word luuk sit phra is a compound: luuk means son or daughter, sit means pupil, and phra means monk. The original meaning, therefore, included the sense that the monks in accepting the child were assuming the roles of parent and teacher. The monks who accepted the teaching responsibilities were called luuy phoo where phoo means father.

Before beginning their studies, the children would perform a ceremony whereby they would offer themselves formally as pupils to the monks who would be their teachers.

After the establishment of the school system, the Waai Khruu ceremony, Ceremony Paying Respect to Teachers, was incorporated as an annual ceremony performed at all levels of education from kindergarten to university.

In this paper I will discuss the Waai Khruu ceremony stressing its characteristic and how it is performed in schools.

The ceremony is conducted on a Thursday at the beginning of the school year. In Thai, Thursday is <u>wan</u> <u>phrarunasarodii</u>; <u>wan</u> means day and <u>shrarusiatsakodis</u> refers to the Hindu divine tutor of the gods.

The setting for the ceremony is usually in the school auditorium or a suitable area for a large group. On the stage an altar to worship Buddha is set up with candles, incense, and flowers. There is also a picture of the King and a Thai flag. As in every Thai ceremony, respect is paid to the country, the Buddhist religion, and the King.

The people involved in the ceremony are as follows:

One, the master of ceremonies, usually the principal, and the entire teaching staff. They are seated on the stage.

Two, the entire student body, seated in the auditorium.

Three, outstanding students chosen to represent their particular classes.

The class representatives, usually with the help of other class members, prepare beforehand a floral display which is intricately and artistically made. The floral display is carried on a tray as traditionally used when passing anything to elders, and includes a candle and three incense sticks.

In former times even the kind of flowers was prescribed because they were dramatically symbolic. There were flowers buds, sharp needle like flowers representing a sharp intellect and a salty kind of grass representing cleverness.

On the day of the ceremony, when the master of ceremonies arrives, the student body stand up to greet him. He then proceeds to the stage and lights the candles and incense at the altar and says a prayer. The students then sit down. The class representatives then come forward one by one with their floral offerings. Following this one of the class representatives begins to chant a poem to honor teachers and the entire student body follow chanting in chorus.

The chanting of the students all dressed neatly in their school uniforms as the faculty sits silently on the stage creates an atmosphere of solemnity.

The chant roughly translated is as follows:

Let us pay respect,
To all the teachers
Who have given us knowledge and skills.

On teachers today and yesterday
Who have taught us
To respect others and conduct ourselves,
Let us pay respect.

Let us recall the goodness of our teachers,
With our heart filled with respect and honor.

We ask for wisdom that we may have
Success in our studies;
We ask for long and healtny lives;
We ask that we may live good moral lives;
Let us be benefit and credit
To ourselves and our country.

Finally, the class representative will chant in Pali-Sanskrit requesting that the students have their wishes fulfilled.

The meaning and chanting of this poem creates a feeling of appreciation for teachers and expresses a belief that teachers are able to impart knowledge to students.

It has the psychological effect of motivating students to endeavor to be better students. It is a way to remind them to conduct themselves mindfully and responsibly in their role as students.

The teachers, themselves, reflect on their role with a resolve to do their best in their teaching job.

At the end of the Waai Khruu ceremony, the principal will express thanks to the students for performing the ceremony and will often, in addition, give a speech concerning the role and responsibility of the students in society.

# Reference

Anuman, Rajadhon Phya. *Life and Ritual in Old Siam: Three Studies of Thai Life and Customs.* Translated and edited by William J. Gedney, New Have: HRAF Press, 1966.

# INTERCULTURAL COMMUNICATION
## by
### Christine Turkewych

Cultural pluralism is a reality of our society, our schools and our communities. The term "multiculturalism" describes the diversity among the ethnic, Francophone, Anglophone and Native cultures which comprize Canadian society. In fact, some argue that Canada has always been ethnically heterogeneous, from its time as a territory comprising fifty distinctive Indian and Inuit societies (Burnet, 1981). The federal multicultural policy by its inception in 1971, as well as several provincial policies, gave political consciousness to this diversity and acknowledged cultural pluralism as a positive force. Briefly, these policies aim to create a democratic society in which every individual will receive opportunities and encouragement to achieve his or her legitimate personal goals and contribute to the pursuit of such goals by others. Multiculturalism is a humanistic concept based on the strength of diversity and human rights.

Education in a culturally pluralistic society becomes challenging in its complexity. The main operants are:

1. <u>We are not all alike</u>.

Our behaviour and attitudes are influenced by the values of our culture. Groups can be formed around categorizations such as race, ethnic loyalties, nationalities, special interest, social classes, religious beliefs and minority status within a country dominated by another group whose members hold power. Thus "culture can be explained as an identifiable group with shared beliefs and experiences, feelings of worth and value attached to those experiences and a shared interest in a common historical background" (Brislin, 1981). Educators who are committed to quality education and equal opportunity for every individual to attain his/her potential, must expand their concern for individual development to include the more difficult task of understanding individuals within the context of their unique cultural experiences.

## 2. Every culture is equally valid.

Further, when the concern for maximizing individual development is viewed in light of cultural context, then it is apparent that there is no single criterion of human potential which can be applicable to all, nor any curriculum which will be equally effective for every culture. Educators cannot operate from a value base which exonerates "our way is the best way" and promotes assimilation. Curriculum development must promote integration through which individual and group goals are achieved.

## 3. Every discipline area is affected.

Prior to the inception of multicultural policies, ethno-cultural groups had established private schools, operating as after-hour and weekend schools which fostered the language and cultural traditions particular to the group. Bilingual programs within regular institutions provided partial immersion. Both "ethnic" schools and bilingual programs promoted cultural heritage, increased the students' sense of identity and served the community goal of cultural retention. Since World War II, English As A Second Language (ESL) programs were developed to assist immigrant students in acquiring the language skills necessary to function successfully in the larger society. Although these programs were and still are effective for the needs of particular groups, they do not address the needs of mixed communities.

With the inception of the Federal Multicultural policy, several provinces (i.e., Ontario, Saskatchewan, Nova Scotia) followed suit with official documents on multicultural education. Ontario's "Special Populations in Education" document encouraged "general system sensitivity" toward meeting the "common needs" of all students, while "facilitating full participation by all students in the educational opportunities of the system". This document promotes multiculturalism as an ethnic that pervades the entire educational system. Over the last twelve years, efforts have been made to promote a "sharing" of ethnocultures which aim at increasing understanding among individuals of diverse cultural backgrounds. An attempt to promote linguistic sharing is exemplified in Ontario's controversial "Heritage Language Program which provides for the teaching of languages other than English and French on an extended school day or after school hours basis" (McLeod, 1981). This program provides students with not only the opportunity to study their own heritage language but also, to study the languages of other ethnocultures.

Frequently, history curricula began to incorporate ethnocultural components and extracurricular activities birthed multicultural festivals through which participants learned about the costumes, foods, immigration and settlement patterns of ethnocultural communities in Canada. These were useful at a consciousness-raising level, but were limited because although they provided the opportunity for knowledge acquisition, there was little or no provision made for application of this knowledge.

More recently, programs have been developed which focus on enabling individuals to function effectively in a pluralistic society. Examples of these are "Multicultural Leadership Camps" for students and "Training for Intercultural Communication" for professionals from a variety of disciplines such as health care and law enforcement. These programs promote self-awareness, knowledge of cultural values and their effect on behaviour, and aim to develop the skills necessary to interact in more than one culture. This approach, referred to as "intercultural", provides for the application of knowledge through simulation activities or problem-centred curricula. Importantly, the intercultural approach transcends compartmentalization.

These new developments served to highlight the inadequacy of teacher training. Teachers could readily become familiar with ethnocultural subject matter, but were unprepared to assess students within a cultural context to accommodate diverse learning patterns. Flexibility in instructional methodology is critical in making a successful transition to a genuinely multicultural curriculum.

## 4. Rolemodelling is highly impactful.

The operational base for every school committed to multiculturalism must expand along three dimensions, simultaneously: (1) structure: the inclusion of ethnoculturally diverse decision-makers and comprehensive policies on education in multicultural contexts. (2) context: resource materials and textbooks which reflect the multicultural components of the society. (3) process: those aspects that exemplify the day to day interactions, the "hidden" curriculum.

Educators' attitudes and assumptions must be congruent with the goals of multicultural policies and programs. Educators' behaviour toward students and colleagues, their verbal and non-verbal communication, their approach and treatment of content, the emphasis and examples used during instruction, all have the potential of contradicting and/or substantiating the goals of multicultural policies. Thus, the development of educators who are effective intercultural communicators is crucial.

## What are the characteristics of an effective intercultural communicator?

An underlying assumption in these educational developments is that a culturally pluralistic society makes new demands on individuals and that the attributes necessary for effective intercultural interaction can be learned.

The field of intercultural communication in North America is new, dating its genesis in post World War II developments around international exchanges and expanded to address domestic interethnic relations. During this 35 year period, the field has developed along several dimensions: (1) the growth of a body of theory and research literature, (2) the emergence of a felt need for culture learning and for skill building in intercultural relations, (3) the formation of organizations to collect, synthesize and distribute theory and research findings, (4) emergence of experiential training programs and courses in intercultural communication in colleges and universities. Individuals from a variety of disciplines such as anthropology, psychology, social psychology, communication, linguistics and business have contributed in creating the study of cultures interacting (King, 1979).

A central idea in the study of intercultural communication entails the investigation of culture and the difficulties of communicating across cultural boundaries.

"Intercultural Communication occurs whenever a message producer is a member of one culture and a message receiver is a member of another" (Porter & Samovar, 1976).

The greater the cultural diversity between "message producer" and "message receiver", the more difficult it is for the message to be accurately understood and appropriately responded to. The cultural context of the message entails such variables as differences in age and sex, differences in values and beliefs, differences in assumptions and expectations, differences in social status, differences in non-verbal behaviour, etc. An effective intercultural communicator is able to deal with high levels of complexity, i.e., numerous variables (Pedersen, 1981).

A review of the research and theory suggests that certain skills are crucial to effective intercultural communication. Among these, the most frequently sighted are:

1. learning how to learn - the ability to continuously seek new information about oneself and others, and to utilize this information constructively.

2. non-judgmentalness - to accept that there is no absolute truth, that one's own opinion is <u>not</u> most worthwhile and to exhibit this in posture, at least.

3. tolerance for ambiguity - the ability to react to new and ambiguous situations with little visible discomfort.

4. respectfulness - the ability to express respect and positive regard for another individual, both verbally and non-verbally.

5. empathy - the capacity to obtain and reflect a reasonably accurate sense of another's thoughts, feelings, experience; to "put oneself in another's shoes".

The development of these skills should become a major goal of education in a multicultural society in an attempt to promote harmonious interaction.

The issues facing educators are:

1. To identify the most effective methods of teaching intercultural communication.

2. To implement these methods in every curricula.

3. To assure that every sphere, from administrators to support staff, have the opportunity to develop these skills.

# BIBLIOGRAPHY

1. Burnet, J. "Multiculturalism Ten Years Later" in <u>The History and Social Science Teacher Journal</u>, Vol. 17 No. 1, Fall, 1981.

2. Condon, J. and Yousef, F. <u>An Introduction to Intercultural Communication</u>, Bobbs-Merrill Publishing, Indianapolis, 1975.

3. McLeod, K. "Multicultuarl Education, a Decade of Development" in <u>Education and Canadian Multiculturalism: Some Problems and Solutions</u>, ed. D. Dorotich, Canadian Society for the Study of Education, Saskatchewan, 1981.

4. Renwick, George <u>Evaluation Handbook for Cross-Cultural Training and Multicultural Education</u>: Intercultural Network Inc., LaGrange Park, Illinois.

5. Samovar, L. and Porter, R. <u>Intercultural Communication: A Reader</u> Wadsworth Publishing Co., Inc., California, 1976.

6. Pedersen, P. (ed), Draguns, J., Lonner, W. Trimble, J. <u>Counselling Across Cultures</u> University Press of Hawaii, U.S.A., 1981.

7. King, Nancy "Intercultural Communication: An verview of the Field" in <u>Multicultural Education: A Cross-Cultural Training Approach</u>. ed. M. Pusch, Intercultural Network, Inc., LaGrange Park, Ill. 1979.

8. Brislin, Richard <u>Cross-Cultural Encounters: Face to Face Interaction</u>. Pergamon Press, Toronto, 1981

Response To:   MULTI-CULTURAL PANEL
by
BOB BARTON


During International Year of the Child,
author P. L. Travers (Mary Poppins) wrote an
article in the New York Times, entitled
"Adventures Into Childhood."

In the article, Travers told a story about
three young boys, all brothers and newcomers to
her London neighbourhood, who tried to stink-bomb
her mailbox and were caught in the act. In conversation later with their father, Travers said
of the boys, "It's just that they don't know
where they are. They're lonely. They need a
sense of place."

She urged the father to spend more time with
his sons and to help them develop a sense of
locality.

Among her suggestions to the man was the idea
of personalizing the neighbourhood by linking
character, place and artifact with story .... any
story. She provided examples of what she meant
but the man was puzzled.

"Never heard of the Trojan horse.  What's he?
A Derby Winner?"

"Well Johnny Appleseed, Paul Revere,
Hiawatha....anything!"

Travers persisted and enthused that the man
should invent stories about local shopkeepers, a
hole in the road, public works of art. "This way
you build your personal world like a bird building a nest. A straw here....a memory there...."

As I listened to the papers presented today
and contemplated the rituals described in several
of them I found myself recalling the Travers article and thinking about the importance served by
those rituals in helping the individual to develop a sense of place and a feeling of belonging.
Moreover I thought about the position such rituals occupied in helping the individual to move

289

from the particular to the universal - from self to a greater understanding of the external world.

It is this awareness of the "otherness of things" which drama in education seeks to develop, for in drama the self concept of the learner will be stretched to incorporate other people, other things, other attitudes and other modes of behaviour.

Christine Turkewych highlighted in her paper the kinds of skills crucial to the fostering of intercultural communications. She indicated that these skills included learning how to learn, non-judgmentalness, the ability to react to new and ambiguous situations, the ability to express respect and positive regard for others and the capacity to obtain and reflect a reasonably accurate sense of another's thoughts, feelings and experience.

When children are engaged in drama, they are called upon to practice all of these skills and more. A class of ten-year olds, taking the roles of beleaguered serfs on a medieval manor, who must grapple with the problem of sowing the spring crops while their baron's errant knights interfere with the work, must employ imagination, identification, empathy, commitment, spontaneity and creativity if the dilemma is to be addressed to the best of their ability.

Much has been indicated in the papers presented today about the values of process - process which enables forms of knowing to be translated into the individual experience of the learner...

Process is what drama in education is all about. By means of this process time can be slowed in order to activate personal imagery and experience and to enable the unfamiliar to be absorbed into the realm of the personal. For those ten-year olds struggling with that problem back at the manor, drama will buy precious time - time to understand what they know and time to discover how to apply their knowledge to an entirely unfamiliar situation.

The words self discipline, concentration and precision have occurred with regularity in the presentations we have witnessed on this occasion. Although the words have been uttered within the context of mastery of specific skills, they apply equally to drama in education.

In drama the learner is required to bring full concentration to bear on questions for which there are no pat answers. The learner is also required to think deeply not only as an individual, but as a member of a community. In such instances the teacher does not furnish the answers but instead poses the difficult questions and challenges the learners' assumptions.

We have heard also today about the importance of building attitudes - attitudes of respect for knowledge, for excellence and for openness to learning.

Because drama in education leads the learner into unchartered territory it reinforces the idea that there is always more to be discovered about things if we are willing to think about them and about our thinking with respect to them.

Along the way, drama can help to develop language and writing, to build self confidence and to provide practice in problem solving, decision making and working co-operatively.

Central to drama, however, is the development of the imaginative thinking of the learner. The challenge to the learner is to produce the ideas.

# BIBLIOGRAPHY

Courtney, Richard    The Dramatic Curriculum, London, University of Western Ontario.

Davies, Geoff    Practical Primary Drama, London, Heinemann, 1983.

Greene, Maxine    "Literacy For What" in Phi Delta Kappan, January 1982, pages 326-329.

O'Neill, Cecily & Lambert, Alan    Drama Structures, London, Hutchinson, 1982.

PART II

TOWARDS A THEORY OF DRAMATIC INTELLIGENCE

# TOWARDS A THEORY OF DRAMATIC INTELLIGENCE
## An Edited Transcript of a Speech
### by
### Howard Gardner

Thanks very much, Bob, I am very pleased to be here, and I'm frankly delighted that the symposium is taking place. It's good for me to have the opportunity to come here because I have a chance to learn something about theater and drama. If memory serves me correctly I have never even been in a play and that's pretty amazing because, as I think about my kids, they all have been in numerous plays: if I was ever on stage, it was so long ago that it's really buried in the recesses of the unconscious. I love to go to the theater, but like many people I don't have as much time to do that as I would like.

I suppose that the reason Bob Colby was kind enough to ask me to come here is because at our research project, Project Zero, we have spent a lot of time thinking about how to conduct developmental psychological research in the arts. What I'm going to do is to share with you some of the lessons which we've learned: Dennie Wolf will give you another version based on her many years at Project Zero.

When one hears about the concept of developmental psychology of the theater or of drama, the first thing that strikes an outsider like me is that it's an extremely broad topic to look at. It's a bit as if you talked about the "developmental psychology of school" or "church" or "television" - some kind of an institution that is very widely represented in the society. So broad a sweep tends to make researchers uncomfortable. We like to be as narrow as we can, and so if you said the "developmental psychology of syntax" or "discrimination of pitch," I would feel more at home: that's something that's narrower and there's less of a chance of making a fool of yourself. Just in associating to the words <u>theater</u> or <u>drama</u>, it occurred to me that one could be thinking about acting, directing, producing, being an audience member, being a stage hand; no doubt many other kinds of roles also exist in the theater. One is talking about many media, not just the stage, but also television, radio, video disks; about all different kinds of performers from Marcel Marceau to Laurence Olivier, to Jerry Lewis, Richard Pryor, Marilyn Monroe, or a star of the soap operas. I mention all of these alternatives because I think it's very important in doing research to try to find some dry land, to try to narrow it down some, so that you can at least have some feeling that you're talking with your colleagues about the same thing. Otherwise if I say theater and you say theater, we might have very different kinds of conceptions in mind.

In my remarks today, I'm going to have in the back of my mind the developmental psychology of a skilled classical actor or actress. That doesn't mean everything I say pertains exclusively or primarily to that individual, but I think it gives some kind of focus if you examine one kind of sociological role.

As for today's game plan, I'll begin by talking about the developmental approach in general. Then I'll discuss a more specific variety of developmental psychology which we call the symbol systems approach; and even an even more specific one, which I have been developing recently, which I call Multiple Intelligences, or MI Theory. Next I'd like to give you some expectations of what might turn out to be similar to what we found in other art forms, and some speculations about how things might be different. Finally, I'd like to talk about some of the educational implications of the position.

DEVELOPMENTAL PSYCHOLOGY

One of the precepts of developmental psychology is that you have some kind of an end state. You can't talk about development unless you're talking about development towards something. Everybody who studies developmental psychology at least agrees about that. However, within developmental psychology, there are a number of different approaches. For instance, you have psychoanalytic case studies, the clinical approach, the information processing approach, and the Piagetian approach. It's the Piagetian

296

approach that I feel the closest to: and when you "buy into" that approach, there are a number of methodological and substantive assumptions which you make. One very important assumption is epigenesis. What that means is that there are certain developmental progressions which every individual is going to go through by virtue of being human. Still one has to live in an environment which affords certain opportunities for exploration, for activity and so on, for that growth to take place. If you took an organism and simply put it in a box or in a closet and fed it, there wouldn't be much development: development pre-supposes some activity in environment. There is also fidelity in the Piagetian approach to what's called the clinical method. This means you don't just give multiple choice questions or take electrophysiological measures: rather you work in an intimate and intensive way with individual children -- asking questions, watching them do things, exploring how they interact with materials, trying to get a "real-life" sense of what they're like as developing organisms.

This is not to say that the other developmental approaches are not epigenetic and do not use clinical methods, but Piaget has focused on this more comprehensively than other people. There are also more aggressive claims within the Piagetian tradition. One is that individuals go through a series of qualitatively different stages, and each of these stages has a structure. By a structure Piaget means an ensemble of operations which will be present in any organism who is at that stage, and these structures have a great deal of power. They cut across all different kinds of materials. A strong Piagetian approach assumes that there are stages like concrete operations and formal operations, and there are structures, which are brought to bear on any kind of activity that the organism is working with. Anybody who considers himself a card carrying Piagetian would adopt this position. Now having said what the approach is, and having indicated to you that I feel this is the most powerful approach we have in developmental psychology, I want to mention where many of us here depart from Piaget. One reservation is that Piaget has a very specific notion of what the end state of development should be, and that is the scientist. In fact, it's probably the physicist more than any other kind of scientist, but it certainly is a scientist. (Most developmental psychologists, being scientists, or at least wishing that they were scientists, are comfortable with that end state.) Obviously for individuals who are involved in the arts, that's not an adequate kind of end state, so there is objection to Piaget's notion about what it means to be developed. There is also a feeling that many of us have that there are vital aspects of personality and of emotional life which Piaget (for quite deliberate purposes) decided not to focus on: that is at least an insufficiency in his position.

Two other criticisms are ones which we of Project Zero are more likely to level than most other people. One is an increasing suspicion of general structures. General structures are these operations which are supposed to cut across all kinds of materials. Piaget says, when you're at concrete operations, you're at concrete operations with everything, so it shouldn't make any difference whether you are working with language or with logic, or with spatial reasoning, or with interpersonal relations, morality, or social development, you should always be at the concrete operational level; otherwise the theory doesn't hold water. We challenge that assumption. As you will see, the core assumption of multiple intelligence theory is a critique of the notion of general structures.

The second criticism is that Piaget doesn't pay sufficient attention to individual variations. He's interested in the norm, in the kind of developmental progression that everybody goes through: this is a very important initial approach for a scientist to take, but if you miss too much of the difference among individuals, then you may be missing the boat.

One of the things that I'm talking about is a word which shouldn't give people in this room any trouble and that's talent. People can be very talented at certain things. They can even be prodigies. There is no way within Piagetian Theory to account for a prodigy. If anything, the whole notion of general structures which cut across all materials would imply that if someone is a prodigy, he's got to be a prodigy in everything. We know from David Feldman's work that most prodigies are not omnibus prodigies --- they're prodigies in one or two things, and that causes a lot of difficulty for the Piagetian position.

## THE SYMBOL SYSTEMS APPROACH:

Anyway this prologomena amounts to saying that we take some general guidelines from Piaget, like the clinical method and the epigenetic approach. We are interested in stages and in general structures, but we are not willing to take them on faith. We need to be shown them, and this has led to the development of a position, which I am going to call the symbol system approach, which those of us in Project Zero, Dennie Wolf and many other people, including myself, have been exploring quite intensively over the past decade. We have also worked in collaboration with scholars elsewhere. I want to mention particularly the work of David Feldman at Tufts University, author of the book, Beyond Universals in Cognition Development. I also mention collaboration with David Olson from the Ontario Institute for Studies of Education and Gavriel Salomon from the Hebrew University, who is visiting us this year at Harvard.

Through discussions, writing, exchanges, and so on, we've come to the conclusion that what you really ought to do with the Piagetian position is to apply it to particular symbol systems, or what we sometimes call domains of knowledge. The general notion here is that there are various kinds of things that human beings can be good at, such as dealing with language, pictures, music; one calls them symbol systems from the individual point of view, and that what one ought to be doing is looking at how development occurs within each of these symbolic realms. So it then becomes an empirical question whether somebody's development with music has as much to do with the development of language or development of spatial skills. It might, but it might not. You don't assume it at the beginning as Piaget did.

There are other implications of the symbol systems approach, and I want to mention a few of them. One is, that within a symbol system, there may be certain abilities which are universal in that you expect everybody within the species to develop them. There are certainly aspects of language which everybody is going to develop, but there are others which only people who either have a lot of gifts, or work very hard, or do both, will develop, like having the skills to be a good poet. Feldman talks about a continuum from the universal to the idiosyncratic, to the unique, the unique being those skills which only a very few people, or only one person develops. If you think about this in theatrical terms, there are certain aspects of role playing or role assumption, which we expect everybody who is human to be able to develop to a certain extent. I throw out the term <u>politeness</u>, which is something that I think everybody - except perhaps people at Harvard! - develop to a certain extent, but obviously this can be developed to a very fine degree. You can be able not only to have extreme diplomacy, and finesse like a king or queen, but also to be extremely good at role assumption, and that's not something you could expect of everybody.

From the point of view of research, there are some other assumptions, which are worth mentioning. We find it very useful, within a particular symbol system or domain, to take a look at those skills which are particularly central in that domain. In the area of the arts, we've looked at things like the ability to represent - to have something stand for something else. This is obviously very important in symbolism and in art. We've looked at expression - the potential of a symbol to convey some kind of mood; sensitivity to reality and fantasy, which is important in many art forms - certainly very important in theater; sensitivity to style, composition, or balance. These are the things most psychologists would ignore because they aren't things that make any difference in the sciences. Indeed if you took a look at a psychology journal for things like expression or style or reality/fantasy or texture, composition or balance, you wouldn't even find it in the index: but these are things that are very important in the arts, and if you

300

want to understand what the development of skill in the arts entails, it is good to look for those kinds of things.

This leads to what may be the most important message that I can bring to those of you interested in doing research in this area. It's a message which I've issued before: you can't do good developmental psychology in the arts without collaboration between people who know something about psychology, and people who know something about the arts. I think virtually every effort to do good developmental psychology which hasn't involved such collaboration has foundered. In general, if it's simply a scientist who does it, he or she tends to become so microscopic, so concerned with the minutiae, that the kinds of findings that are obtained strike people within the arts as missing the phenomenon: I can give you hundreds of studies of music, for example, which were so focused on whether you could hear the difference between a D and a D flat, that they just bypass what's important in the area of music. The risk of restricting research to people who know a lot about the art form is that often they aren't very well trained in the sciences and so they don't do research which would withstand critical scrutiny. The other thing, though, which is more insidious is that people who are very involved with the arts usually love the arts and they are very afraid of doing anything which might violate what's important to them, but you can't do scientific research unless you are willing to leave stuff out. You can't look at everything. Einstein once said that the purpose of doing a chemical analysis of fluid is not to recreate the taste of the soup. (laughter) You can't do that recreation in science and you can't do analysis of the theater and make it feel like opening night. It's just not going to work, and I guess if it does feel like opening night, you might be in trouble anyway when the reviews come out.

Anyway we've had the most success at Project Zero when we've worked closely with the people who are knowledgeable in the arts and who aren't afraid of doing this kind of reflective analysis, and I think they would agree that it's been a symbiotic kind of relationship.

301

A final point I want to make about the symbols system approach is that it has a very nice agenda for arts research and arts education embedded within it. It's disarmingly simple, but I think it opens up a world and this was a world that was opened up for me by Nelson Goodman who founded Project Zero. Here is the insight: when you talk about symbol systems, you can essentially buy into the whole metaphor of literacy. Everybody knows about literacy with language and we all know it's important in education to learn how to read and how to write. That's what literacy is about, and we know that there are steps to help take and that people can become good at it and some people probably have more talent, but everybody can become better, more literate. I think it's extremely productive to think of every artistic realm, indeed, of every symbolic realm as involving literacy, so that an educational goal is to be able to make individuals, or to allow individuals, to be skilled in reading a symbol system, making sense of it. You can read music (by reading music I don't mean reading scores but rather knowing how to listen to it.) You can read paintings and know how to look at them; you can read drama, etc., and you can also write it. Again by writing it, I don't mean taking a paper and pencil, but rather creating something out of the medium: everybody has the potential to do something in the visual arts and musical arts, in dramatic and creative arts. We may not all have the same potential, but we all have some. So if you think about education as the development of skill in the symbolic activities involved in an art form, whether it be theater or music or literature, I think you forge a bond to a whole viable educational tradition and you also bind to a viable research tradition.

There's another corollary to this approach. Much research in the arts has foundered because people are insistent that they want to talk about quality and what's good and bad. I'm not saying that quality is unimportant - in the end it's the most important thing, but there is such a disagreement about quality, and there are so many skills which you need before you can even get into the question of quality, that I think it's very valuable for the researcher not to focus directly on quality, but instead to focus on the

302

skills tnat you need to be able to do anything. After all, you're not going to be able to write a good piece of music unless you can write music period and know something about harmony, composition, instrumentation and that kind of thing. Similarly, you can't listen to a work of music unless you know something, at least passively, about sonata form. That doesn't mean that you're going to be tne greatest connoisseur or the greatest composer in the world, but without those skills you can't even enter into the conversation. Moreover, I think it's a very useful thing for researchers not to worry so much about whether Johnny's play is better than Sally's play on some ideal dimension, but rather what are the skills that are involved in being able to produce a play at all.

Now, one of the problems with the symbols system approach is that there is no way of limiting how many symbol systems there are or how many domains there are. Essentially, you can go on creating them ad infinitum because there are no rules about what doesn't count. Therefore, in my own work I became interested in seeing whether one could, in fact, limit this endless source of symbols and domains. My own work, as Bob mentioned, has been divided between working with normal and gifted children, and looking at their development, and working with individuals who had brain damage as a result of a stroke or other kinds of pathology. I've been looking at these two populations as a way of understanding what's involved in high-level mentation of any sort, and in a sense children and brain damage patients have been a window for me to think about cognition.

MULTIPLE INTELLIGENCES:

As a result of this work over many years, I came to the conclusion some years ago that, in fact, there is a limited number of intellectual competences that people have the potential to develop, and I decided to call these things intelligences. The way I arrived at my list of intelligences was by bringing together information from a lot of different sources, information which, to my knowledge, hadn't been combined

before. In addition to the information about
development and information about breakdown
(breakdown proves particularly valuable because
it involves studies of what happens to the brain
as a consequence of various kinds of damage), I
also looked at what we know about exceptional
populations, -- prodigies, autistic children,
idiot savants, children with learning disabilities, indeed anybody with an uneven intellectual
profile. I looked at a lot of information about
cross-cultural cognitive abilities: What skills
are valued in cultures other than our own? I
think that our own view of intelligence is very
skewed towards what's been important in the West
in the last few hundred years, and it's not a
good representation of all the things that human
beings do well. I looked at what we know about
cross-species intelligence, the difference between humans, primates and other organisms. I
surveyed what we know about the evolution of
cognition over millions of years from the patho-
logical record and other kinds of records. And
last but not least, I examined what we know from
psychological research -- both experimental
research where we look at what kinds of abilities
transfer and which ones don't: and at psychometric research, at what we know about which
tests correlate with which other tests.

Anyway, this produced a very big bouillabaise
and I performed what I call a "subjective factor
analysis." Instead of putting all the data into
the electronic computer, I put it into my own
computer, which is smaller, and I came up with a
list of seven different intelligences, the so-
called mutliple intelligences.

Now, I'm not going to be able to persuade you
that mine is the right list. I don't even know
that it is myself, but I am convinced that human
beings are capable of a number of different
things, and perhaps most important for these purposes, I think that the symbol systems which we
use and the cultural domains which we value are
products of these intelligences, either viewed
together or separately. Some symbol systems and
some cultural domains really focus just on one
intelligence, but many others of them are combinations of intelligences, and on your right side,
on the board, I've listed the Magnificent Seven

304

(laughter); also known as the Seven Dwarfs
(laughter) and by even less positive characterizations by some of the researchers who had to
deal with this.

I'm going to mention what they are and give
you one or two examples so you can have a proto-
type in your mind. The epitome of linguistic
intelligence would be found in a poet. Musical
intelligence resides in a composer. Logical-
mathematical intelligence is found in a physicist
or mathematician, and I claim that what Piaget
has studied is logical mathematical intelligence
even though he would like to claim that his
theory would account for all of them. Spatial
intelligence entails the ability to negotiate
one's way around large-scale space and to build
and manipulate mental models of space. Spatial
intelligence gives me the opportunity to say that
no intelligence maps one-to-one onto an adult
role. Still if you know that somebody has a
highly developed form of intelligence, you can
predict the kinds of things they're going to do.
Somebody with a highly developed spatial intelligence might become an engineer, a surgeon, archi-
tect, choreographer, sculptor, aviator, and is
less likely to become a lawyer, an accountant or
conductor. Bodily - kinesthetic intelligence
involves skilled use of gross and fine motion
movement. Dancers and athletes who are using
their bodies to very different ends in many ways
exhibit the same kind of intelligence in my terms.
I also talk about two personal forms of
intelligence: an interpersonal form, which is
basically oriented outward to other people,
toward understanding other people, what they're
feeling, how they work, what makes them tick; and
intrapersonal intelligence, the same kind of
sensity directed inward to your own person.

I could go on and talk a lot about intelligences. That would be a mistake because that's
not what I'm here to talk about today. Instead
I'll say something deliberately provocative. I'm
going to speculate about what intelligences would
be important for an actor. It might even get in
the way because I don't think deductive reasoning, which is the keynote of logic, is of the
essence. I don't think spatial intelligence is
important either. Musical intelligence is also,

I think, irrelevant - not obviously if you want
to be Gwen Verdon, but for the average classic
actor.  On  the  other  hand,  bodily-kinesthetic
intelligence is extremely important.  In fact, in
my chapter on bodily-kinesthetic intelligence in
Frames of Mind, I begin with several pages on
Marcel Marceau from whom I learned a lot about
bodily-kinesthetic    intelligence.     Linguistic
intelligence is obviously important, though maybe
not for Marcel Marceau or Harpo Marx.  I think
the  personal  intelligences  are  also  of  the
essence, though I think it would be very revealing to discover which aspects of personal intelligence are most important.  For example, I am
not  so  sure  that  intrapersonal  intelligence  is
that important for an actor.  You need to know
the world of others but not necessarily the world
of yourself.

When we think about the development of these
intelligences, it may be that the intelligences
can be detected at a very early age.  In the
bodily-kinesthetic and linguistic areas, I would
look at how good kids are at imitating what other
people say; how they sound and and that kind of
thing, and what they do with their bodies; how
they walk, their fine motor and gross motor movements, and the child's ability to recognize how
other people are feeling.  This is hard to put
into   words,   but   interpersonal   intelligence
entails the capacity to recognize what's going on
in  the  situation,  and  similarities  which  cut
across  apparently  disparate  situations.    For
example, people can feel embarrassed in very different  kinds  of  situations.    I  think  it's  the
mark of somebody with a highly developed interpersonal  intelligence  to  be  able  to  recognize
that embarrassment is going on in both those
situations, and if they want to be an actor, to
be able to use their bodies, their language, and
whatever else to recreate embarrassment, independent on the particular incident in which that
embarrassment happens to be forthcoming.  I think
these would be early markers of a flair for the
dramatic.

Anyway, as I said earlier, in different cultural roles you have different blends of these
intelligences.  I claim that spatial intelligence
isn't very important for an actor but certainly

for a director or a choreographer, I think it's very important. I said logical-mathematical intelligence wasn't important for an actor, but I think the producer had better have some; the finance manager better have some, and probably the author had better have some too. I think it's also worth just footnoting that in different cultures or sub-cultures, theater might call in different blends of intelligences. I don't know anything about the theater in Bali or in Japan, but I wouldn't be surprised if a somewhat different blend of intelligences, for instance spatial intelligence might be much more important in Japan, so I wouldn't want to pre-judge that.


THEATER AND OTHER DOMAINS:

The next thing I want to do is to mention some of the things which we found out in looking at the development of artistic skills in other areas. One could use these to generate developmental hypotheses - - a list of findings which you might expect if you look at the development of theatrical abilities. One thing is that you might find a period between the ages of 4 and 7 where children have what I call first draft knowledge of symbol systems, like language, drawing, and scripts - what it's like to have a birthday party or go to a restaurant, or go to the dentist. Children would have these forms of knowledge in a high degree of readiness, so to speak. They could produce them quickly, and fashion interesting kinds of combinations among them. They might well be chaotic and they wouldn't be tremendously well organized, but the children would exhibit a certain imaginative flavor in the kinds of things they do in any art form, including the theater. These abilities are not subject to introspection by the child: rather they are a sign of having a new muscle that you're trying out to see all the different things it could do. This is the age in which figurative langauge is always very interesting, and I think the kinds of dramatic play which children do on their own or in some ensembles might display that kind of flair as well.

We find in middle childhood a period which I often call the literal stage. Now children are reluctant to be adventurous, to go out on their own, to combine things sort of spontaneously, much more interested in developing skills, learning how to do things the "right way"; and so in drawing, children want to learn how to draw in a representationally accurate manner. They want to know something about perspective. They want to be able to draw how someone looks, or what's it like for something to move. Similarly, in language they want to be able to make a poem that rhymes, has good meter, conveys a certain mood. I would imagine that if kids were involved in drama they would want to know what's the right way to act out a certain role or, to tell a joke so that it gets a laugh, that kind of thing. They would be very skill-oriented and I think that people who are involved educationally should be aware of that need at that particular time.

In other art forms when children become adolescents, there often is much more of a blending of their own personality, of what's important to them; their own emotional life becomes melded with the kinds of skills which they've acquired in the previous years. If they haven't developed skills, they probably will become very frustrated and they may cease altogether to be involved in the arts. If they do have enough skills, they will no longer want merely to marshall the skills without having a personal involvement with the materials. Rather they want this repertoire of skills to speak to who they are and what they want to achieve in life.

This leads to what Jeanne Bamberger has called the Midlife Crisis in the life of performers. It happens early in musical prodigies. I don't know about the theater, but I would imagine that as your voice changes literally, the way you think about yourself in the theater may also change. Anyway, this sequence of an early flowering, followed by an interest in the skill of building, and knowing how to do things the right way, and finally by a crisis where you try to combine your skills with the issue of who you are and what you want are the kinds of things which seem to recur in other art forms. I think one would do well to be on the lookout for them in theater.

What things might be different between theater and other art forms? Here, I become even more speculative. In the other intelligences, one is looking for sensitivity to fairly particular kinds of patterns -- sounds, to music, to words, and langauge, to visual configurations in the spatial area. I think that the kind of sensitivity that would be important in the drama is the sensitivity I spoke about before: Sensitivity to situations; how to size up what's going on quickly. Researchers haven't studied that because it's hard, but I have a feeling that this is going to be something that is particularly important in many other areas. I think the fact that you're always interacting with others, with an audience at least, and with other members of the troop, gives a very special flavor to the theater, and again makes it hard to study. It's the inherently interpersonal nature of the theater. You find prodigies in areas where kids can do things alone, like in music or in math, and where there isn't much knowledge of the outside world required. Obviously theater is entirely opposite on both of those realms.

I think in our own society the fact that theater is so charged with Hollywood, money, success and the "star syndrome" gives an additional flavor too. Children make a connection to being successful in the outside world, which you don't do if you're a mathematician; after all who knows what being a good mathematician can lead to when you're grown up? I think the whole relationship between who you are and the skills you're carrying on in enacting other roles, is going to be more acute in the theater. You can dissociate being a great chess player from your identity outside of the chess match, but I think it's increasingly difficult to do that in the area of theater. My own guess is that people with theatrical flair are acting all the time and they are trying out things all the time. We all know about the theatrical personality, and so the line between the skill and the profession on the one hand, and what's going on in other corners of one's life are more difficult to draw -- except in a society where there's a very specific cadre called acting.

I wanted to put it formulaically in terms of developmental psychology. To understand the theater you have to understand the kinds of symbolic skills that I'm talking about, but also the kinds of life crises that somebody like Erik Erikson studies. It's very hard to try to combine those two approaches, but I think it would be necessary.


## EDUCATIONAL ISSUES:

I want to say a few words about education -- not so much about theater in this instance, but about the sort of things relevant to the educating of intelligences. I think you can assess intelligences very early because in the first instance they are simply pattern recognizing and generating abilities. I have already suggested what I think some of those pattern recognizing abilities would be in theater. They would involve dealing with persons and situations -- not as microscopic as some of the pattern recognition abilities which might be important in logical-mathematical intelligence or in musical intelligence. I think the particular milieu in which somebody gains theatrical skills would also be very important to think about. Who are the agents that transmit the requisite intelligences? Where are they transmitted? Does a lot occur naturally in the every day world just by watching people? What is the role of the teacher? The role of explicit tutelage as opposed to just watching a great performer on stage? How much of the teaching takes place in terms or theory, or principles, or philosophy --- the method? or a method? To the extent that it takes place that way, people do need to have formal abilities of a logical mathematical sense, so that they can deduce what to do in a certain situation. That's very different from an educational philosophy where apprenticeship is featured and you just work with somebody, watch what they do, they correct you, and so on. Then a formal logical approach would be much less important.

My own notion is that in any intelligence, there are crystalizing experiences. These are situations in which a person becomes involved and discovers the sorts of skills that he or she has, the sorts of skills that he or she lacks, and begins to think about how to remedy the lack: From the point of view of the observer, what you want to do is to look at markers -- the things at different ages and stages which indicate who has average ability, who has exceptional ability, etc. In the area of drama, if you'd be on the lookout for people who once you say to them - "look you've got to hold your body the way x does" -- they will never do it any other way because it just instantly translates into the correct movement. You'd want to be on the look-out for people who seem to have that ability, but at a certain point get derailed: somebody may be fine until the age of 12 or 13, and suddenly something goes wrong. All of a sudden a new kind of skill is encountered -- maybe the difference between children's theater and adult theater -- and that can't be handled any more.

What I'm trying to say here is that there's a certain set of assumptions which go with multiple intelligences theory in the educational realm. First of all potentials can be assessed early. You ought to be paying attention to the usual loci where skills are imparted. Who is the usual agent? How much explicit training as opposed to more informal or formal tutelage or just observation? What are the crystalizing experiences where skills come together and can be recognized as such by the person themselves and by teachers and others? And, finally what are the markers? What are the things which you as an educator can pay attention to, to show that somebody has exceptional skill or is about to go wrong, if we knew exactly what wrong was?

I've been talking a lot about how developmental psychology and multiple intelligences theory might help to carry out research in theater and the arts, particularly about what it takes to become an actor, but I hope I've implied something about other skills as well. The final point I want to make is that it's a two-way street. I think that one of the problems with intelligences theory is that it talks about a lot of different intellectual potentials, but doesn't talk much about how they get put together. I think that studies of theater can be particularly useful in this regard because, after all, when a person appears as a performer, he is appearing as a whole person and he isn't just exhibiting one intelligence at one time and another intelligence at another time. He is really orchestrating, blending them together, making them work effectively, kind of as a troup all encased within one skin. We don't have any way of thinking about how that glue takes, about what kind of an organizing principle allows someone to work very effectively with his different intellectual skills and make them cohere. I hope that the kinds of ideas that people at Project Zero have been developing, might be of some help to those of you who are trying to think about analogous issues in the theater. At the same time, it's my expectation that to the extent that we understand what's involved in the theater in becoming an effective performer, it really should help us understand how people in general work even if they are not in the theater, and how any of us manages, so to speak, to get our act together.

DRAMATIC IMAGINATIONS
by
Dennis P. Wolf

## Introduction

It seems interesting to me that we have as
many different words as we do which describe what
human beings do with their minds. On the one
hand, we talk about the flashes of insight as
compared to rumination and problem-solving as
compared to intuition. But surpassing this sense
that there are different "flavors" of thinking,
language also hints at the fact that there are
distinctive forms of thought. We speak of mathe-
maticians problem-solving, painters sketching out
their ideas. In this essay I want to explore the
very particular way in which drama calls on
individuals to exercise their thoughts. By the
end of it, I hope to have outlined some of the
special qualities of theatrical imagining which
set it apart from imagination as it ticks away in
the brains of physicists, city planners, even
novelists or dancers.

Right away, there are some definitions that
need sorting out. I use the word "imagination"
rather than "intelligence" in order to make it
clear that the skills I will be talking about may
have little to do with knowing Christopher
Marlowe's birthplace, Restoration conventions for
scene changes, or the publication date for
"Little Foxes". This is knowledge about the
dramatic world; and I want to explore knowledge
in the dramatic world -- the thinking and imagining which actually makes a production unfold.
There are many forms of dramatic imagination --
the playwright's dialogue, the director's conception, the actor's interpretation, the making of
sets, the amplification of characters through
costumes, the creation of mystery, harshness, or
magic through lights -- these all count. However, here I am going to think aloud about just
two of those many kinds of dramatic imagination:
1) what I will call the enactive imagination of
an actor and 2) the linguistic imagination of a
playwright.

One way to pursue the question of what's special about drama or dramatic imagination is to develop a pedigreed description of it -- turning to the greats to see what Aristotle, Aristophanes, or Shakespeare wrote in their letters, announced to their students or wrote in their diaries. But those sources are familiar and well-used, whereas other, equally valuable, insights are untapped. For example, it's possible to look at theater in other cultures, Noh drama, Balinese rural theatre, North American ritual performances and, by comparing these different dramatic forms, try to distill the core or the essence of what a performer or playwright must be able to achieve. Closer to home, there is the option of examining the evolution of dramatic understanding within individuals, asking what it is that remains the same and what it is that changes as the "drama" of a peek-a-boo or chasing game becomes skilled performance or theatrical writing.

## Insights about artistic learning from children

For more than ten years, a group of researchers, some of them psychologists and some of them artists, all of us housed at Harvard Project Zero, have been studying children's ability to represent experience to themselves and to other people. Throughout this period, we have looked at those aspects of symbol use that matter to all human beings in the course of everyday life: the ability to form sentences, calculate with numbers, or make drawings. At the same time, we have been particularly interested in studying the more specialized sides of symbol use which artists articulate most clearly. In looking beyond the ordinary and necessary forms of symbolic development, we have investigated children's use of metaphor, their songs, and the small dramas they create in the midst of make-believe play. By watching children of different ages invent songs, poems, and plays, we have otained a glimpse at the way in which a general capacity for symbol-use gradually becomes specialized into the visual imagination of a painter, the kinesthetic sensitivities of a dancer, or the dramatic imagination of an actor. By comparing the performances of young children, adolescents and adults we have begun to outline the steps according to which the specialization of imagination occurs and the characteristic ingredients of a number of the different types of creative work. One of our most robust findings concerns the way in which even five year-olds (never mind older children) are aware of the particular demands within each of the different artistic domains. By way of example, I want to turn to our research findings on two distinctive types of imagination active within drama, the actor's "the enactive imagination" and the "linguistic imagination" of the playwright which I mentioned earlier.

## The development of enactive imagination

What do I mean when I talk about "enactive imagination"? Here an example is illustrative. Early in the Royal Shakespeare Companys' production of "Nicholas Nickleby" there comes a moment when Nicholas stands by watching Wackford Squeers teach the young inmates of Dotheboys Hall. The lesson is a torment and a travesty; Squeers delivers each question as if it were an insult rather than an inquiry, bullishly insisting that the boys spell "window" as he says it, "winder". The boys respond in a leaden, montonic chorus devoid of any individuality or spontaneity, eyes fixed and staring. From a balcony, Nicholas looks on -- while he says nothing, his eyes move back and forth between boys and Squeers, the tiny muscles that hinge his jaws quiver, the knuckles of his hands are white as he grips the railing. For me, this moment is an excellent example of what I would call "enactive" imagination. The actor is able to stand, breathe, even use his eyes as Nicholas might at that moment. Hence, it is difficult to dissect "enactive intelligence" into separate ingredients. But in a peculiar way, children's play, because it builds its sophistication gradually, may help make a list of the ingredients.

## Suspending the "here-and-now"

The willingness to suspend the priority of the actual or real circumstances in favor of "alternative realities" occurs in a range of human interchanges. In its simplest form we can discover it in peek-a-boo, when both partners experience the thrill of disappearance and search

315

even though both are still really seated face-to-face. Later, it takes more sophisticated forms -- the willingness to go on believing in the fiction of a puppet theatre, even when a hand reaches down from above to disentangle the strings, or to be involved by Cyrano's sword play, even though the foils are rubber-tipped.

The ability to produce and sustain this suspension comes quite early. Sometime between 12 and 18 months most children learn to pretend. In the second year this ability remains mild, children can drink out of empty teacups, pretend to take a bite out of a block, "drive" a pillow as if it were a car or bus. However, between the ages of two and five, children's capacity to create vivid pretend performances grows rapidly. Consider, for example, how many four year-olds are able to turn a living room into a harbor, with a couch for a boat and carpet waves. Their sense of an alternative reality is vivid enough that when you enter the living room to pick up your newspaper, they call out "Don't step there, you'll drown!" By five years, children are even able to preserve the "theatre" of their play by absorbing intrusions. They make accidents, stray visits from the dog, even phone calls, a part of the fiction, rather than letting these intrusions tear the fabric of pretense. For example, one four year-old we observed was playing birthday when her younger brother wandered through the space she had laid out as her party table. Rather than have her fiction break, she announced, in her best Irene Worth fashion, "This is the baby brother and he is always coming to bother the birthday party."

The way this four year-old hangs onto the illusion of theatre is impressive. It alerts us, as adult observers, to the centrality of the ability to pretend in an actor's intelligence. However, the child's handling of the boundary between theatre and life still has growing room. Beyond the four year-old's ken is the whole realm in which more sophisticated actors learn to play with the boundary between theatre and "real life", making it electric and illuminating. To offer an example: Once in a performance of "Waiting for Godot", I saw two women walk out noisily in the midst of one of the long dialogues about patience and waiting. Unphased, one of the actors rose to the occasion, and announced, "You know, Didi, not everyone is like us. I've known people who just don't understand there are things worth waiting for." At a level beyond impromptu response, much modern theatre after Brecht -- "Marat Sade" or "Nicholas Nickleby" -- plays with the suspension of disbelief, using asides, chases through the theatre, actors within the audience, costumed stage crews as means to enhance or joke about the theatre as a "world within a world." The example from "Nicholas Nickleby" contains a brilliant conception of how to create an alternative reality through theatre. The play's action is laid out so that the audience is in an envelope of fiction between Squeers and the boys on stage with Nicolas poised above them.

## The whole dramatic moment

A three year-old who is acting the part of a "parent" may drag a "child" around by any available limb, even while softly whispering "I'm going to put you to bed now." Similarly, a four year-old pirate can slash the air with a broomstick-cutlass and say "I'll cut you up" in a voice that sounds annoyed, rather than deadly. An eight year-old playing "The Little Princess" may sound sad enough as she cries herself to sleep in the attic, but she may look like she is lying on a beach chair getting a sun tan. During the school years, "enactive intelligence" faces a new season in which a major challenge is to harness many modalities -- voice, posture, gesture -- into increasingly <u>integrated</u> system for portrayal.

Our observations of socio-dramatic play during the early elementary school years suggest that children begin to think about the "whole" dramatic moment. Consider the example of Jeannie who, at age 6, is playing out an episode about putting on a birthday party. For a while she goes about her business of being the "mother" talking, whistling, and bustling about noisily. Suddenly, she has an idea, she whispers to her partner (who is playing the child) that she is going to make it a <u>surprise</u> party. From that moment forward the texture of the dramatic cloth changes: Jeannie tiptoes, whispers and lays

317

plates down so slowly you think that time has almost frozen. The particular dramatic moment -- that of the birthday preparations -- has become like a glass of clear liquid in which a particular emotional tone spreads, coloring voice, gestures and large-scale movement. Possibly, Jeannie is precocious, and certainly at six, she doesn't command a wide range of affects, nor can she convey complex states like ambivalence or remorse. But even if young actors harness words, voice, body, and props only in bold, familiar emotional landscapes, they begin to understand the way that separate modalities can echo and amplify one another.

During this same period, children etch out another understanding about the "whole dramatic moment". Again, Jeannie provides a clear illustration: One morning in the middle of her hallway, she is acting out the moment in Snow White when the witch comes with the apple while the dwarves are away at the mines. Jeannie has taken the role of the witch. Another player has the role of a dwarf. Together, they have agreed that Snow White "is behind the closet door." Jeannie is tottering toward the closet door with a blanket around her shoulders and an old Easter basket over her arm, cackling all the way. The "dwarf" stops to watch her. Jeannie notices and hisses out in a stage whisper, "No, don't stop. You have to go on doing the picking. You can't know I am coming." Incipient in her remark is the understanding that any one moment in a play is a slice across <u>all</u> the characters on stage. If an actress is in the scene, even though she is silent, her actions and presence must contribute to the whole. Just as voice and gesture are integrated into the portrayal of anger or suspense, all the different lines of action must add up to one whole dramatic moment.

The end result of understanding that a single dramatic moment is composed of many strands or threads is -- or may be, many years later -- the kind of moment in which Nicholas watches from the balcony. The actor playing Nicholas has harnessed all the channels -- intonation, glance, posture, and movement -- to "speak" the "enactive" language of drama. Even though it is Wackford Squeers who is doing the talking and the moving,

while Nicholas says nothing and stands outside
the central focus of the scene, Nicholas' silent,
agitated watching is an integral part of the dramatic moment.

Young actors, at least of Jeannie's calibre,
have a handle on what could be called the engi-
neering of a dramatic moment. At least intuitively, they know that drama makes use of many
"languages" at once -- speech, intonation, gesture, objects and that any one dramatic moment
arises from the tension between and across actors.
However, they may not be particularly able to
turn isolated dramatic moments into a continuous
flow of dramatic action which binds one scene to
another. Between six and twelve, children may
imagine their way into novel human situations --
they may be quite successful at acting, almost
breathing in character at highpoints -- but less
successful at keeping characters alive in slower,
more ordinary moments. However, development of
their ability to sustain dramatic actions seems
to me to be a matter of gradual expansion. A
remaining quantum leap for young actors lies in a
different direction.

## Metaphors, concretizations and interpretation

Many elementary-school actors concentrate
narrowly on realism, in the sense of detailed,
but straightforward recreations of the literal
details of characters, words and actions. However, as Polonius would have it, there is a way
in which actors can "by indirections find directions out". There is a level of acting which is
metaphoric rather than realistic. It has to do
with inventing elements of performance, outside
the already written dialogue, which "say" who the
character is or where the character is at that
moment in the dramatic action -- by showing
rather than by blurting out the information. In
the episode from "Nicholas Nickleby", the actor
has found ways to show Nicholas' horror at the
Squeer's school. Nicholas' silent position up in
to the balcony, at a great distance from the
classroom, signals his moral and emotional separation from life-as-usual in the school. Though
Nicholas is teacher at Dotheboys Hall, he will not
and cannot take part.

This faculty is interesting among enactive abilities -- while it is sophisticated, it is not abstract, in the usual sense of that term. To master this skill, an actor (or director), like a poet, must find what T.S. Eliot called the "objective correlative" -- a powerful, visible, often physical embodiment for an inner state. At their best, these "concretizations" are not straightforward "reports" on psychological information, instead, they are behavioral metaphors for what is going on within a character or between characters. Because these concretizations lie outside the script-as-written they provide the means for the interpretation and re-interpretation of even the most classic plays. The actress playing Ophelia, for example, can portray an innocent who is almost pre-adolescent in her naivte. In that case, the madness has a fragile, girlish quality. That mad Ophelia sings privately, but prettily, to herself, toys with her hair, dances in a wandering, helpless way. If Ophelia is played as older, intuitive, and full of feeling -- then her madness is made of shattered promises and deceit. To carry out that madness quite different concrete signs have to be invented -- torn clothes; a gesture of beheading flowers; cracked, driven singing. Clearly, in this ability to concretize a conception of the character lie the roots of interpreting not just of individual characters, but of whole scenes or works. Behind this interpretive ability lies a still broader notion that scripts are really only the beginning points for performances, they provide the bare bones over which a number of different dramatic anatomies can be fitted.

This ability to conceptualize and reconceptualize dramatic materials does not occur in the context of improvised socio-dramatic play. Instead, it is urged into existence when children make the transition from dramatic play to the performance of scripted works and when adults set young actors the problem of deciding "how they will play" the princess, the swineherd or the villain. Take for example the group of 10 or 11 year-olds who were working on a production of the "The Mikado". They knew the story and many of them had seen a televised performance. Still, they were somewhat at a loss to understand the notion of the Japanese court. In the course of

320

coming up with "stage business" the chorus members intuitively experimented with a number of different conceptions for the court and courtiers. Some of them wanted to take off on their ideas of Japanese tourists by wearing Sony Walkmans and fiddling with cameras. An Asian teacher argued that those images were derogatory, and the ten year-olds were back to square one. She showed them Japanese screens and scrolls. The children tried to capture their sense of the formality by moving very stiffly, but that led one child to comment "you look too much like robots and this isn't Star Wars, you know." They talked about what would make the slowness seem elegant instead of automated. Eventually, they combined slow movements with a kind of exaggerated courtesy. No great re-conceptualizations of "The Mikado" evolved, but the instance does provide a sense of the tentative way in which even ten year-olds can experiment with hunting for the right behavioral metaphors to back a performance.

The ten year-olds were limited by their supply of ready-to-hand metaphors and images. They had only cultural stereotypes, materials from Star Wars, or Brothers Grimm notions of court life to back up their dramatic experiments. With practice, training, and exposure to "real" theatre--all of which often come in adolescence-- these limitations may break apart. Take the example of a twelve year-old who was given the part of Sylvia in "Two gentlemen from Verona". In the early stages of learning her part, her characterization wobbled--she could not get a hold of a particular Sylvia, only various pale versions of a haughty princess. Several weeks into rehearsal, she was working on the scene in which she catches Proteus in his double-dealing ("You may have your wish, my will is even this/ that presently you hie you home to bed,/ thou subtle, false, perjured, disloyal man/..."). "Sylvia" and "Proteus" were working on the staging of the scene and had agreed that in the earlier portion, he would accompany his wooing and flattery with a long-stemmed rose. At that juncture, "Sylvia" stumbled on a way of concretizing her response to "Proteus". She took the long-stemmed flower from him--elegantly, as if genuinely taken. Then with a snap and gathering

321

speed, as she moved through her retort, she shredded the rose.

The point here is less whether this is the "right" or even an "insightful" dramatic device on "Sylvia's" part. The point is that adolescents are engaged by this kind of dramatic problem as actors. At least at an intuitive level, "Sylvia" recognized the expressive power of her gesture. The physical shredding was a strong visual analogue to the retort and had symbolic value (she was tearing up one of the conventional symbols of romanticism, a long-stemmed rose). As in other art forms like poetry or painting, adolescents have the capacity to see the several aspects, layers, or possibilities within an enterprise. "Sylvia", like other serious adolescent actors has re-defined the problem of acting. It isn't any longer just a problem of creating an illusion, or a whole dramatic moment, it also involves showing what the dramatic moment <u>means</u>.

## The linguistic imagination of the playwright

Clearly there are varieties of dramatic imagination within the theatre. Besides the enactive intelligence of actors, there are the visual intuitions of set, lighting and costume designers and what I will call the linguistic intelligence of a playwright. In this next section, I want to talk about this kind of linguistic intelligence and what we can learn about its essence if we look at its roots in childhood.

As a first step, it is important to get a sense for what sets the dramatic use of language apart from everyday speech or storytelling. Figures 1 and 2 present two versions of the early childhood of a famous German folk hero, the trickster, Til Eulenspeigel. The text in Figure 1 describes Til's infancy in the language of a folktale, whereas the text in Figure 2 presents the same events in a dramatic form.

Figure 1: A modern folktale version of Til Eulenspeigel's boyhood.

Only days after Til was born, it was clear he was no ordinary baby. Even Til's own grandmother said that in all her one hundred and ten years she had never seen a child the likes of Til. He bellowed and hollered and ate jam out of the pot with his bare hands.

In desperation, his poor mother put Til together with his two well-mannered, rosy-cheeked, clean-as-the-laundry, cousins. The instant Til caught sight of them, he knew they were more starch than soul. With a glint in eyes, he dashed out and wrapped his fat little jammy little arms around them. They, being much too polite to escape, were soon just as sticky as Til. What pleased Til even more than the jammy handprints on their backs, was the way his demure little girl cousin began to sling jam, too.

Figure 2: An excerpt from "The Marvelous Adventures of Tyl" by Jonathan Levy

Grandmother.
      I'm your grandma. Kiss Grandma.

      (She leans between Father and Mother, holds Tyl's head, and kisses him loudly. Tyl howls, turns, and bites her hand. She yelps).

      OW. He bit his grandma.

Doctor.

      He bites everybody.

Tyl.

      (Aside.) What can I do? I'm too young to explain.

Grandmother.

      (To Mother.) Marjory, I have to tell you something. I'll be a hundred and ten years old in March and I've seen a lot of children in my time. But I have never seen a child like this one.

Doctor.

>    And neither have I.

>        (Music. Tyl comes downstage and eats
>        jam out of a pot with his hands. The
>        Grandmother and Doctor are shocked.)

Doctor.

>    Look at your cousin Dietrich.

>        (Dietrich, a cut-out figure on wheels,
>        is rolled to the middle of the stage.
>        He is hinged at the waist and bows
>        politely.)

Grandmother.

>    And look at your cousin Sue.

>        (Suzanne, very ladylike, comes
>        downstage as if on wheels. Music out.)

Suzanne.

>    Little boys made horrid noise
>    And get in scrapes and messes.
>    Little girls wear cultured pearls and
>    long expensive dresses.

>        (Tyl smears jam on her outstretched
>        hand. She pauses, turns, then smears
>        the jam on his face. He put both hands
>        in the jam pot and is about to smear her
>        dress when the Grandmother takes her
>        hand and drags her away.)

Grandmother.

>    Suzanne! (The Grandmother slaps her
>    hand. Beat. She turns and slaps Tyl.)
>    Don't lower yourself.

>            (Music in.)

If we contrast these two renditions of Til's
pranks, what emerges is that the drama presents a
"present and particular moment" in contrast to
the story's "recollected and explained moment."

In plays, the language represents the talk of people caught in an immediate situation. In stories and tales, language, while it may capture some conversation, often concentrates on the organizing perceptions of an outside observer, the narrator. In drama that organizing activity belongs largely to the audience.

Thus, playwrights use words in special ways: Since they are writing "talk" they use a kind of immediate language which occurs largely in the first person and present tense and exhibits the structures and rhythms of oral speech. (With the exception of Suzanne's ditty, all the characters in "Tyl" speak conversationally). Second, because they are writing speeches for characters inside a situation they can write language which is context dependent, even elliptical. (When Grandmother says "Don't lower yourself" to Suzanne, we immediately understand what she means because we have just seen Suzanne smear jam on Tyl.) Finally, as the example of Suzanne and the jam pot indicates, words are only part of the drama, the writer also has movement, props, silence, music as raw materials.

## The kinds of language play: Dramatic and narrative

Many children in Western, middle-class cultures have the opportunity to engage in, not one, but two kinds of make-believe play. The first kind of play is often called socio-dramatic play. It occurs when children become actors and have to cope with either transforming real spaces and objects into imaginary ones or inventing the needed costumes and props from whole cloth. Anyone who recalls childhood remembers playing "store", "school", "Batman", "mothers", or more mysterious scenes. In this kind of play, children are involved in both composing and enacting episodes (e.g., what Batman and Robin will do and how best to simulate those superhuman feats given two pillows, a broom, and two old bath towels as props). The strong emphasis on "here and now" action means that this type of play opens an especially wide window on what I've called the playwright's linguistic imagination. A second form of play occurs when children project the imagined actions and dialogue onto small figures such as Smurfs, doll-house people, or stuffed animals. Although sometimes this kind of play takes on the dramatic format of a puppet-show, more frequently, the child uses the figures to act out or amplify a story-like narrative.

If we compare socio-dramatic play with replica play, we get a kind of natural laboratory in which to ask what even young children recognize as the special genius of dramatic as compared to narrative forms of language use. In a way, that sensitivity to the differences between "dramatizing" and "narrating" provides insight into children's hold on the playwright's particular skills and intuitions. By looking at age-related changes in these two kinds of play, we can achieve a kind of "time-lapse" view of how children come to understand the distinctive properties of dramatic language.

## Immediate language for "here and now"

Between the ages of three and five years, when children engage in socio-dramatic play, they speak in the first person, present-tense dialogue of participants. If they are playing out a chase, they may run from doorway to chair and back again, punctuating their darting back and forth with comments like "Hey, you. Come back here." By comparison, when children narrate the actions of small figures in replica play, they speak in the past tense about other persons, "The boy yelled at them to come back." Thus, by the time of kindergarten many children can distinguish a fundamental quality of dramatic as compared to narrative language. Basically, even young children intuit that in drama the words belong to participants, whereas in stories (even where there is conversation) many of the words are those of an observing narrator outside the flow of action.

## Talk vs. Explanation

During the early school years, the distance between dramatic and narrative language seems to widen still further. As they learn about written language, children (at least in literate settings) realize that the language in stories is meant to be "independent", while the language in dramas is meant to be "dependent". In a story, a narrator creates situations entirely out of words. Thus everything--even pauses and silences--must be committed to words. Since the words work alone to portray the scene, the characters, the actions and the talk, narrative language operates independent of props, gestures, or special effects. By contrast, dramatic language is often richly "dependent" on the situation being acted out. It is "right" for a character in a play to pick up an object, fondle it and say nothing more than "I see." But in order to create the "same" event, a storyteller would have to write, "When the old man entered, he saw what had once been his vase sitting on the rich man's table. He held it gently and murmured, "I see."

In order to demonstrate that even elementary school children have a feel for the difference between the dramatic and narrative uses of language, we have been showing kindergarten, first, and second graders a silent film about two children playing tricks on another child in a park. We have asked our subjects for both dramatic and narrative renditions of the film. Figures 3 presents the responses of one seven year-old girl.

Figure 3:

Portions of one seven year-old's dramatic and narrative renditions of a silent film.

The dramatic rendition (using small figures)

Boy 1:    Hey, quick here he comes.

Girl 1:   Let's hide in the bushes.

(Makes Boy 2 walk down the path through the park)

Boy 1 (whispering):  We can throw this hat out at him.

Girl 1:   He'll never know it's us.

(Makes Boy 1 heave the hat out onto the path)

(Makes Boy 2 stoop to pick it up)

Boy 2:   Hey, where did this come from?


### The narrative rendition

Once there were three kids in the park.
Two of them wanted to play a trick on the
other one.
They hid in the bushes until he came.
Then they threw out this funny-looking hat at
him.
He didn't know where it came from.
So he was surprised.


These renditions (and others like them) demonstrate how clearly elementary-school children
understand the rich interweaving of language,
motions and effects in drama.

Currently, this is as far as our research on
the language skills of drama has progressed.
Where older children are concerned, we have only
anecdotal information. But even such informal
observations suggest something about the task
which belongs to later stages in the development
of the linguistic imagination necessary to play
writing. First, there is the problem of writing
"in character". If you look at the seven year-
old's dramatization of the film, you notice that
the three children's lines are virtually identical. There are no clues in their speech as to
what makes one mean, another weak-willed, and the
third one innocent. The devices of accent, particular imagery, or an individual set of topics
haven't occurred to seven year-olds. Even
further ahead is the task of trying to make something larger happen in the course of making the
characters talk. Here I mean the way that Chekov
reveals the sisters' resignation in the closing
scenes of the "Cherry Orchard" or the way that
Fugard reverses the relation between Master
Harold and "the boys" just through what the characters say. These dramatic writing tasks build
on the foundation discoveries of younger children, but they are probably work for adolescence
and adulthood.

Conclusion:  A long-term view of dramatic imaginations

In discussing "enactive intelligence", I
sketched three fundamental abilities which appear
in a staggered fashion throughout childhood. The
ability to create an alternative dramatic world
appears first, showing up in the dramatic play of
pre-school children. The concept of a whole
dramatic moment can emerge during elementary
school, in young actors who have the opportunity
and the interest to try out, observe, and absorb
instruction. This sense for the whole dramatic
moment means that the young actors realize their
roles through voice, posture, gesture and movement and sustain that hold even when they are not
the focus of action. Finally, the notion of
interpretation and the ability to concretize a
particular interpretation of a dramatic moment
seems to belong to adolescents. Similarly, in
describing the early evolution of a linguistic
imagination, I pointed out how preschoolers
recognize the immediate qualities of dramatic
language and then how school-age children realize
the rich interplay between talk, gesture, motions,
and objects in drama.

I want to point out that these sequences are
additive:  no matter how early a particular skill
or intuition arises, actors and playwrights never
outgrow working on it. Children may "turn on" to
the possibility of creating an alternative world
as early as age three, but mature actors are
still involved in the problem. In that way, the
young child's transformation of the living room
couch into a boat evolves into the older actor's
ability to play with departures into the audience, turning them into a dramatic joke about
the separation of the fictional and actual worlds.

In talking about two distinctive kinds of dramatic imagination, I've used research from cognitive and developmental psychology to unravel and
describe some of the distinctive skills of performers and dramatists. At the end of looking at
these two distinct skills, I am struck by what an
interesting natural laboratory the theatre is.
First, it provides a very vivid illustration for
the fundamental diversity of human intelligence--
even within the microcosm of a closely-allied set

of professions. But, in addition, the theatre provides a powerful antedote to our usual conception of individual intelligence. Given the way productions combine the imaginative work of playwright, actor, and designer, the example of the theatre should provoke us to insist upon understanding, not just individual genius, but collaborative forms of intelligence and invention whether they occur in plays, architecture, or scientific research.

References

While this is not an academic paper carrying references to scholarly works, for those readers who are interested in reading more about the research into the development of artistic skills which is conducted at Project Zero, I would like to recommend the following:

Gardner, H. (1983). Frames of mind. New York: Basic Books.

Winner, E. (1982). Invented worlds: the psychology of the arts. Cambridge, Ma.: Harvard University Press.

Winner, E. and Gardner, H. (1979). Fact, fiction, and fantasy. New Directions for Child Development, 4. San Francisco: Jossey-Bass.

Wolf, D. and Gardner, H. (1979). Early symbolization. New Directions for Child Development, San Francisco: Jossey-Bass.

A publications list which includes numerous specific articles can also be obtained by writing: Project Zero, 321 Longfellow Hall, 13 Appian Way, Cambridge, Ma. 02138.

META-THINKING:
THOUGHTS ON DRAMATIC THOUGHT
by
Virginia Koste


First, thank you for the honor and plague of
this burdensome opportunity to give a small talk
on a large subject, to venture some finite
responses to infinite questions. I am helplessly
in love with these questions, and with the very
idea of a symposium about them. When you stop to
recall that at its root "symposium" means "a
drinking party" (ah, those Greeks!), you realize
that this is a kind of cerebral celebration of
the addictive thirst which inebriates but is
never quenched. Thought-oholics Anonymous, high
on ideas. Thinking about thinking: a heady chase.
Symposium -- a drinking party at Harvard, the
found week-end; it makes you see afresh the lusty
reality of metaphor in human history. Which
brings us to our questions -- questions which may
not be difficult to answer, but impossible. And
so, of course, irresistible. Like Saroyan's Joe,
in The Time of Your Life, "I'm in love with the
possibilities." Passionately.

A symposium draws us together by what Dr.
Pamela Rooks calls the passion to find out, a
basic motivation in all arts and sciences, though
details and languages differ. Artists and scientists are bound by audacious humility: that
paradoxical state of mind which is at once awed
and emboldened by the urge to conceive the in-
conceivable and know the unknowable, the siren
call that makes the famous, infamous temptations
of the flesh seem pretty mere.

So what is the nature of the dramatic intelligence, if there is such a thing, and how does
it work (and play), and what/where are its
origins? Well, it is some comfort that Einstein
used to say, "Ladies and Gentlemen, if I knew
that, I would know everything." (Bronowski,
1978, pp. 102-103). And Abraham Maslow, after
one typical outpouring of provocative notions,
suddenly confessed, "What this means I don't
know" (1968, p. 114). Like Button-Bright, the
always lost-and-found child wandering through Oz,
we must go on saying "I don't know" to certain

hard questions. In both science and art it is essential to maintain the skill of suspending judgment, to resist the temptation to give false answers when we are just getting good at asking true questions.

At the core of my own life work is a statement that I happened on in a <u>London Times</u> liner twenty-odd years ago: "Understanding the atom bomb is child's play, compared with understanding child's play." As we keep on stubbornly trying to figure out a little more about these complex processes, I feel the sense in Henry Miller's remark that "understanding is not a piercing of a mystery, but an acceptance of it, a living blissfully with it, in it, through, and by it" (1941, p. 181). That may sound evasive and far-artsy, but it may be instead a useful refusal to be seduced by habits of dichotomizing, rubricizing, and counting phenomena which decline to be thus apprehended. In studying the nature and functions of dramatic play and thought, orthodoxy must yield sometimes to paradoxy; the ways to knowledge are less likely to be straight and narrow than curved and wide, especially in the high-wire act of the human mind presuming to study itself. Bronowski says:

> We none of us know. And what is so exciting about research on the brain at this moment is that although we do not know, we can see how it must go. It is clear that the mind can get this enormous richness because it has a huge number of connections. And these connections are not of the push or pull type, but of some other type in which every connection modulates every other. The result is that the brain must be using some kind of statistical language which is quite unlike human language...different from any statistical language that we use; we do not know how it goes, but this is what we have to discover. I guess that the discovery will take us the rest of the life of the universe. But meanwhile, I hope that we shall make some progress (pp. 103--104).

Working in the world of drama and theatre, I suspect that dramatic thought eludes the merely conscious, straight gaze. Maybe one way into

studying dramatic thinking is through thinking
dramatically; maybe one way into studying play is
to think playfully. That, I hope, only _sounds_
simple-minded, because I have a hunch that _it may_
include a wider range of processes than a first
glance reveals. Anyway, here is a cluster of
clues, in no particular order, because they are
not linear or sequential or ranked but instead
seem to exist simultaneously and inter-
connectedly.

I continue to surmise that the processes of
natural dramatic play in childhood are the
sources of mature creative processes and may be
essentially identical to them. Perhaps they are
separated only by degree points along the same
continuum, and perhaps they can be studied in
parallel and inter-connectedly. To some extent
this is already happening, of course.

I suspect that dramatic thought, whether in
child's play or adult dramatic work, is centered
in the mental act of transformation. Further, I
think that most natural play is, by that definition, dramatic--even manipulative play, if the
blocks, rocks, etc. are made (perhaps silently,
internally) symbolic, so that imaginative projection takes place; even such games as tag, if the
players (perhaps unconsciously) experience
escape/pursuit interactions metaphorically. Such
transformational thinking, we now recognize,
begins early. How do five-month-old babies so
quickly become expert at playing peek-a-boo, that
precocious drama about what Dr. Louise Kaplan
(1978) calls "the enigma of disappearing and
reappearing" (p. 144)? To thus internalize the
metaphor of being lost and found, of separation
and reunion, is an awesome symbolic experiment in
grasping inter-related planes of reality through
transformational enactment--a playing out with
the whole body/mind of that problem-solution plot
which is the paradigm of so much life experience.
This amazing capacity to think symbolically by
means of the dramatic imagination is noted by Dr.
Kaplan, who writes in her book _Oneness And_
_Separateness_, "The baby who once in a while prefers the illusion of his security blanket to the
actual presence of his mother is neither madman
nor cynic--he's on his way to making metaphors"

(p. 156). I submit that in fact he may be already living a metaphor.

Bronowski says that "all the paradoxes of literature arise from our attempt to speak simultaneously of ourselves as both knowing selves and as known objects" (pp. 94-95). Dramatic play, dramatic thought are at home with such paradox; simultaneous subjectivity/objectivity occur as in dreaming. Jamake Highwater, in The Primal Mind (1981), maintains that such dichotomies are in fact inventions rather than natural divisions. The convention of regarding objective and subjective as polarized perspectives fogs the lens. Mike Nichols (1978) says of Elaine May's improvisational performances that she could "simultaneously comment from without and fill it from within...being completely real, saying things for the first time. She's clearly just thought of them and she's really feeling the things, but also she's outside saying, 'Did you ever notice this about this kind of person'" (p. 87). I bet that such multiple simultaneous viewpointing is intrinsic to dramatic thinking. For further light on this and related ideas read Dr. H. Giffin's The Metacommunicative Process In Collective Make-believe Play (1981).

Similarly, divergent and convergent thinking seem to me to be simultaneous in dramatic thought, or at least interlaced in speed-of-light rhythms, with freely experimental ideas soaring off multidirectionally, perhaps flung, flown from a focal thought which both launches and magnetizes them back from their fancy flights like bevies of boomerangs. That is, dramatic thought can both "wander" and also choose its points of departure and destinations holistically, spontaneously.

And dramatic thought, I believe, is holistic and spontaneous. It takes place in the primal realm where all natural resources are available, where past and future are contained in the present moment, where no dichotomy between mind and body, memory and foreseeing exists. Inner and outer fuse, as do what we call conscious and unconscious (or preconscious), affect and cognition, emotion and intellect. Right and left collaborate; intuition and analysis combine.

336

Sweat and cool conjecture commingle without contradiction.

Now, such thought burns juice but does not
waste it. The extravagant expenditure of energy
characterizing dramatic thought (whether in
child's play or adult work) relaxes thought flow,
and the consequent accelerated thought-flow cycl-
ically further energizes.

Also, the emotional, physical, and mental
catharsis of playing through dramatic situations
and actions--both expressed and internal--purges
inhibiting tensions and disarms mental censoring.

I see curiosity (the passion to find out) as
both a cause and effect in dramatic thought processes. Curiosity is both temporarily satisfied
and recurrently aroused; here again, fulfillment
and drive intermit or coexist.

Break-through thought (whether only for the
individual himself or for others as well) is
allowed, both internally and expressed, because
of the psychic safety of the promise and premise
that everything is "unreal". The impunity
guaranteed by this "otherly real" tacit tenet
catalyzes connections otherwise forbidden; conventional distinctions between "possible" and
"impossible" are transcended. (For instance,
requirements for belonging to a ten-year-old's
witch club included "Take a bath once a week" and
"Know how to fly through the air.") Advanced
adult creative thinking also involves such seemingly incongruous juxtapositions. In this meta-
world closed, imposed patterns need not be tole-
rated, so that unrestrained invention is
empowered. Freedom of choice and the license--
the necessity--to originate are not only permitted but required by dramatic play and
thought. I wonder if the child in Piaget's so-
called pre-operational stage might be abler to
imagine certain concepts of time/space than are
most older minds, because his thought modes are
as yet less contaminated by imposed patterns of
linear, logical reasoning.

Another inherent component of dramatic
thought and play is empathy, permeating both imi-

tation and transformation. The mind enters into what is observed; the recording of stimuli is instantaneous and can be accomplished without such physical materials, delays, and skills as are required for drawing, for example. This mental, kinesthetic indentification with otherness (not only other persons, but also natural forces, conditions, objects, ideas, images) seems to be a main means of understanding. Internalizing, absorbing of observed phenomena as a way of knowing connects with the functioning of dramatic empathy.

In pure dramatic play the process itself is all; it is enough. There is no product, nothing material to keep. There are often relics, of course: collected bits of costumes, scenery, props, where such materials are used. But the playing itself, like live theatre, is absolutely ephemeral. The implications of this fact are rarely recognized fully enough. The purity of genuine dramatic playing in childhood arises from its imperviousness to material record; the child knows intuitively and surely that moth and rust cannot corrupt it nor age wither it; it cannot be stolen or borrowed, used or abused. The child himself completely controls and owns it; he can risk giving himself totally to his dramatic play because no one can possibly examine it, judge it, or take it away from him, and because he cannot be proved responsible for it. All of this because it vanishes instantly in time and exists completely in the present. Of course, this is fully true only of play which is private, unselfconscious, and in a self-selected place and time. If so (like Dr. Margaret S. Mahler, among others), we may need to reconfirm the value of that mode of research which is grounded in careful observation of ordinary human behavior occurring in natural settings, as one essential means of studying these processes.

Maybe dramatic play ignores or transcends categories. Maybe dramatic thought pervades the child's play, sometimes externalizing itself as spontaneous dancing, singing, writing, painting, building, costuming, sculpting, as well as acting. The mind experiments with symbolic thought, transforming sand into castle or garage into theatre, and transforming itself into multiple

338

rotating identities, situations, and forces. Symbolic thought. Transformation. Empathy. Holistic exploration, connecting known and unknown. "The very existence of play," says Huizinga in <u>Homo Ludens</u> (1950), "continually confirms the supra-logical nature of the human situation" (p. 3). Dramatic play releases thought streams in all of their varied forms and modes, suspending them in a mental fluidity conducive to spontaneous invention and discovery, catalyzing connecting of aspiration with realization, later with now, known with unknown, legend with life.

Now, if it is in the nature of these processes to function holistically and to some degree invisibly and inaudibly, they are not easily accessible to analysis. Besides, they are, of course, always in motion, and made up of myriad, inseparably interconnected parts which naturally resist isolation and identification; the relationships between them and of each to the whole are likewise elusive. This spontaneous streaming of symbols--imaging in motion--is not yet very graphable or photographable. To study the mind, the mind's eye as well as the camera eye is needed. To the extent that it is possible to see the inner dramatic play of one's own mind, whether the total body/mind sensation of a moment from childhood or from last night's dream or from a present, waking dramatic thought, we can glimpse insights into these processes. In my book on this subject (1978) I tried to capture the dramatic play of children dramatically, through its observable manifestations: recorded narratives of actual scenes, scenarios, and scripts of and by children themselves. I have great expectations of other ways being used in various disciplines--including our own--and of still other methods yet to be found. Maslow wrote:

If it is our hope to describe the world fully, a place is necessary for preverbal, ineffable, metaphorical, primary-process, concrete-experience, intuitive and aesthetic types of cognition, for there are certain aspects of reality which can be cognized in no other way (p. 208).

If dramatic play and thought will not hold still to be categorized and labelled, if it is not linear and cannot be perceived within the strictures of Aristotelian habits which are inherently at odds with the phenomena being investigated, it may nevertheless be characterized by a high, internal order. I recently read that "in a quantum leap for physics, researchers are recognizing...'chaos'--a previously unknown side of nature...'Because chaos may in fact be a higher form of order, the science of chaos,' says mathematician Ralph Abraham, of the University of California at Santa Cruz, 'represents a new paradigm, a turning point in science'" (Begley, Carey, and Kahn, 1983, p. 53). It is exhilarating to hope that the complexity of our subject need not intimidate us, even in what Bronowski called "an age in which most nonscientists are feeling a kind of loss of nerve" (p. 112). If dramatic thought is not irrational but what might be called metarational, if it is multidirectional rather than simply sequential, if it is multi-levelled rather than plainly planed, if it is mobile rather than stable, then perhaps our ways of contemplating it must be all of these as well. I do realize the joke--the intrinsic irony--of this paper, trapped in the verbal mode, struggling to touch on, hint at some small part of the restless realities it talks about, using words to say that words and such are not enough.

And at last, why my word meta-thinking? Well, getting back to origins and connections, the Greek meta denotes change, beyond, after, among, over. And the Old English word thought means both thinking and feeling combined. To me it is a significant and useful fact that millenia ago such different languages were already struggling to create words that could suggest mental transformation and the commingling complexity of the mind's motions and emotions. So my observation/experience of thinking in night and day dreaming, in playing, in writing, acting, directing leads me to suggest that meta-thinking involves maximal mobility and simultaneity of multiple image and idea formation and transformation out of a holistic sense and sensibility of a high, chaotically conceptual order, freely fusing concrete and abstract, psychic and sensory, temporal and spatial, cognitive and intuitive. By

340

whatever names we know, these multiple modes merge and mesh around, interact, overlap, recombine in ceaseless mental motion. Detached and involved, embracing first, second, and third-person viewpoints, they at once crystallize past sums of memories and future-focussed hypotheses in merged time, looping, leaping, spiralling in the always present present. Adults whose childhood practice in private, natural dramatic play and thought has been sufficiently strong and sustained to maintain and transmit this meta-thinking have the power to include, absorb, and transform other minds in that mature playing which we call dramatic art.

# REFERENCES

Begley, S., Carey, J., & Kahn, R. (July 18, 1983). Finding the order in chaos. Newsweek, 53.

Bronowski, J. (1978). The origins of knowledge and imagination. New Haven: Yale University Press.

Giffin, H. L. N. (1981). The metacommunicative process in collective make-believe play (Doctoral dissertation, University of Colorado, Boulder).

Highwater, J. (1981). The primal mind: vision and realty in Indian America. New York: New American Library.

Kaplan, L. J. (1978). Oneness and separateness: from infant to individual. New York: Simon and Schuster.

Koste, V. G. (1978). Dramatic play in childhood: rehearsal for life. New Orleans: Anchorage Press.

Maslow, A. H. (1968). Toward a psychology of being. New York: D. Van Nostrand Company.

Miller, H. (1941). Reflections on writing. In Ghiselin, B. (Ed.) (1961). The creative process: a symposium (pp. 179-186). New York: The New American Library of World Literature, Inc. (a Mentor Book).

Rooks, P. A. (1982). Man in his wholeness wholly attending: D. H. Lawrence and aspects of modern thought (Doctoral dissertation, University of York, England).

Sweet, J. (1978). Something wonderful right away. Interview with Mike Nichols (pp. 72-88). New York: Avon Books.

# A FEW RELECTIONS ON "DRAMATIC INTELLIGENCE"
## by
## Jonathan Levy

Goethe said "The Will cannot do the work of the Imagination;" to which I would add, "And vice versa." There are simply too many true ways of knowing for any one of us to pretend to know it all. Who, for example, would we say knows more about Shakespeare: Harry Levin, Harvard's great Shakespearean emeritus, or Sir Lawrence Olivier? We wouldn't say, if we had any sense, because the question has no right answer. They both know Shakespeare profoundly, but they know him in different and -- and this is really my point -- in complementary ways.

I am convinced the best way to approach a new question is to gather different kinds of knowers in one place and let them talk at each other, on the theory that the common ground they find between them will become beachheads to further investigation of the question. That is what Charles and Bob have done today, and I am grateful to them for doing it. For, clearly, the stated subjects of today's conference need as much light shed on them from as many diverse quarters as possible. "Toward a Developmental Psychology of the Theatre" and "On the Nature of Dramatic Intelligence" are huge subjects. Either of them (to paraphrase the Passover service) would have been enough: enough to keep us here, talking, for weeks.

But the subject this conference implies is greater still. For our implied subject is no less than "Children and the Theatre: What happens when these two mysteries are combined?" And that is a subject I am sure you'll agree which would keep all of us in this room occupied for the rest of our working lives.

Therefore, before I respond to Howard, Denny and Jinny, let me respond to this occasion. Let me suggest that this be the first of many such gatherings; that we agree to meet regularly to pursue our subject, and that we add to our future meetings other kinds of knowers, from historians of education to working actors. I say this because I believe that we are very possibly at the beginning of something grand, in both senses of the word: something big and something splendid.

I thought a great deal about what I could usefully add to today's discussion. I decided immediately to avoid anything vaguely scientific, especially Psychology. I am no psychologist and don't pretend to be one. (As I have learned today to my shame, I can barely speak the language).

What I am is a playwright and a teacher. I have written lots of plays and watched them worked on in rehearsal. I have worked with colleagues on their plays. And I have taught playwriting, both to gifted young professionals and to stray dull-normals who wandered into my classes because they had been closed out of "Sex and Society" and "Elementary Calculus."

I have also had a good deal to do with theatre for children because many of the plays I've written have been children's plays. And I have spent time thinking about what I suppose could be called Education for the Theatre, both for my classes and, more broadly, at Lincoln Center, which supports an Institute for the Arts in Education with which I was associated for some years.

What I finally decided to do is to make three quite different points, each arising from a different part of my theatrical experience; all, I hope, touching in some way on today's subject. Today, as I conceive it, is a day to lay whatever cards we think we hold on the table. Later we can try to match them by suit and sequence.

First, I'd like to put a few questions to the company at large. (I have already asked a couple of them to Howard and Denny in private). They are questions which came out of my practical work in children's theatre. I had to put them aside at the time they occured to me because of more pressing questions: e.g., Would the turntable work tonight? How would we keep the character man sober between the matinee and the evening performance? But the questions stayed with me and today, I thought, would be a good time to ask them.

Second, I wanted to offer a little unsupported conjecture on the nature of Dramatic Intelligence.

And third, I thought I would show you, for what it is worth, a hypothetical school curriculum for Education for the Theatre which my colleagues and I at Lincoln Center drew up. These last remarks will take the form of an anecdote with snapshot.

First, the general questions about children and the theatre. I can put them very briefly. Since I seem to be taking my text from the Passover service, let me ask four of them:

1.  When we say an audience of children "loses" itself in what is happening on stage, what do we mean?

2.  When we say a child "identifies" with a character on stage, what exactly do we mean? (Perhaps this is a corollary of the first question).

3.  What do children understand about character? How subtly and deeply do they see it?

4.  Since so much of children's theatre is implicitly or explicitly didactic, how much of what is taught is learned? For how long? How deeply, compared to experience in real life? (I am asking this about child actors as well as child audiences). In short, since it is generally assumed that the theatre can teach, I am asking: can it? And, if it can, how and what?

Second, a quibble and two thoughts on Dramatic Intelligence.

The quibble is only this. The phrase "Dramatic Intelligence" bothers me. I think in (and through) words, and the words "Dramatic Intelli-

gence" don't help me get nearer the fact. Quite
the contrary. I find I have to put the words out
of my mind in order to think about the fact. I
do understand that Howard uses the word "intelligence" in this context as a technical term, as a
term of art; and that the term is usefully parallel to the other sorts of intelligences he has
identified. Still, at least for my private use,
I would like to find another word or phrase, a
nickname possibly, which might, like some nick-
names, make the subject more approachable. Perhaps you will say that those of us who make
things out of words get into the lazy habit of
expecting the words themselves to do half our
thinking for us. If so, I plead <u>nolo contendere</u>.
In any case, I will gladly and gratefully keep
using the phrase "Dramatic Intelligence", until,
as the song has it, the real thing comes along.

So much for the quibble. The first thing I
really want to say about Dramatic Intelligence is
that, as I understand it, it operates almost
exclusively in the conditional and the subjunctive, which will make it hard to observe and to
measure. Actors, unlike writers, don't leave
drafts. And playwrights, who do leave drafts,
leave in them only a thousand-thousandth of what
has passed through their minds. Dramatic Intelligence appears most characteristically not in
the work finally forged but in the sparks thrown
off in the forging, and you cannot collect sparks.
You can only collect gray ashes which were once
sparks. A finished play, reduced to its published version, or a finished production, frozen
on the Stage Manager's cue sheet, can be an
admirable artifact. But we must realize that the
Dramatic Intelligence which fashioned it is long
since gone, probably into hiding, where it is
teasing itself into another foray.

The second thing I want to say about Dramatic
Intelligence is that an essential part of it --
perhaps <u>the</u> essential part of it -- is double
vision. It is always in two places at once.
From the outset it incorporates the simultaneous
sense of doing and being seen doing, of making
the gesture and calculating the effect of the
gesture. It incorporates both the dancer at the
barre and his mirror. Dramatic Intelligence
requires the presence of an implied observer.

346

Indeed it is perhaps the presence of this implied observer which, in the prototypical case, distinguishes acting from simple play.

What I am talking about, I suppose, is self-consciousness, because self-consciousness implies (perhaps requires) a simultaneous consciousness of others. So here is my first unauthorized hypothesis of the day: If Self-Consciousness is a developmental stage -- and if it's not, what is? -- perhaps there can be no fully developed Dramatic Intelligence until after the onset of Self-Consciousness.

Third, the hypothetical school curriculum: the anecdote with snapshot. Perhaps, as is the case with most snapshots, it will be more interesting if you know a little about who is in the picture.

Lincoln Center has always had an Education Department. For years it did little more than send performers into schools, where they would play their Brahms or do cut Romeo and Juliets and go, leaving (it became increasingly clear) very little behind. Then it occured to someone to send artists -- artists, not teachers -- into the schools to introduce the work before it was performed and answer questions about it after it had been performed. This arrangement turned out to be much more satisfactory for everyone concerned -- students, teachers, and performers -- and Lincoln Center did more and more of it until the extended residencies of artists in schools became at least as important as the touring performances.

Those were the days when there was public money for a variety of Artist-in-the-Schools programs, and many flourished. But in the mid-seventies it became clear that this was very soft money and would not be around forever. The immediate problem then became how to design a program which would continue in the schools after government money had run out and Lincoln Center established an Institute for the Arts in Education to address itself to this problem. I worked at the Institute for several years.

The program we developed was, I think, theoretically a good one. We teamed working artists -- performing artists, mostly, because the performing arts are Lincoln Center's strong suit -- with interested teachers. Together, relying on one another's expertise, they were asked to devise and test small bits of what eventually we hoped would become a program in Aesthetic Literacy which would then become a regular part of every school's curriculum.

I don't have to tell you that this did not happen. The reasons why I think it did not happen are not germane to today's discussion. What is germane, I believe, is the thought that went into inventing the curriculum. It is germane partly because over the years some very good artists put their minds to educational questions working artists rarely have occasion to consider; and partly because what we are fumbling to do seems in many ways complementary to the work Project Zero has been doing so remarkably for years. To put it simplistically, it seems to me that those "intelligences" they have been seeking to study and understand, we were trying to elicit and refine.

In any case, one spring day the Institute assembled three groups of artists at Juilliard: dancers, musicians and theatre types. Our brief was outline an overall curriculum in our own art which could then be reduced to small units and tested in the schools. Each group met alone for most of the day. In the late afternoon, the three groups came together to compare results. I remember being astonished at the number of ways in which the three curricula were similar, especially theatre and dance.

I don't know where the music and dance curricula are. I hope someone thought to keep them, as I kept the theatre curriculum. It is the product of the imaginations of the five people whose names appear under the copyright sign in the lower right-hand corner of the chart: Tom Bullard, David Shookhoff, David Trainer, Andrew Wolk and myself. I gave you my credentials. The other four are all working directors, and Trainer and Wolk are playwrights as well. All of us had had some experience working with children, and Bullard and Shookhoff had a great deal. Everyone but me was then in his early thirties and thus

348

fairly close to his own Education in the Theatre.

This is the curriculum we drew up. Most of it, I think, is self-explanatory. There are, though, one or two points that need some explaining.

1.   What appears in brackets seemed possible to us but not necessary. What appears in brackets followed by a question mark seemed questionable.

2.   We assumed the availability of a variety of professional plays for the students to see and of good young artists who could be brought to the schools from time to time to exemplify an idea or illustrate a principle. Obviously, this assumption is not true in all places in all times.

3.   It may seem that we were trying to do too little over twelve years. We were assuming that the schools would give up one, or at most two forty-minute periods for Aesthetic Education per week, and that theatre was only one of the arts to be considered. If the schools gave us more time, clearly we could plan to do more.

4.   I need hardly say that each half-sentence in each box on this chart would take several fat books to develop in any kind of workable detail.

I realize our hypothetical curriculum may be absolute nonsense. None of us who drew it up knew anything technical about curriculum planning or developmental psychology. If we had, I'm sure the chart would look entirely different. Still, I offer the curriculum without apology for what it is: a first draft done in good faith by one sort of knowers. And even if everything in the draft turns out to be wrong, it is nonetheless useful. What is written down can be changed, refined, corrected or replaced, which is what I hope will happen to this curriculum -- indeed, to everything that has been said this morning -- when we next meet.

| GRADE | 1 | 2 | 3 | 4 | 5 |
|---|---|---|---|---|---|
| I. RUBRIC | STORYTELLING<br>Done by professionals, teachers and children, both alone and in groups<br><br>The point is to create a theatre in the mind. | | | FORM INTO FEELING<br>Short scenes built from the students' own experience. | |
| II. EXERCISES | Physicalizations (e.g. "Who, What and Where;" "Space Walk;" etc. | | | Improvisations on particular situations | |
| III. PERFORMANCE | E.g. Mummenschantz (Physical transformations, fantastical images, short segments)<br><br>(Short improvised-skits?) | | | Minneapolis' Little Mermaid (Longer and more coherent plot, stronger and more complex feelings)<br><br>(Class play?) | |
| IV. OTHER | Other kinds of play<br><br>N.B. No explicit connection is to be made among I, II and III. | | | Ordering space, in Art class, but no explicit connection made with I, II and III. | |

PROFESSIONAL TRAINING: PARALLEL BUT NOT CONNECTED.

| 6 7 8 | 9 | 10 | 11 | 12 |
|---|---|---|---|---|
| **CHOICES** Intensive study of theatrical moments, perhaps as long as a scene. | **THE WHOLE PLAY (I).** Intensive study of one or two plays. | **PERFORMANCE** Creation of a collective, ensemble piece, culminating in performance. | **THE WHOLE PLAY (II).** Intensive study of one or two plays, different in as many possible ways from those studied in ninth grade. | **GOING TO THE THEATRE** As much as individual injustifies, but at least some for all. |
| Changes of words, blocking, space etc. and discussion of the effect and implication of each change. | Transformation of character, development of mood, language and imagery, etc. NB. The focus is now on the whole, not parts. | Body, voice, memory etc. exercises toward the piece. | Historical, textual, etc. studies relevant to the play(s). Exercises toward the piece. | Talk about, analyze, read plays for all, as interest warrents. Lesson in technique for those interested. |
| (Go to the theatre, ideally to see plays they've done pieces of) (They perform play(s) they've done pieces of) | See the play or plays and perform at least scenes, ideally all. | Several performances of the piece, if possible in different spaces and for different kinds of audiences. | See the play or plays and perform at least scenes, ideally all. | _Ad lib_, as interest warrents Class Play |
| Discussion of and opportunity to learn skills and crafts, e. g. mime, lighting. NB. This must be rigorous and specific. | Coordinate with other subjects, e. g. Art, English, History. | | Coordinate with other subjects, e.g. Art, English, History. | 1980 Thomas Bullard Jonathan Levy David Trainer David Shookhoff Andrew Wolk |

PROFESSIONAL TRAINING: PARALLEL BUT NOT CONNECTED

351

# TOWARDS A DEVELOPMENTAL PSYCHOLOGY OF THEATRE:
## A CONFUSION OF CONFUSIONS
### A Position Paper
### by
### Roger L. Bedard

The Children's Theatre Association of America exists as an organization to unite people who work with drama and theatre with and for young people. This group is united only by its common focus on young people, but unfortunately, more unity is often assumed. The common use of the term, "Child Drama," to include both Creative Drama and Children's Theatre is an explicit manifestation of the degree to which these separate disciplines are often considered the same, or, at least, inextricable bound together. The problem of this forced unity becomes apparent with the confusion raised when many different perspectives (reflecting the wide range of practices inherent in drama and theatre with and for young people) are focused on a topic such as that used for this symposium. Until this confusion is addressed, there will be little meaningful work accomplished in articulating pressing research questions in the field as a whole.

In an attempt to clarify definitions of theatre/drama with and for children, a CTAA committee, in a report published in 1978, suggested that drama/theatre be viewed for the perspective of a continuum, wherein drama in its natural state would occupy one pole position, while formal theatre would occupy the other pole position. It was further stated that "The natural propensities of children located at the far left of this continuum, are seen to be the basis of, and to infuse, all the forms of drama and theatre."[1].

This continuum provides a graphic comparative analysis of the disparate forms of theatre and drama. It is unfortunate, however, that many practitioners have taken this same continuum as a definitive illustration of the "developmental" nature of drama and theatre. They deduce from this -- and other inappropriate sources -- that young children naturally move from being a participant to being an audience member, and that drama (participation) is appropriate for young children that theatre (child as audience member) is appropriate for older children. Such a perspective is neither based on tested theories nor on an accurate description of the actual status of the field. Such a "developmental" perspective is not explicit in this continuum, but the untested assertion that drama and theatre are linked by the "natural dramatic properties of children" invites wholesale misinterpretation and confusion.

This confusion was graphically illustrated when theatre practitioners, drama specialists and child psychologists all focused on the question of a developmental psychology of theatre. The theatre practitioners were interested in the child's response as audience members; the drama specialists were interested in child psychologists (particularly Howard Gardner) approached the subject from the perspective of the child as artist (in this case, actor). All discussion was informed by the unspoken assumption that there exists a common thread to unite these disparate perspectives. As the discussion progressed, it became very clear that all parties in the discussion were tenuously joined by a thread that consists of vagaries an unfounded (or, at least, untested) assumptions.

The link between the child as participant in drama, as an audience member and as a theatre artist, has never been clearly articulated or, much less, tested. Yet, this very idea forms the basis for most of our work in drama/theatre with and for children. Until this link is clarified and tested, the field will continue to build confusion upon confusion, and an aesthetic that truly embraces drama and theatre with and for children will evade our grasp.

[1]Jed H. Davis and Tom Behm, "Terminolgy of Drama/Theatre With and for Children," Children's Theatre Review, XXVII, 1 (1978), p. 10.

# ABOUT THE AUTHORS

WILLIAM BAIRD is a Ph.D. candidate, Applied Cognitive Sciences Centre, Ontario Institute for Studies in Education.

GISELE BARET, Ph.D. is Professor of the Faculty of Education, University of Montreal, Montreal, Canada.

ROGER BEDARD, Ph.D., teaches in the theatre department at Virginia Polytechnical Institute and is Vice President for Education & Theatre Development of the Children's Theatre Association of America, and Editor of <u>Dramatic Literature for Children: A Century in Review</u>.

BRADLEY BERNSTEIN received his Ph.D. for a study of Viola Spolin's improvisational techniques used for classroom learning. He has conducted improvisational workshops in Canada, the United States and Australia.

DAVID BOOTH is Professor, Faculty of Education, The University of Toronto.

RICHARD COURTNEY, responsible for graduate Arts & Education at Ontario Institute for Studies in Education, is cross-appointed to the Graduate Centre for the Study of Drama (Toronto). Past president of CCYDA-DRAMA CANADA and of the Canadian Conference of the Arts, his books in print include <u>Re-Play</u>, The Dramatic <u>Curriculum</u>, <u>Drama in Therapy</u> (2 vols), and <u>Play, Drama & Thought</u>.

HOWARD GARDNER is affiliated with the Boston Veterans Administration Medical Center and Harvard University Project Zero. Author of many books, his latest is <u>Frames of Mind, The Theory of Multiple Intelligences</u>.

ROBERT GARDNER, Ed.D., is in the Radio and Television Department, Ryerson Polytechnical Institute in Toronto.

HOLLY GIFFIN, Ph.D. is Director of Dramatic
Education, Mt. Altos Institute for Human
Education.

PORANEE GURURATANA, lecturer, Srinakarinwirot University, Bankok, is the author of Pre-School
Children & Learning and the only Thai book
on Creative Drama, Creative Dramatics for
Elementary School Children.

VIRGINIA GLASGOW KOSTE is Professor and Director
of Drama and Theatre for the Young at
Eastern Michigan University Department of
Communication and Theatre Arts.  Author of
Dramatic Play Rehearsal for Life, and
numerous articles and plays including Alice
in Wonder.

JONATHAN LEVY is Professor of Theatre at the State
University of New York in Stony Brook, and a
well known playwright for children including
The Marvelous Adventures of Tyl.

DR. JOHN MCINNES is an Associate Professor at
Ontario Institute for Studies in Education
and the senior author of reading and
language programs, used throughout Canada,
published by Nelson, Canada.  He has written
both trade books and texts for children, and
has taught extensively from primary grades
to graduate school.

PETER MCLAREN teaches at Brock University, St.
Catherines and was a classroom teacher for
six years, a press columnist since 1979, and
is the author of Cries from the Corridor.

SUE MARTIN, Ph.D., Professor of Dramatic Art,
University of Windsor; producer of Actor's
Trunk Company, has published many articles
and is co-author of Sprouts: Projects for
the Creative Growth of Children and Treasure
Hunts: A Creative Discovery of Classic
Literature.

HIROKO NORO received her M.A. in Japan and has published articles in Japanese on language teaching and Japanese art and has taken tea ceremony lessons for eight years.

LAWRENCE O'FARRELL is Associate Professor and Chairman of the Arts, Faculty of Education, Queens University, Kingston, Canada.

PAMELA RITCH, Ph.D. is Associate Professor, Department of Theatre, Illinois State University, Normal, III and Vice President for Research and Publication of the Children's Theatre Association of America. She is former Editor of the Research Issue of the Children's Theatre Review.

DR. H. HOWARD RUSSELL is Professor and Chairman, The Department of Curriculum, Ontario Institute for Studies in Education, and was formerly responsible for the Arts and Aesthetics Program of CEMREL, St. Louis. He is the author of many distinguished research reports.

RINA SINGHA, M.A., is a leading Kathak dancer, toured with Ram Gopal, and is founder of the Kathak Institute, Toronto. Co-author of Indian Dances and author of multicultural teaching kits, as a dance ethnologist and dance educator in multicultural education she has delivered addresses in Sweden, Hawaii, India, etc.

JUDITH SILVER received her Ph.D. (Toronto) for her study of folk dance as therapy and she is a leading Canadian folk dancer. Counsellor, therapist and researcher, she is the co-author of the important paper, "The surrogate function of lines in visual perception" (Perception, 1974)

SANDRA SHINER, Past President of the Association for Bright Children, researched the curriculum for gifted students for her Ph.D. She has consulted on two films and lectured widely about the gifted (including York and Toronto Universities and OISE) and is the author of Gifted & Talented Children.

CHRISTINE TURKEWYCH, M.A., was a consultant with Alberta's Cultural Heritage Branch, and with Citizenship and Culture (Ontario) where she was responsible for training programs in multicultural communication; she is now an administrator, Women's College Hospital, Toronto.

DR. OTTO WEININGER is Professor in Applied Psychology and Chairman of the Early Childhood Program at OISE. He has developed a number of films on children's play, is the editor of the Journal of the Melanie Klein Society, and is the author of Play and Education and Out of the Minds of Babes.

JOYCE WILKINSON, Ph.D. is Associate Professor, Faculty of Education, University of Lethbridge, Alberta, Canada.

DENNIS WOLFE is Professor of Psychology and Senior Researcher for Project Zero. She is the author of many articles and co-author of the book, Early Symbolization. New Directions for Child Development.

# ABOUT THE EDITORS

JUDITH KASE-POLISINI is Professor of Theatre Education and Artistic Director of the USF Educational Theatre at the University of South Florida. A former President of the Children's Theatre Association of America, she is currently a member of the Commission on Theatre Education for the American Theatre Association and Region III Chair of the Alliance for Arts Education of the John F. Kennedy Center for Performing Arts. An author of many articles, she has published two plays and is listed in Who's Who of American Women and Who's Who of the South and Southwest.

ROBERT WILLIAM COLBY is Director, Graduate Institute for Drama-in-Education, Head of the Drama/Theatre for the Young Program and Director of Youtheatre at Emerson College and Board Member-at-Large for the Children's Theatre Association of America.

CHARLES E. COMBS, Ph.D. is Director of Theatre at Plymouth State College, and Editor of the Research Issue of the Children's Theatre Review, a quarterly publication of the Children's Theatre Association of America.

RUTH BEALL HEINIG, Ph.D., President of the Children's Theatre Association of America, is former editor of the Children's Theatre Review, and author of Go Adventuring! A Celebration of Winifred Ward, America's First Lady of Child Drama. She teaches in the Communication Arts and Sciences Department at Western Michigan University.

LIN WRIGHT, Ph.D., former President of the Children's Theatre Association of America is Chair of the Department of Theatre at Arizona State University, Editor of Professional Theatre for Young-Audiences, Board member of the Arizona Alliance for Arts Education and author of numerous articles.

359